JUST THIS SIDE OF MADNESS

Creativity and the Drive to Create

JUST
THIS
SIDE
OF
MADNESS

Creativity and the Drive to Create

Carol Ann Beeman

UCA Press
1990

ISBN 0-9615143-9-6

There is really no such thing as a sole accomplishment. Thanks goes to many patient and persevering people who made this study of creative drive possible in this form—most notably, Dr. Robert E. Lowrey, Dr. Jeff Henderson, Ms. Kathleen Hart, and Ms. Kim Kelley.

Thanks to my ever-patient family and friends, especially my son David Morizot, and his roommates, Ken Fortenberry and Martin "Buddy" Eggensperger.

Thanks to my priest and therapist, respectively—Rev. Lawrence Maus and Dr. Laura Dubuisson Morrison.

God bless you,
Carol Ann Beeman
7/23/89

CONTENTS

PREFACE

So ends the last lesson of a nondivisable ignoramus: a double lesson—outwardly and inwardly affirming that, whereas a world rises to fall, a spirit descends to ascend. Now our igno-ramus faces the nonanswerable question, "who as a writer am I?"...

I am someone who proudly and humbly affirms that love is the mystery-of-mysteries, and that nothing measurable mat-ters "a very good God damn": that "an artist, a man, a failure" is no mere whenfully accreting mechanism, but a givingly eternal complexity—neither some soulless and heart-less ultrapredatory infra-animal nor any un-understandingly knowing and believing and thinking automaton, but a naturally and miraculously whole human being—a feelingly illimitable individual; whose only happiness is to transcend himself, whose every agony is to grow.

—e. e. cummings

This book and I have come a long way in the past fifteen years. I am on the one hand grateful for this opportunity to reassess and reorganize my thinking, but on the other hand almost at a loss as to where and how to take hold of it again in order to update and revise the information. So, in order to simplify and clear out the dead wood, I will begin again at the beginning.

The concept of a drive to create which is genetically transmitted and separate from creativity itself presented itself to me in the spring of 1973. I was a mother of young children, married to a psychiatrist, and living in Monroe, Louisiana. I was attending graduate school in psychology and peeping about looking for a topic suitable for a master's thesis. I had been a closet poet for many years, a fact I shared with very few people. I had been a classroom teacher and had volunteered for work at the local mental health clinic and with various charity organizations and cultural events in our town.

Another fact of my life made me fascinated with Virginia Woolf and all the literature coming out during the early seventies about her, her work as an artist and writer, and her illness—manic-depressive or bipolar disorder. Manic-depressive illness did not "run" in my family—it galloped!

I had recovered from a depressive breakdown after the birth of my second child. Emotional balance seemed an impossible dream. My mood swings were so volatile that on any given Monday morning I might wake up at the point of suicide but by Tuesday afternoon might feel like going shopping. This made life difficult.

I wanted a literary lifestyle so that, perhaps without having to constantly live under the strain of excuses and explanations, I might somewhere find the balance that would make me accessible to life and life accessible to me. Today I am fortified by a relationship with a Higher Power that was only superficial during those years. I am learning with the help of many in our society to understand dysfunctional families, the battered wife syndrome, alcoholism, and mental illness. I am a survivor. All these things have happened to me, been the fabric of my living on the way to becoming the poet and writer I had hoped I could be in 1973.

Given the perspective of the past fifteen years, I am interested in learning if this book and my experiences are still validated by the common experiences of others attempting the creative life. Reviews, as well as responses from readers and to lectures given when the book was first published in 1978, indicated these ideas held value and validity. The advantage of a little maturity makes the original intentions of this book seem to me rather pretentious and self-serving. My hope now is that more thought and perspective may be generated here that will be of use to others in this adventure called life.

The original concept of this book was generated by an argument I had with my late husband Dr. John P. Burton. I had been piling through Leonard Woolf's memoirs and reading Quentin Bell's *Virginia Woolf*. Over drinks one evening, after dinner and putting the children to bed, we were discussing the Woolfs and their lifestyle—the enormous part her illness played in how they lived and worked. We naturally and really naively fell to discussing the "insane artist" myth and "just what role Virginia's illness played in her writing."

John seemed to think the insanity may have provided periods of relief from ordinary reality and become a source of inspiration for her writing, much of which is deadly real and yet surreal at the same time. I disagreed, mainly on the gut-level feeling that it was her struggle with the illness that made her sane functioning all the more precious to her. Then, there was the fact of her accomplishments—all those volumes of literary criticism and biography which set her apart from a mere fanciful or even distinguished fiction writer. There was so much solid achievement there—

lucid, intelligent, carefully written and accessible, extremely inspiring and hopeful.

It seemed to me that most insane people have enough to do just to keep their heads above water. Most highly creative people ignore society and in their rushes of ego and ego gratification have little desire to be of help and service to others. But here was a woman, a couple, interested in world economics, politics, literary achievements, and community improvement, as well as the daily things of living which happened to include mental illness.

I began to argue passionately for a factor in the situation which promoted this world view and the constant effort on Virginia's part both to describe her world and to communicate with that "other" world not afflicted or affected by her madness. The fact that she could not have made any impact on that world nor any dent in her illness without her rational functioning as a writer seemed huge to me at that time and still does. Like most of us, I had rejected the "insane artist" theory, but getting around the influence of Virginia's illness seemed unavoidable. Leonard Woolf had identified it as the single most important fact of their life together. He had thrown his life and energies into the balance for her sake.

Reflection on the physiology of the body and how the body properly struggles for homeostasis and balance in health made me turn toward the mind. Wasn't there as important an effect in the mind, something equally physiological that turned the mind toward health and balance? John told me to look up the book by Clifford Beers, *The Mind That Found Itself*. Mr. Beers was a contemporary of Virginia Woolf who lived in New England and suffered from an acute manic illness during which he was incarcerated in a mental asylum for nine years. A Yale graduate and a highly articulate and literate man, he wrote about his illness after being released and restored to a life of normal functioning as a businessman. In the book he described the sudden onset of his mania, his life and mistreatment in the asylum, and his recovery. His book helped open many doors to the mental health movement in this country.

What mainly impressed me about Clifford Beers's account was that his illness came on suddenly and without any real external precipitating factors and that its course and his recovery seemed equally without external reference. The Woolfs had made similar observations about Virginia's illness. At the time I was writing the first edition of this book, manic-depressive illness was not yet established as a genetically transmitted disorder. Today that is being established on a scientific basis. Also, we have increasing evidence that alcoholism and other mental disorders are at the least genetically influenced if not transmitted via the DNA encoding on the chromosomes.

What is proposed here and what is still under investigation is the possibility that a genetic factor exists and operates that predisposes certain people toward the artistic life. Certainly, everyone has a drive to be creative, to express things about their lives in a creative way. This is seen on every hand in the interest children have in arts and crafts and with our adult hobbies. We like to "make" things.

To my mind, especially today, this is a pure reflection of our Creator in us—a desire to give from within ourselves, to add things to our surroundings that reflect our inner lives and being. However, in the life of the artist this drive to be creative and to function in a particular creative area seems to override all other drives and functions, even other ambitions which might be socially more rewarding.

The fabric of life is woven tightly and loosely around major life events. We are still coming into this world and leaving it in the same manner in which our ancestors thousands of years ago entered and left. The mysteries we encounter are subject more to moments of reflection and illumination than to scientific scrutiny, and yet as moderns we can evoke both to synthesize and express our common experiences.

Our new buzzwords revolve around "quality" of life and "quality time," but what prompts us to give expression to these inner motivations, to seek a new language, a new metaphor, to reach beyond the limits of language to touch each other in new and more satisfying ways? This is the work the artist in our society attempts, often at grave risk of personal stability and health.

In the past the artist was blamed, set apart, often misused and abused because of his excesses. I believe it to be true that he abused himself at the expense of his work without regard to the risks he was taking. The lack of balance would then give rise to a complex range of health problems which today we are beginning to view as the result of varied and interdependent genetic components influenced by physical and environmental factors.

Human growth and change are the essence of the artist's message. The common awareness of who we are bridges many gaps in our world. The ability to see, hear, feel, and be human enables us to respond to others in a caring and beneficial way. The artist's gifts are subject to the same laws and rules as any other abilities here on earth. The problem of being a gifted individual is not identical with being a driven individual, but often we are enlarged and advanced by the contributions of a driven, gifted person.

At the time of the first edition of this volume, there was a great controversy beginning about new technology in gene-splicing and manipulation of genetic material. Fear and confusion attended the process then as now. The propensity for mankind to turn any new possibly beneficial alterations of our world toward destruction concerns most of us. It is time to consider the evidence of uniqueness as a gift, not a burden. To eliminate at will and at random various genetic qualities, even those considered "defects," could put at jeopardy closely linked or otherwise poorly understood genetic material. This is the time for caution.

Fear and prejudice continue to lock us into our prison of pre-conceived ideas and continue to push our artists into asylums and self-destruction. Perhaps it is possible for our society and our world to grow beyond destruction and nihilism, but to me the evidence shows this is clearly an individual process as well as a community responsibility. Commitment to life for me means acceptance and surrender to my Creator. In this way creative functioning in daily life is neither a fringe benefit nor an option, but a part of a much larger process which involves all of us—a process of relinquishment and in a very particular way—healing.

Works Cited

cummings, e.e. i: six nonlectures. New York: Atheneum (by arrangement with Harvard UP), 1962.

PART I:
The Dilemma of the Creative Person

Chapter One
Introduction

The wheel of history must not be turned back, and man's advance towards a spiritual life, which began with the primitive rites of initiation, must not be denied. It is permissible for science to divide up its field of inquiry and to set up limited hypotheses, for science must work in that way; but the human psyche may not be parceled out. It is a whole which embraces consciousness, and is the mother of consciousness. Scientific thought, being only one of its functions, can never exhaust all the possibilities of life.

—*C. G. Jung*, Modern Man in Search of a Soul

Our libraries and bookstores are filled with books containing theories of creativity. Analysis after analysis of the creative process has been written up in recent years. What is it? How do we measure it? How does it operate? Who is creative? Why are they creative? Are there genetic determinants for creativity? How can each individual maximize his creative potential? What is required to be creative? Ad infinitum, researchers have explored the surface of the matter only occasionally probing into a crack or crevice of the cavern, which sprawled below their basic inquiries. It is to open the mouth of that cavern to public view and discussion that this book is written. The *how*'s and *why*'s of creativity will be swallowed within these pages by the enormous question of *whether*: to create or not to create.

In order to get a handle on this puzzle I have divided this study of creativity and the artist's drive into four sections which are separate but interdependent facets of the discussion. Part I is devoted to the modern artist: his work and his dilemma, the problems that attend the creative lifestyle. Part II turns the focus of the book to **propose** a new theory of creative drive that may help modern artists face with understanding a few of their problems and in so doing increase both the quality and quantity of their creative production. Included is a chapter on the history of treatment of mental diseases and a chapter on the most recent genetic and therapeutic advances. Part III shifts to Virginia Woolf—a case in point. Coming as she did at a critical time in history, Virginia Woolf exemplifies many of the modern complaints of artists in general. Her life, her mental illness, and her writing served as harbingers of the contemporary era in which to live the creative life is to deliberately and methodically place one's own consciousness on the chopping block of an insensitive, materialistic society. Virginia Woolf's suicide was in the broader sense a creative martyrdom to which she was driven both internally, by the timebomb of a genetic disorder, and externally, as an artist living in the twentieth century.

Part IV is devoted to the social data and applications of our new information about genetic disorders, education for the gifted and talented, and recovery programs for alcoholics, addicts, mentally ill people, and dysfunctional family systems. The whole idea of systems in society and therapy is something that has come about since the first edition of this book and is a great help in finding new ways to think about ourselves and our social underpinnings. We are in the social sciences and in the medical world awakening to the reality of how interrelated and interdependent our social structure and systems of modern living are. The past five years have seen an explosion in self-help and recovery programs, especially those using the 12-Step Plan of recovery initiated by Alcoholics Anonymous. As our world community has shrunk and consolidated, so our denial about the need for the spirituality Carl Jung called for early in this century has been and is being broken.

Social scientists have established concepts about the ever-pyramiding structure of human psychological needs and drives. Some have curiously suggested inherent patterns of behavior while others as a side issue of scientific investigation have ranked, filed, and explained away our humanity as only a function of our biological and social needs. They have taught us we need air, that we get thirsty, that we need sleep, that we are driven to make sense out of our environment, that we will fight over territory, children, or even a set of principles acquired through a process of socialization, that we must have sex, that we cannot survive without food, and so on. Far from challenging the validity of these observations, their primary assumption that man is susceptible to innate biological drives and equally compelling psychological drives will serve as the jumping-off point for this discussion of the artist and his drive to create. This drive is inherent in every human being, but quantitatively it appears to be more forceful in certain of us. When the exceptional drive is combined with exceptional artistic ability and power, then we can observe the emergence of an artist.

Our knowledge of drive behavior and creativity will serve as a flashlight to help us enter and challenge the Labyrinth of creative drive, motive, desire. It seems almost a cliche that creativity, however the term is defined or applied, is a universally applicable quality of life, but when we talk about the artist and his work, there is a discernible difference. In the arts the quality and quantity of creative production lies somehow within the experience of the artist himself. Many highly creative people are content never to enter a field of artistic endeavor and others seem limited by obstacles that obviously less-talented people are driven to overcome.

We talk around these enigmas and make noises about the "artistic temperament" or the "insane viewpoint" essential to artistic production. Only occasionally do we get down to the nitty-gritty that what we are actually seeing in the person who adopts a creative lifestyle is the operation of an overriding "drive" toward creative expression.

A work of art is the product of a drive to create something tangible which rises out of the artist's unique perceptions of the world. Like any other biologically or psychologically functioning drive, the creative drive is produced by the tension of opposite poles exerting their influences on the personality or consciousness. At one pole is a deficit and at the other is an overabundance, a satiation. The drive is pure energy, either physical in biological drives or mental in the psychological realm. In the most critical sense the artist in contemporary life cannot possibly reach the level of satiation, because his basic creative needs are so continuously being drained by the demands of a complex and impersonal society that he must forever operate under the strain of a deficit. This deficit requires constant creative effort in order to maintain the ever-increasing energy levels of his internal drive. If for some reason his creative functioning is impaired or thwarted, then the course of the drive is deflected and the energy may turn to self-destructive ends, such as mental illness, alcoholism, drugs, other compulsive behaviors, or even suicide.

Understanding the interaction of an inherited illness such as bipolar disorder, alcoholism, addiction, or obsessive-compulsive disorders with the demands of artistic insight and sensitivity may help in the process of healing and self-discovery. Creative problem-solving enhances the possibility of human survival and spiritual development. Learning to enhance and cultivate our creative drive in this new era of personal adventure is worthy of study and exploration. This book is a part of that process.

But artists have always suffered, you may say. How do the pressures of contemporary life enhance the probability of destructive ends for the artist? Carl Jung zeroed in on the answer to this crucial question in his book *Modern Man in Search of a Soul*:

> The disturbing vision of monstrous and meaningless happenings that in every way exceed the grasp of human feeling and comprehension makes quite other demands upon the power of the artist than do the experiences of the foreground of life. (157)

In former centuries the creative vision of the artist could range from the minutely personal to the externally gargantuan without exceeding the grasp of the human mind, but what living person can grapple with all the painful elements of chaos, cataclysm, and confusion that attend human existence in this modern era? The complexities are overwhelming—the technology of modern warfare, the incredible grief of the holocausts of this century, the extremes of economic flux which seem frivolous and unpredictable, and on the other hand, the dramatic potential for man's welfare and benefit which has been presented to us by explosive advances in scientific knowledge. The artist in the modern world wrestles not only with the pain and frustration of his own individual life as a mortal passing through a valley of fantastic delights and unpredictable terrors, but through his artistic vision he is apprenticed to all the agony and idiosyncrasy of the abyss which opened before man in the breakdown of law and order in the early years of the twentieth century and which is still being played out before our eyes. It was a Hiroshima survivor who asked the question which epitomizes the quandary of contemporary man: "What guinea pig can come to grips with the terms of his own existence?"

And yet this is exactly what we expect from our artists and what the artist himself must attempt to translate not only for himself, but for society. Is it any wonder that art forms depicting neurotic- or psychotic-like themes of disaster and dissolution are so prevalent in every area of art—graphics, writing, plays, videos, films, painting, sculpture, the dance?

What the books on creativity seem to do is build up for all of us a conscious acceptance that man is not doomed to self-destruction. There is hope. There are positive outcomes to our human struggles. Indeed, we have been fashioned in the image of our Creator who looked on His creation and said, "It is good."

The goal of this book is to examine the strains on creative functioning, the role of the artist in our midst, and the existence of psychological principles that govern the operation of creative drive. To be able to address the positive aspects of a drive for creativity and to enhance constructive outlets for that drive seems to me a basic human developmental task. Self-destructiveness and impotency are the alternatives. Surely self-destructive behavior robs us of our artists and robs our artists of their work.

Just as from primeval times the role of the medicine man or holy man was to render the irrational impotent in order to augment the spiritual healing and continuity of the society, so today in certain ways each of us may enter into that process through the creative experiences within us. In the recreative and reconstructive works of art and faith, order, growth, and human potential are viewed as the extensions of a loving, wise Creator. Each living, working artist is empowered not only with the nightmare of man's primordial nature, but he carries simultaneously the vision and the hope of a new heaven and a new earth.

We must release the artist from our preconceived and limiting notions about his lifestyle and his creative work. We must release ourselves from the impositions of personal isolation and gross materialism that precludes a life of faith and creativity.

In his 1970 acceptance speech for the Nobel Prize in Literature, Aleksandr Solzhenitsyn reminded us:

> . . . it was not a slip of the tongue for Dostoyevsky to say that "Beauty will save the world," but a prophecy. After all *he* was given the gift of seeing much; he was extraordinarily illumined. (7)

If the artist is to be able to continue at all in his role as interpreter and visionary of his own age, he must have emotional and psychological freedom to follow the dictates of his heart, to develop fully his creative talents. The central issue of the theory proposed in this book is that the drive to create energizes the basic elements of creative perception, that it comes naturally and genetically, and that it may be linked to genetic factors which research scientists believe are responsible for certain biochemical dysfunctions in brain metabolism. These dysfunctions are found in alcoholics, addicts, certain mental illnesses, and possibly other obsessive disorders.

We hopefully are living on the edge of a new era of human development, but we may be approaching catastrophe so great that life on this planet could be annihilated. Therefore, it is even more imperative that we pursue healing and community, faith and creativity. Our artists can assist us only to the degree they themselves are freed from the inherent psychopathologies that plague them and us. If our creative energies can be directed toward reconstruction and regeneration, modern consciousness will benefit.

Each new work by a contemporary artist whether in the visual arts, belle-lettres, music, or the performing arts is but a small part of the framework of that reconstruction. But for the catharsis to be effective, it must aim toward that creative peak we identify as art, that level where man exists not just as himself, but as Man—a human being with all the potential for evil and for good with which he has been endowed. The critical issue is choice.

Yehudi Menuhin, the world-famous violinist active in the International Music Council of UNESCO, wrote:

> I look upon great works of art not only as isolated gifts and benefactions from heaven but also as high points emerging from a continuing living process. It is upon this view that I base my belief in art as hope for humanity. (82)

To insure the "living process" to which Menuhin refers and through which artists create, creative functioning must be better understood. We are people of varied gifts and talents. If we discover and develop our gifts in service of one another, mankind will benefit. That service begins with attention to what ails each of us, what afflicts us personally and as a society, what binds us. Every positive step of self-discovery insures that these "gifts and benefactions from heaven" need not be wasted or destroyed.

Works Cited

Jung, C.G. *Modern Man in Search of a Soul*. New York: Harcourt, Brace & World, 1933.
Menuhin, Yehudi. "Art As Hope For Humanity." *Saturday Review/World*. Vol. 12/14/74.
Solzhenitsyn, Aleksandr I. *The Nobel Lecture on Literature*. trans. Thomas P. Whitney, New York: Harper & Row, 1972.

Chapter Two
Creativity: A Process and a Product

Whereas moral courage is the righting of wrongs, creative courage, in contrast, is the discovering of new forms, new symbols, new patterns on which a new society can be built.

—*Rollo May*, The Courage to Create

The most salient mark of a creative person, the central trait at the core of his being is, as I see it, just this sort of courage. It is not physical courage of the type that might be rewarded by the Carnegie Medal or the Congressional Medal of Honor, although a creative person may have courage of this kind, too. Rather it is a personal courage, a courage of the mind and spirit, psychological or spiritual courage that is the radix of a creative person: the courage to question what is generally accepted; the courage to be destructive in order that something better can be constructed; the courage to be open to experience both from within and from without; the courage to imagine the impossible and try to achieve it; the courage to stand aside from collectivity and in conflict with it, if necessary; the courage to become and to be oneself.

—*D.W. MacKinnon*, Creativity: A Discussion
at the Nobel Conference

Recently at a convention I was approached by a young man who had heard I was working on the second edition of this book and wanted to discuss it with me. His first question was a well-focused, "How do you define creativity?"

I tried to emphasize that my idea for this book was more to examine the motivational aspect involved in human creativity, and most particularly, in the artist in our society. Since he seemed acutely interested and personally related some of his own experiences in seeking the creative lifestyle, I "blessed" him with a summary of my ideas about creative drive and its possible relationship to mood disorders including alcoholism and addiction.

Throughout our discussion, this young man repeatedly made the statement that I was describing creativity as a process rather than a product. I finally gave a rather uncomfortable but not unqualified "yes" to that observation. I didn't want to get caught up in the whirlwind of semantics. Honest differences of perspective, however, are generative.

It will be virtually impossible to survey the literature on creativity and the history of creativity research in this one chapter. What I hope to do is to selectively describe the bases of that information using subjectively what seems important to me. And, I confess, I am more interested in the "process" than the "product" in this volume. The drive I am claiming exists is an observable and definable reflection of the process involved in the creative act and resulting product.

Creativity in a generic sense seems to me the voice of the human spirit—the heartcry of a living being coming to terms with itself, its place in the order of things, and its relationship to its Creator. Forgive the use of the neuter gender, but in a real sense, the spirit embraces masculine and feminine and yet it is neither. It is the quintessential essence of being that animates body and soul without which the life of the person cannot be maintained or observed.

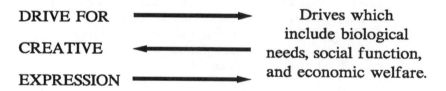

Figure 1:   THE TENSION OF OPPOSITE POLES

I think of the spirit as that part of each of us that sees the work of the Creator on every hand and recognizes its goodness, that sees in itself the vast oasis of hope, love, and faith located in the desert of the physical, and that both travels and transcends its distinctively human road, intensely motivated to share that journey with itself and its fellows.

These three aspects concern me most as I try to formulate and discuss a theory of creative drive—a recognition of and relationship to the Creator, a personal self-awareness, and a commitment to growth through the process of creatively becoming. If as a literary or scientific reader of this book, you cannot relate to what I have said, then please just hear me out.

Ten years ago man was again the center of the universe, pre-Copernican. Even theologians in the past twenty-five years had struggled with the proclamation, "God is dead." Science had undertaken to move into the void. After all, hadn't our best minds agreed, "Nature abhors a vacuum"?

In the eighties, elevated by a desire to understand ourselves and our lives here together in this shrinking world, we have rediscovered the facts of faith, reason, and the reality of life outside the laboratory. Even physics, the oldest of sciences, has returned to the realm of supernatural inquiry by extrapolating quarks and quirks that can only be reasoned and mathematically deduced. Our computers develop "viruses"; our minds find human beings out of control but not reduced to nothingness as once feared by the earlier existentialists.

Compulsion is not equal to drive. Therefore, product cannot in and of itself identify creativity. Reproductivity exists apart from creativity. I think we can talk about creativity when we see a dynamic relationship reflected in the originality, quality, and arrangement of what is produced. The product reflects the creative innovation but never equals it. Energy is required for the process.

Most authorities agree that what is produced must be original—something that did not exist before in form, appearance, or relationship. The result of the creative expression is something new, worthwhile, and human. My simple equation would contain the following elements: observation, unique perception, energy, relationship, production.

In Robert Weisberg's book *Creativity, Genius and Other Myths* (1986) I found an excellent review of the works of the mathematician Poincaré (1970) and G. Wallas (1926). Using the four basic stages of creativity presented by these researchers, he claims creativity has been expressed when "a novel response . . . solves the problem at hand" (4):

1. *Preparation.* This stage is characterized by a long period of conscious work which is unsuccessful. "After this period of preparation, the problem is often put aside, and not thought about consciously."

2. *Incubation.* "The problem is not consciously thought about, but work continues unconsciously."

3. *Illumination.* "If the incubation stage is successful, then in the next stage the person experiences a sudden illumination, a sudden insight into the solution of a problem."

4. *Verification.* "The illumination stage usually produces only a glimmer of the solution, however, with verification . . . being worked out later. . . . According to the view developed by Poincaré, and carried forth by others, the unconscious conducts the mental act of combining thoughts, judges the potential value of each combination and 'informs' the conscious of those that are valuable" (19-20).

Here is an example of these stages given by Poincaré from his own experiences:

> For fifteen days I strove to prove that there could not be any functions like those I have since called Fuchsian functions. I was then very ignorant; every day I seated myself at my work table, stayed an hour or two, tried a great number of combinations and reached no results. One evening, contrary to my custom, I drank black coffee and could not sleep. Ideas rose in crowds; I felt them collide in pairs interlocked, so to speak, making a stable combination. By the next morning I had established the existence of a class of Fuchsian functions, those which come from the hypergeometric series; I had only to write out the results, which took but a few hours. (81)

Weisberg continues his line of thought by discussing the criteria used by the unconscious for evaluation of any given combination of thoughts. This is a useful entry point for the implication of a drive state operating throughout the process. By its very nature the unconscious cannot be observed. Likewise, the energy involved in the stages and for working from one stage to the next is not directly observed, but I believe it can be both intuited and inferred.

> That is, once the unconscious begins combining these thoughts, how does someone suddenly realize that one combination is a potential solution? Poincaré and others believe that such a judgment is an *esthetic* one, based on an individual's sense of beauty. . . . Poincaré emphasizes the fact that scientists and mathematicians often talk about the beauty of a theory or the ugliness of a proof, and this, he feels, demonstrates a similarity between scientists and artists. Scientists also rely on their intuition of beauty when they make leaps of imagination. (21)

Arthur Koestler (*Act of Creation*, 1964) and others refer to the Latin word for "thinking" as a key to understanding creativity in general. *Cogitare* means "to shake together." Again, energy is at least implied if not inherent in our very discussions of creativity. Koestler's metaphor for the stages of creative processing is "bisociation," a two-step activity involving free-form associative thinking (brainstorming) and logical application (evaluative thinking) (21).

In his view of creativity, education is imperative, and he states unequivocally: "I believe one point should be strongly emphasized, and that is that artistic creation is a skill that must be learned" (Koestler 134). Koestler claims that the emotions are responsible for the movement of the mind (subconscious, we might say) through the stages of creativity: "What is happening is, put into our jargon, a series of bisociative processes involving the participatory emotions" (371).

Using my simple formula which includes the drive state, observation and unique perception form during the preparation and incubation stages. Both of these together could be seen as a gestation phase in which the human being at rest is merely concerned with the activities of daily living. A need arises to make sense out of a situation, to problem-solve, or to simply balance emotionally the ledger of the internal stimulation which arises quite normally from life's incongruities and dissimilarities, for example, the wide gap between work, eating, sleeping, social functioning and violent upheavals on an international as well as local and personal scale.

How can our lives be regularly examined and our place in the order of things be reconciled? How do we assess events of difficult rational and emotional content both at home and on a national-international scale? Modern telecommunications has made even the most modest cottage a window on the world.

Emotions are a keen part of our perceptions of ourselves and our world. Energy is required in their repression or acknowledgment. The dissipation of that energy or constructive use is the issue raised in this book. Truly we struggle at times to understand, to make sense, to gain a mental-emotional balance, to maintain emotional or soul equilibrium.

In our modern living this is almost an impossibility if we allow ourselves to process emotionally even the events that directly impinge on our individual psyches—the common ground of local community, neighborhood crises, or personal events. The alternative is to not process emotionally. This leads to dissociation, suppression, or repression. All are unhealthy alternatives to experiencing reality. Each of these ways our minds avoid painful emotions is only a stop-gap measure. Eventually our defenses will wear thin because so much energy is required to continue to suppress, repress, or dissociate from the painful elements we do not want to deal with consciously.

Most of us are familiar with the process of repression—unconsciously excluding from consciousness painful emotional responses to things in our lives we do not want to or cannot deal with. Another common word for this defense is denial. Dissociation is also common in today's economy of existence. Suppression is a process by which we simply "stuff down" feelings that are painful or threatening. This method most often leads to physical stress-related illnesses like ulcers, colitis, or cancer, where by comparison repression most often leads to low-level or moderate depression and feelings of guilt and low self-esteem.

By dissociating or cutting ourselves off from our feelings, we can survive any informational onslaught that is often overwhelming and confusing emotionally; for example, a random murderer enters a McDonald's or an elementary school and shoots helpless and harmless children and adults. How should one respond—anger, fear, resentment, hate? And yet, the farther removed geographically from the incident and the more emotionally removed, the greater the deficit of emotional release and the greater possibility of emotional repression or dissociation. Public rituals such as the funerals or memorial services for the victims become ways of releasing the painful reactions; however, many people may need longer-term support in working through the grief. This is what therapists call a "post-traumatic stress reaction." If the problem continues over more than several months it may be identified as a disorder that requires more specific therapeutic intervention. Many people who have suffered through significant trauma in childhood use the defense of dissociation in order to avoid stimuli that may evoke the fear, anger, or pain of a past trauma.

We live in an age of technological ontology in which living and *being* are contradictory states of affairs. An inherent drive for balance and aesthetic satisfaction pushes us into a process that will hopefully be discharged in a creative rather than a destructive fashion. It is at this point that I view every human being as essentially creative, made in the image of the Creator of life itself. We do have choice, as I see it; the activities of the soul of man coherently affect that choice. Illness, disease, anti-social acts seem a deflection and a result of the negative discharge of creative energy. We can learn another way.

Koestler and others see creativity as a skill that is learned. We are presently in an educational movement to provide appropriate learning experiences for our identified talented and gifted students in the public schools. It seems to me that the quantitative and qualitative expression of creativity including both process and product is proportional to two major factors, both of which operate within the individual—talent and affectivity. The drive state operating in creative expression will be observable in relationship to these two major components. Talent—the innate abilities, including intelligence—determines to a certain degree the level of competence that the person may achieve in creative functioning; affectivity— innate emotional sensitivity—determines the role of perceptions in the building up of the drive state, how much energy is actually required to balance the emotional-mental system of the individual.

Another common way of dealing with emotions we either cannot or do not want to acknowledge is called displacement. By this process we redirect the energy of the painful emotions onto objects or other people unrelated to the original cause of our pain. In this way we find often an "acceptable" release rather than to have to accept the pain or anger or whatever feeling we find unacceptable or inappropriate to our situation. Displacement may lead us into addiction or alcohol consumption in an effort to find some way to discharge the painful elements in our psyche. Often people who use this way to discharge the emotional backlog of their lives find themselves constantly blaming others for their problems or for how they feel. They find it difficult to face their own feelings and accept responsibility for them.

Through early nurturing and creative learning that augments and affirms healthy emotional functioning, every person can learn to maximize his or her talents and abilities. It will, however, still be the highly sensitive person who will find a need to function consistently in a creative process. In a person who has a perceptual sensitivity and hyperacuity, the creative function serves to protect the self and help in the homeostasis of mind and emotions. In the case of an artist, who by definition perceives the world uniquely and sensitively, the drive to create functions at a high level in the hierarchy of both emotional and physical needs.

This model in no way implies mere compulsivity as some may assert. I think compulsivity may be viewed as deflected energy that has not been trained creatively or that cannot be employed in a creative process because some inhibiting reason or limiting factor blocks or prevents creative functioning. Where the artist is concerned compulsivity can destroy creative achievement.

Koestler expresses his view of the process this way:

> Once the artist has acquired sufficient technical skill to do with his material more or less what he likes, the question of *what* he likes, i.e. what aspects of reality he considers relevant, becomes all-important. In other words, of the two variables I mentioned—the limitations of the medium, and the prejudiced eye beholding the motif, the first can be regarded within a given school, as relatively stable, and we can concentrate our attention on the second. There can be no unprejudiced eye for the simple reason that vision is full of ambiguities, and all perception, as we saw, is an inferential construction which proceeds on various levels, and most of it unconsciously. (373)

Accepting this unconsciousness of the first stages of creative functioning, one is able to observe the elemental build-up of energy attendant to the first phase of any drive state in which the organism is at rest but becoming engaged with a deficit in some area of physiological or, in human beings, psychological need. The necessary energy caused by the drive state is designed to promote activity that will bring the individual human being emotional balance, a sense of well-being, and a positive recreation (*re-creation*). And, as with other drive states, when a sufficient and appropriate outlet cannot be found, the energy is deflected toward inertia, illness, destruction.

Creativity is an inherently healthy and productive way of life that most people can learn. It was once believed that artists derived new material or contracted new methods from their distortions of reality. This is not true. Creative functioning has a homeostatic effect on consciousness. By finding a healthy creative outlet, a person is learning to release emotions in a positive way. Sharing what we feel by words, pictures, movement, portrayal becomes a way of connecting with others that brings greater self-esteem and promotes learning and growth. We are part of the ongoing process of living.

"Guard your neuroses," some poorly informed mentors might have urged in the heyday of early Freudian analysis. But today, I believe creativity to be an asset to productive, healthy mental and emotional functioning. Art is not only productive for society as a whole in reflecting what deviations and corrections need to be made in the course of civilization; but art, even on the personal level, is therapeutic and an asset to emotional well-being as it brings the individual into relationship with his or her feelings.

In their book *Creativity, Talent and Personality* (1984), Emanuel Hammer, Margaret Naumberg, and Leo Rosten report the results of their testing for creativity and relate that to personality inventories and affective measurements. The primary work they did was with children using the Rorschach Test, the Thematic Apperception Test, and the House-Tree-Person Test.

> Creativity, we have seen, is a many-vectored thing. But what may we expect in a generic way, as an answer to the question raised in the first chapter of this book: Is the creative person a first cousin to the madman?
>
> It is hard to give a categorical yes or no answer to this question. It is true that the subjects judged "truly creative" show, on the psychological techniques (noted above), greater inner distress and agonies than do the control group of subjects judged "merely facile." The creative youngsters also suffer from a sense of emotional disequilibrium within. Although we have just begun to scratch the surface in understanding the complex process of creativity, it can be safely assumed that, among the many variables, emotional conflict is a frequent one—not to be equated with mental illness which is defined more by the manner of *handling* emotional conflicts than by their presence. (111)

Robert A. Prentky in his book *Creativity and Psychopathology* (1980) addresses the question, "What is a creative product?" Citing the work of some of the giants in the field of contemporary creativity research—Koestler, Barron, Arieti, Gardner, MacKinnon, Pavlov, Cattell, McConaghey, Bronowski—Prentky identifies what seem to him by research and consideration the most important aspects of creativity both in process and psychopathology:

1. The key element of a creation is originality (Bronowski, 1970).

2. The creation is typically a synthesis and reformulation of already existent experiences or ideas.

3. The creation is spontaneously derived. It is not labored over.

4. In spite of the revelatory nature of the insight, there is an incubation period. During incubation raw material is sorted through, reshuffled, mulled over.

5. The creation occurs within a social context, influenced by the times, the environment, and a community of colleagues.

6. It is assumed that there is some worth inherent in the creation. Something artistically or scientifically sterile would not be deemed creative. This is reality orientation. A triviality is not seen as creative. The creation must achieve some identifiable goal (22-23).

On this point, I disagree. In the model I have proposed, because mental health is part of the benefit of creative functioning, even a triviality if it serves that purpose for the person producing it would not be considered trivial at all. And I would use the words "aesthetically pleasing" rather than "artistically and scientifically." However, even in this respect, I am not sure a hard-and-fast rule may be applied. A friend of mine who is a counselor keeps on her desk a sculpted head which one of her daughters created in a college art class and gave to her. The face is distorted in an agonized silent scream of pain and rage. Obviously, a catharsis occurred during the process of its creation and the message encoded into the product. This is creativity in action for the mental health and emotional business of the person whose energies entered into the work.

7. Whatever change derives from the creative insight must be sustained. This excludes the "creative happening" or any experience born of whim that quickly dies.

The most fertile imagination is little more than fanciful thinking when served only by quixotic and utopian dreams. Interestingly, this is one characteristic of the creative product that says that the product must be produced (23).

Again, I am not certain I even understand this point. Seeing creativity as I do more from a "process" orientation than the "product" viewpoint, I am reminded of the dozen blind men trying to describe an elephant by touch. Each held to an entirely different description because they were running hands over distinctively different parts of the animal.

8. The most rigorous and least-encountered characteristic is that the product in some way changes the human condition. The product must go beyond what we know and create a new, transcendent aspect of human experience.

Most of us could probably count on two hands the number of individuals who have accomplished such a feat: Copernicus, Newton, Darwin, Freud, Marx, Einstein, da Vinci, Michelangelo, Goethe, Shakespeare, Beethoven, and Mozart are obvious candidates (23).

Obviously here, I strongly protest. I don't think I am arguing "art for art's sake" when I say that any creative functioning is worthy and should be encouraged in the individual. Talent education is not an alternative. It is essential to mental and possibly even physical health and well-being. Creativity education should be a part of the regular curriculum. We have as a society approved golf, tennis, jogging, and other recreational activities for the body which used to be taboo. It is time to release the mind and spirit from superstition and bondage.

Prentky reflects on the possible relationship between creative functioning and pathology:

> There is a marked resemblance between the cognitive styles characterizing creative thought that Cattell and his colleagues sought to define and the psychotic loosenings (or tightenings) of ideational boundaries that McConaghey described. In the latter case (McConaghey), the disorder may be called over- or under-inclusion, and in the former case (Cattell), the gift is creativity. The apparent difference between the divergent thinking, loose associations, and irrelevant themes of psychotics and the amazing conceptual leaps, cognitive flexibility, and serendipitous discoveries of creative artists and scientists is one of control. Psychotic thinking is unbridled and capricious, while creative thinking is rationally directed and purposeful. In sum, it appears that there is reason to suspect a *continuity* between normal and pathological thinking, a point convincingly argued by Claridge (1972). . . . The existence of such cognitive styles may facilitate creativity as well as reflect a genetic predisposition to psychosis. (48-49)

Other factors that have been studied or associated with creativity in general include the following:

1. *Intelligence.* "Creative persons are, in general, intelligent, whether their intelligence is estimated from the quality of their accomplishments

or measured by standardized tests. Yet we have found essentially zero correlation between the measured intelligence of our creative subjects and the judged creativeness of their work; and similarly, little relationship between their academic performance both in high school and in college and their judged creativity" (MacKinnon 127).

This is an important insight since we do have the phenomenon of the so-called *idiot-savant*. In actuality a high level of creative drive combined with sensitivity and talent could produce exactly the effect of an idiot-savant where circumstances would allow the creative activity to flourish.

2. *Eccentricity.* Many researchers refer to the child-likeness and nonconformity of obviously creative people. Some even identify the quality of strangeness with genius. This is the observable result of unique perception and sensitivity to external and internal stimulation.

3. *Courage and independence.* To this attribute Rollo May has devoted an entire volume, *The Courage to Create* (1975). Others have written on the obstacles facing the artist approaching a new project, referring to the problem of facing the blank page or the blank canvas as "overcoming the power of the white."

4. *Thinking styles.* This would relate to the predominance of associative, evaluative, convergent, or divergent thinking patterns.

5. *Originality.* In an article for the *Journal of Abnormal and Social Psychology* (1955), Frank Barron discussed this aspect of creativity:

> If we consider the case of a human being who develops strongly the disposition toward originality, we must posit certain personal characteristics and personal history which facilitated the development of such a disposition. In our hypotheses, the term "dominance" was used to describe one trait of the regularly original individual. This may be translated as a strong need for personal mastery, not merely over other persons, but over all experience. It initially involves self-centeredness, which in its socialized form may come to be known as self-realization. One aspect of it is the insistence on self-regulation, and a rejection of regulation by others. . . .
>
> The disposition toward originality may thus be seen as a highly organized mode of responding to experience, including other persons, society, and oneself. The socially disrated traits which may go along with it include rebelliousness, disorderliness, and exhibitionism, while the socially valued traits which accompany it include independence of judgment, freedom of expression, and novelty of construction and insight. (484-5)

Many writers discussing the artist and creative research refer again and again to the facts of trauma in the early childhoods of many generative, creative people. The constant attraction to these incidences as causative factors can be included in the concept of a creative drive. Surely, all our biological and physiological drives are to promote our survival and health. In the case of the psychological drives, social conditions do impinge to restrict or modify creative functioning.

Human beings do learn to accommodate social requirements and restrictions. However, as we can understand the socially derived aspects of creative functioning and allow the drive to create to serve its life-affirming purpose in augmenting mental health in the individual, then we can have a more healthy society. Physical fitness is related to exercise and social support for good health habits. Likewise, we must have social approval or acceptance for mental and emotional fitness.

A person who has been abused whether as a child or an adult will be under an extreme need to express what feelings he or she has repressed or dissociated from. In a later chapter, I will discuss art therapy and how the psychiatric pioneer C.G. Jung advocated it, as well as how it is being employed today with psychiatric patients, especially with children who do not have the verbal skills to work through their problems and need other avenues of creative expression.

Relationship and production close the circle of the creative process. As John Donne so famously observed, "No man is an island." And every artist and genius echoes that theme. It is sad, indeed, when the society at large fears, opposes, regiments, represses, and isolates the highly driven person so that mental health suffers often irreparable damage. Nothing is created in a vacuum. In a very real way as I will discuss in later chapters, the drive to create is operating in each of us for sickness or health only to the degree that we have learned to accept our social environment and operate within it. Flexibility and adaptability determine production to a great degree.

Works Cited

Barron, Frank. "The Disposition Towards Originality." *Journal of Abnormal and Social Psychology.* 51:1955.

Hammer, Emanuel F., W. Margaret Naumberg, Leo Rosten. *Creativity, Talent and Personality.* Florida: Robert E. Krieger, 1984.

Koestler, Arthur. *Act of Creation.* New York: Dell, 1964.

MacKinnon, D.W. "Creativity: A Multi-Faceted Phenomenon." *Creativity: A Discussion at the Nobel Conference* (Ed. J.D. Roslansky). Amsterdam: North-Holland, 1970.

May, Rollo. *The Courage to Create.* New York:W.W. Norton, 1975.

Poincaré, H. "Mathematical Creation." *Creativity* (ed. P.E. Vernon). New York: Penguin Books, 1970.

Prentky, Robert A. *Creativity and Psychopathology.* New York: Praeger, 1980.

Wallas, G. *The Art of Thought*. New York: Harcourt & Brace, 1926.

Weisberg, Robert. *Creativity, Genius and Other Myths*. New York: W.H. Freeman, 1986.

Works Consulted

Abra, Jock. *Assaulting Parnassus: Theoretical Views of Creativity*. Lanham, MD: UP of America, 1988.

Anderson, Maxwell; Rhys Carpenter, Roy Harris, *The Bases of Artistic Creation*. New Brunswick, NJ: Rutgers UP, 1942.

Arieti, Silvano. *Creativity: The Magic Synthesis*. New York: Basic Books, 1976.

Arieti, Silvano. *The Intrapsychic Self: Feeling, Cognition and Creativity in Health and Mental Illness*. New York: Basic Books, Inc., 1967.

Barron, Frank. *Creative Person and Creative Process*. New York: Holt, Rinehart & Winston 1969.

Barron, Frank. *Creativity and Psychological Health*. Princeton, NJ: D. Van Nostrand, 1963.

Gardner, Howard. *Art, Mind, and Brain*. New York: Basic Books, 1976.

Kagan, Jerome. *Creativity and Learning*. Boston: Houghton-Mifflin, 1967.

Kneller, George F. *The Art and Science of Creativity*. New York: Holt, Rinehart & Winston 1969.

Kubie, Lawrence. *Neurotic Distortion of the Creative Process*. New York: Noonday P, 1958.

Ribot, Theodule Armand. *Essay on the Creative Imagination*. New York: Arno P, 1973.

Chapter Three
Dilemma of the Creative Lifestyle

It is my impression that in the last 25 years we have done quite enough research on the characteristics of creative acts and the environmental conditions that facilitate their emergence. In the future, our efforts should focus upon the personality and motivational factors which, when present, literally force the person into creative endeavor, no matter what the cost in strenuousness and risk. Only when we have done this will our conceptualization of creativity be such that we can convincingly understand the lonely, driven giants whose efforts shape their own and our worlds.

—*Salvatore R. Maddi, Ph.D.*
Perspectives in Creativity

It seems more and more difficult to avoid the fact that the "driven" creative person is different from other people. It really cannot be any other way. His or her thinking, emotions, relationships with others, even the lifestyle are tied irrevocably to the all-pervading images of the subconscious mind. To project and control these images is the primary compelling factor in the lives of such individuals, their raison d'etre.

Without free access to a way of life which promotes their living in harmony with the subconscious and the enormous build-up of creative energy involved, problems arise. Some effective means for dealing with the tensions that occur must be found because an innately more sensitive perception of external stimuli is combined with an inherently strong drive to express that perception creatively. Inevitably, if thwarted or repressed, the energy of the drive to create will turn inward with destructive results—alcoholism, drug addiction, mental illness, suicide or some other premature death from stress-related causes. Even when an outlet sympathetic to the direction of the creative person's drive is available, living is still a precarious balancing of extremes in perception and behavior.

Compare the predicament of the artist or creative person in contemporary society with the plight of the tightrope walker or trapeze artist in the circus. This metaphor may help enlarge our perspective on the problem of creative drive. A sense of balance is paramount, and this sense of balance can only come from training, skill, and conscientious effort. Yet, the creative work is often achieved in impossible circumstances by monumental efforts under life-threatening conditions. Afterwards, the contributions of our creative people are often misused or misappropriated. Rewards are more often meager, except for the intrinsic value of the work itself to the person who created it.

Seeking balance many highly creative people turn to various alternatives—drink, drugs, self-indulgent displacement activities, or compulsions. They may experience a lapse in ego defenses, such as, projection (blaming others), displacement (substituting a less rewarding activity), repression (sealing off and hiding desires and problems from the self), dissociation (splitting off the emotions from the reality of experience). Any of these if overtaxed may result in neurosis or psychosis. Whereas it is good for most people to have recreational activities and hobbies, for the artist or "driven" creative person, any activity, no matter how benign, which is used to relieve the anxiety and frustration of the drive-state without allowing the energy to be discharged in the creative process can lead to more denial and illness.

When we are deprived of food, water, oxygen, it is easy to see the basic physiological response appropriate to the drive-state because these are elements of survival. Not so easy to recognize are the struggles of the mind when psychological life and balance are threatened. The evidence becomes more obvious when the unmanageable life reveals the stress of the unrelenting build-up of drive energy. What is being proposed in this book is that the drive to create is as observable and operative in the human being as the more apparent drives for food, sex, comfort, emotional stability, or any other need related to health and well-being.

On the other hand, suppose the creative person, the artist, does try to weld his drive for creative expression to the demands of the society in which he lives. If he can do this and remain faithful to the direction and development of his own psyche, well and good, but in most instances this is not realistic. Fortunately or unfortunately, however you might think about it, the artist's function as interpreter of his age places him ahead rather than in step with or behind the society as a whole.

In the United States today the style of living required to promote the public successes in most areas of the arts runs counter to the creative living which enhanced and supplemented the creative work in the first place. An almost "heads you win, tails I lose" predicament prevails. Once a person attains recognition for his work, he or she is not only expected to outdo himself or herself at every turn of the calendar, but the recognized artist must also become involved in the treadmill of promotion of his own work. Intense and agonizing psychic frustration and dissociation from his creative self is inevitable.

The problems facing the artist who must work under the strain of an intensive and internal psychological drive to create become even more circular and devastating, because every activity which keeps the artist or "driven" creative person from meaningful work doubles the intensity of his drive state, making avenues of escape more and more attractive. Then, the whole gamut of drug abuse, sex addiction, alcohol abuse, psychopathology, or suicide simply reinforce society's view that creative people are inherently unstable.

The economics of the situation cannot be denied, since they are inevitable facts of life just as real as the creative drive. We have generated a much-touted "consumer society"—insatiable, but bored by its own consumption. Things take precedence over ideas and emotions. In fact we find most of our ideas and emotions being pegged and analyzed and then used to commercially promote products. That "average" person so dear to consumer-oriented research is more likely to see his identity tied to a house, a section of town, a type of automobile, or a corporate image. It isn't women alone these days who must complain with Sylvia Plath's "Amnesiac":

> Name, house, car keys,
>
> The little toy wife—
> Erased, sigh, sigh.
> Four babies and a cocker!

In effect, the small businessman (which most artists are forced to be), the private entrepreneur, is discouraged from enterprise by the impossible competition with mega-corporations. Even our private farmers are faced with the vast enterprising of agribusiness which owns everything from feed to marketplace and can more easily control and streamline production for lower costs and higher profits.

In the professions requiring higher education, people are often labeled by those degrees and expected to restrict thinking and opinions to codified areas selected during advanced studies. This is one of the major problems among our creative researchers, especially scientists—not a lack of communication, but a discouragement of inter-disciplinary dialogue and cross-fertilization of projects. Even the method of funding large grants to institutions officially inhibits the creative and generative interaction of researchers in different areas.

And the artist is at the bottom of the barrel. His choices are even more limited and prohibitive. Unless he inherits wealth, the individual workman of art in this day must find himself or herself denying the consumer-oriented lifestyle in order to "afford" the time and materials required to pursue the work of art. It was Virginia Woolf who in the thirties complained bitterly about the economic hardships facing young artists, or those who submitted emotionally or physically to the demands of consumerism. Always particularly concerned with the problems of the woman artist, she made this observation in her essay *A Room of One's Own*:

> It may seem a brutal thing to say, and it is a sad thing to say: but, as a matter of hard fact, the theory that poetical genius bloweth where it listeth, and equally in poor and rich, holds little truth. . . . It is—however dishonouring to us as a nation—certain that, by some fault in our commonwealth, the poor poet has not in these days, nor has had for two hundred years, a dog's chance. (111)

As a steady stream of magazine and newsletter articles insist on reminding us, the modern poet, fiction writer, or visual artist—the problems of the performer have been documented and made sacrosanct—is only rarely able to support himself or herself without supplementary employment. So add to the artist's "towering inferno" of emotional liabilities the psychological and emotional toll of such stringent economic facts of life. Another whole realm of problems with destructive possibilities superimposes itself on the already much-assailed individuality of the artist.

If he or she accepts a lower standard of living or a hand-to-mouth existence, then by the very nature of this society and the economic principles which govern our effective membership in the society, the working artist reduces his actual power to deal adequately with contemporary life to a critical level. There are no economic advantages to being on the bottom. Faced with fewer tax breaks, no health insurance benefits, no cost of living increments, the artist pays the required price of competitive economic functioning. He or she must seek out the limited funds available through endowments and prizes, most of which are shrinking every year and which are usually reserved for those who have already attained national recognition. But, even when eligible for financial assistance, the artist in our society may lack access to information essential to application for such funds or lack ability to apply.

Frank Barron gives this example in the preface to his book *Creativity and Psychological Health*:

> Not long ago I was walking down a street in Berkeley and I met another subject in the study of writers, a poet also, who was making a living by typing manuscripts for undergraduates. He happened to be flat broke at the time and

needed carfare back to San Francisco, so he asked me to lend him a dollar. I started to do so, but he interrupted to say that he had another idea: he could sell me a copy of one of his books of poetry, which he happened to have with him. "Oh, yes," I said, "do that," so he sold me the book, for the filthy dollar I had taken from the pockets of the steel workers, and he drew a picture in the book besides, and inscribed his name and the date there. Poetry is its own reward, but we could wish that all those whose task and pleasure it is to create beauty in the world, and who can do so if the world will only give their time back to them, might have leave to do for an ordinary living wage the work their heart desires. (x)

Considering the complicating social, psycho-emotional, and economic forces at work on the individual artist, it seems evident that an inherent drive for creative expression, more intense and personal, more integral to the ability of the personality to survive, is involved in the active production of art or the creative power generated by artists in any society. The maddening craze for artistic growth and creative perfection cannot be understood or tolerated by the effete or the insensitive. When the artist breaks down or destroys himself or herself, it is at least in part a demonstration that the things of living have exhausted his resources, diminished his strength, and broken his spirit to the point that he is robbed of his art— his life has lost the focus of his work.

Works Cited

Barron, Frank. *Creativity and Psychological Health*. Princeton, NJ: D. Van Nostrand, 1963.

Maddi, Salvatore R. "The Strenuousness of the Creative Life." *Perspectives in Creativity* (Ed. Irving A. Taylor & J.W. Getzels). Chicago: Aldine, 1975.

Plath, Sylvia. "Amnesiac." *Winter Trees*. New York: Harper & Row, 1965.

Woolf, Virginia. *A Room of One's Own*. New York: Harcourt, Brace & World, 1929, 1957 by Leonard Woolf.

Works Consulted

Drives, Affects, Behavior. Vol. 2 (Ed. Max Schur, M.D.). New York: Int'l. UP, 1965.

Sherif, Muzafer and Carolyn Sherif. *Social Psychology*. New York: Harper & Row, 1969.

Social Psychiatry. Vol. 1 (Ed. Ari Kiev, M.D.). New York: Science House, 1969.

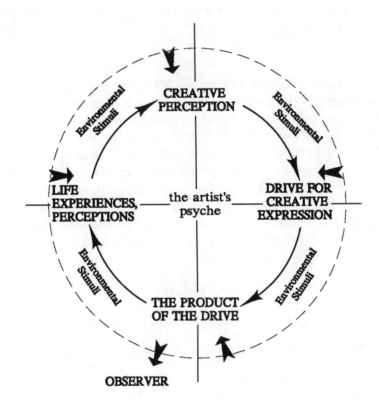

Figure 2: THE INDIVIDUATION OF THE CREATIVE PROCESS

Chapter Four
The Cutting Edge and Creative Drive

The fact remains that the processes of illness block and corrupt the creative act. Moreover, just as illness produces neurotic symptoms which becloud the very conflicts which they aim to express, so the creative product of science and the arts can mask and disguise the very processes of the illness to the clarification and expression of which modern art, literature, music, and science are currently if unwittingly dedicated. This indeed is the paradoxical dilemma of the precise moment of culture through which we are passing.

—*Lawrence Kubie, M.D.*, Neurotic Distortion
of the Creative Process

Modern art, music, theatre, dance, and literature are filled with emotional outburst, lament, violence, and insanity. We are caught culturally in a social crucible unique to our time in history. Why?

During the Victorian era sex was a taboo subject and the society was involved in a kind of repression and social formality unknown and almost inconceivable today. Basking in the teachings of Freud and his followers, we in the twentieth century are learning to release our sexual fears and inhibitions. Our "how-to" books on sexual comfort and release have expanded our knowledge to a level which is boggling to consciousness, and still the volumes continue to pour from the presses. Media of all forms feature talk shows, call-in programs; phone networks promote sexual connecting. But even more dangerous to our common consciousness has been the violent swing of the pendulum in the other direction. In the rush to release all our pent-up sexual repressions we have closeted the dank opposite of sex—death.

In the process of freeing our minds from one set of prohibitions we have rigidly set up new ones; death and disease, the process of dying, these have become "dirty" in the modern mind. Sex and death sit logically at the opposite poles of this strange medium we call life. Sex is the energy of creation/construction; death is the force of destruction/inertia. A rabid denial on one end sends the pendulum crashing madly toward the other extreme; if we wildly embrace the perception and exploration of one, the other will hang around the fringes as a shadow hinges on the brilliance of the sun.

Freud perceived this state of the psyche when he willed us a death instinct as certain as his well-touted pleasure principle. And today we are embedded in some stage of a mental epidemic that is as incredible a denial of the human condition as were the sexual taboos of our grandparents and great-grandparents. Evidence of what I am saying can be gathered on every hand.

The "beautiful people" we see on television and their euphemisms have wrapped our lives in the cellophane of unreality which denies that death is a partner to birth, that life is not a succession of laundry problems easily resolved by buying the right bleach, that people do suffer the irreversible effects of aging, and that disease and physical handicap are very real parts of many people's lives.

Our elderly are banished to "homes" where they can "rest" and where we can isolate the reality of their disease or decline to death. Even the mortuary is now a funeral "home," and instead of the family member being buried from the living room or the church, he or she is removed to the funeral parlor where the reality of death can only momentarily be inflicted upon his friends and relatives. Our denials of the facts of death and dying are as real as the Victorian denials of the facts of sex and birth. Our use of metaphor in this way removes us from the realities of existence.

Because modern man is faced with the possibility of irrational and unpredictable death on every hand, he has turned almost hopelessly to his intellect in order to deal with the overwhelming emotional content connected with his personal sense of vulnerability. For example, far from winning a true sense of mastery over the chaotic conditions of our twentieth century, the existentialists have given us hardly an escape hatch through which to defend the viciously assailed modern consciousness. Sooner or later the energy required to maintain the denial or shore up the intellectualizations will not be available, will drain the common psyche to the point that a new, hopefully more healthy consciousness must intervene. But, it is a long, hard emotional trek back toward a more balanced public mental health. The therapeutic process is never an easy one. It requires honesty, especially self-honesty. In the state of personal or collective denial, truth becomes a stranger and falsehood, a bedmate. The pain of growth may be necessary, but suffering is optional; the choice is ours.

On the one hand, hanging on the edge of nuclear disaster becomes a habit. On the other hand, we are also faced each day with the personal threat of violent crime in our cities and neighborhoods. Accidents, diseases, terrorists seem to strike without any warning. These things interrupt what we, in our denial, believe is the "natural course of life." What has happened to our acceptance of reality? Viewing the impotence of modern man in the face of such horrors, what has changed is our poor power to deal with our emotional involvement in the process. Our energies are being drained; our health is suffering; our minds are disturbed. We are a nation of neurotics, parceling out our lives in safe, well-packaged assumptions that run counter to the emotional trauma that really makes up our daily fare. And we are doing this instead of reaffirming the truths that have for eons guided faith, hope, and reason. As e.e. cummings asserted: ". . . love is the mystery-of-mysteries . . ." (110).

But, you might protest, aren't the recent books, lectures, and courses on death and dying evidence that the pendulum is already swinging back to a more moderate center? It seems to me that little of this has actually permeated the modern consciousness. Most of these efforts do not return death to its place among the mysteries of life where the more primitive part of the human psyche can deal with it through mystic rites. In some cases they do not augment expression of the personal emotions connected with our individual relationship to life and death. Some even explore clinically, isolate the "facts," and present death as a sterile event to be "studied" antiseptically.

At a time when medical science and research seem to promise a future in which death and disease will be conquered by technology, the imminent possibility of holocaust, some natural disaster, plane crash, insane gunman, or incurable disease like AIDS can seem especially frustrating. This is, probably as at no other time in history, a problem peculiar to the modern mind—more overwhelming than any ever faced. To deal with the emotional threat we may or may not feel on every hand making us personally vulnerable, we embrace a host of philosophies—nihilism, existentialism, communism, dadaism, "New Age," and others—in order to brook the tide and come to grips with the terms of existence.

Our controversies range from cryogenics to abortion, from euthanasia to the death penalty, but we consistently skirt the deeper psychological issue of why these things threaten us personally so much that we are willing to tie up enormous amounts of time, energy, and concentration of mental and economic powers to "solve" them as social problems. Is it possible, as I have suggested, that they aren't really social "problems" at all, but social "symptoms"?

Into this modern state of mental-emotional turmoil steps the artist, the creative person. This is why Dostoyevsky could say, "Beauty will save the world."

Art always intercepts us at the point of our most rigid denials and most frustrating emotions. It soothes as well as awakens. It mirrors ourselves, and we can either fantasize away what we see or take inventory of what is really there in the reflection. If the agonizing process of catharsis and acceptance is embraced we can return to ourselves more mentally whole and intricate, more mentally reconciled with our primitive "instincts." Art walks in tandem with religion. Art is a reflection of the reality of who we are; religion opens the door to a relationship that can restore us through ritual to our Creator. Both are a community experience—an expression of community. The isolation of modern man is another symptom of his malady of faithlessness.

By serving to reflect the state of man's existence, the artist is a conservator of sanity rather than part of any lunatic fringe as he or she may at some time appear. And in western civilization today more than ever before, the artist has also become a "priest." He or she goes into the sanctuary of the human mind, and the work he suffers through there serves as our common catharsis. The artist is not on the cutting edge of the mental milieu of his day, he *is* that cutting edge.

Here is the crux of another difficulty facing the creative artist living and working in our society, and in the West. The farther the collective concepts and attitudes of a society move away from reality, the more rigid will the public philosophy become. The society will tolerate fewer and fewer deviations from the ill-conceived "norm." The artist and generative thinker in such a situation cannot have his art or creative thought and the standards of the society as well; there will be a credibility gap that no amount of explanation can fill. The behavior of the artist will be based upon the fundamental truths from which he or she takes his art. The farther the society moves away from those realities or embraces the distortion and denial rather than seeking truth and healing through acknowledgment and catharsis, the worse it will be for the individual workman of art.

The Swiss psychiatrist Carl Jung noted this effect and for this reason refused to distinguish between "artistic inspiration" and "pathological invasion" (psychiatric disequilibrium) when asked to define each in his Tavistock Lecture Series of 1939 at the famous London clinic. He went on to remark:

> It is not an absolute increase in insanity that makes our asylums swell like monsters, it is the fact that we cannot stand abnormal people any more so there are apparently very many more crazy people than formerly. (38)

In a society that denies the inevitability of death why do you think so many artists are consumed with dying? A. Alvarez in his book *The Savage God* made the following assessment of the modern artist facing his subconscious work in a society without any substantial truce with death:

> This ultimately is the pressure forcing the artist into the role of scapegoat. In order to evoke a language of mourning which will release all those backed-up guilts and obscure hostilities he shares with his audience, he puts himself at risk and explores his own vulnerability. (237)

We forbid people to mourn and yet we are a nation of melancholics. Suicide strikes at the root of consciousness. Murder, war, violence are out of proportion to any other experience of life. Somehow in the midst of all this, we expect the artist to come to terms with not only his own existence, but ours as well. Is it any wonder that given all the problems of the creative lifestyle already discussed plus the added burden of acting not only as a mirror, but as priest and healer to Western man's ailing psyche, suicide is so common in our artists?

It was on this very basis that Virginia Woolf was chosen for this study as a "case in point." I believe that the recent revival of interest in her life and work is a reflection of her pivotal significance. She stepped out of the Victorian drawing room, but looking back over her shoulder at that society, as a modern, she showed us how we are different. In much of her work we can see where the denial of death is leading our society.

Following the thread of her life, poised as it was at the crossroads of the new era, we encounter not only drawing rooms and social conversations, but death, madness, and suicide. In her novels she splashes the canvas with broad strokes to bring her genius to bear on the problems at hand. In some of her essays she tries to reduce the facts of life and death to a size with which the mind can deal. In her essay "The Death of the Moth" she miniaturizes the mystery and permits us like children to stand around quietly, catching a peek at the truth, fluttering and tender in the palm of the artist's hand:

> As I looked at the dead moth, this minute wayside triumph of so great a force over so mean an antagonist filled me with wonder. Just as life had been strange a few minutes before, so death was now as strange and uncomplainingly composed. O yes, he seemed to say, death is stronger than I am. (6)

This consciousness of death was what both blinded and attracted Virginia Woolf as light attracts a moth. And at this level she was a modern person trying to assess the terms of existence. In an age which denies the suffering and vulnerability of the individual, which sends millions into wars and gas chambers, she cultivated her awareness of death. She attempted to reduce it to manageable terms and in so doing became a symbol of the modern person struggling against all odds to remain intact emotionally, psychologically, and spiritually.

In her novels Virginia Woolf reflects the viewpoint of the survivor in life who is at odds with his own survival. Her settings include grief, but her aim seems focused on catharsis, the survivor's stance. Did she consciously do this; was it her premeditated plan to convey it? I doubt it. Mesmerized as she was by her inner drive for creative expression, she was drawn magnetically as any artist is in any age to examine the source of the greatest despair and discomfort.

For example, through the mind of the old maid artist Lily in *To the Lighthouse* she throws a reflecting beam of this peculiar awareness the artist has. She catches Lily in the garden, off-guard. She is painting, and as she paints, she is thinking about the heroine of the book, Mrs. Ramsey, for whom Virginia's own mother was the prototype. Like her mother, Mrs. Ramsey had died young, leaving her family and her life seemingly incomplete. But Lily is distinctively a survivor, and it is from this perspective she looks out on events:

> Without saying a word, the only token of her errand a basket on her arm, she went off to the town, to the poor, to sit in some stuffy, little bedroom. Often and often Lily had seen her go silently in the midst of some game, some discussion with her basket on her arm, very upright. She had noted her return. She had thought, half laughing (she was so methodical with the teacups), half moved (her beauty took one's breath away), eyes that are closing in pain have looked on you. You have been with them there.
>
> And then Mrs. Ramsey would be annoyed because somebody was late, or the butter not fresh, or the teapot chipped. And all the time she was saying that the butter was not fresh one would be thinking of Greek temples, and how beauty had been with them there in that stuffy little room. She never talked of it—she went, punctually, directly. It was her instinct to go, an instinct like the swallows for the south, the artichokes for the sun, turning her infallibly to the human race, making her nest in its heart. (291-292)

In this way Virginia Woolf described her Victorian mother who lived among life's realities from the smallest (the spoiled butter, the chipped teapot) to the largest (the illnesses and deaths of her neighbors). But Lily is not a Victorian—she is a modern. As we follow her thoughts we realize that we have much more in common with her than with the incredible

Mrs. Ramsey. Lily is a survivor, living in a different age with a different perspective, and so—we discover—are we. Mrs. Ramsey with her basket on her arm is not real to us, but Lily's reaction *to* Mrs. Ramsey *is*:

> And this, like all instincts, was a little distressing to people who did not share it; to Mr. Carmichael perhaps, to herself certainly. Some notion was in both of them about the ineffectiveness of action, the supremacy of thought. Her going was a reproach to them, gave a different twist to the world, so that they were led to protest, seeing their own prepossessions disappear, and clutch at them vanishing. (292)

That the artist will be at conflict with the trends and consciousness of the society in which he lives is inevitable. The greater his or her drive to create—the drive to give tangible expression to the images of his mind, the more sensitive that artist will be to the emotional drains of his or her unique position. Virginia Woolf killed herself in 1941 in what became symbolically a one-person protest, a sacrifice unique to an age that embraces "the ineffectiveness of action, the supremacy of thought."

Across the English Channel a madman named Adolf Hitler had captured the thinking of an entire nation. And so on goes the "progress" of man, jerkily and uneven, but whether we realize it or not, on the spot where the artist or creative person stands today will be built the schools and institutions of tomorrow. The work of the artist in this age is peculiarly terrifying and personally devastating, and what about tomorrow?

Carson McCullers captured a glimpse of the creative society for us in her short story "A Tree. A Rock. A Cloud." The protagonist in the story makes his appeal to the sex-surfeited, dreary society of a sleazy all-night cafe, but he is speaking directly to a newspaper boy:

> The old man still held the collar of the boy's jacket; he was trembling and his face was earnest and bright and wild. "For six years now I have gone around by myself and built up my science. And now I am a master, son. I can love anything. No longer do I have to think about it even. I see a street full of people and a beautiful light comes in me. I watch a bird in the sky. Or meet a traveler on the road. Everything, son. And anybody. All strangers and all loved! Do you realize what a science like mine can mean?" (291)

Works Cited

Alvarez, A. *The Savage God: A Study of Suicide*. New York: Random House, 1972.

Jung, Carl G. *Analytical Psychology*. New York: World, 1953.

Kubie, Lawrence. *Neurotic Distortion of the Creative Process*. Lawrence, KS: U of Kansas P, 1958, 1961.

McCullers, Carson. "A Tree. A Rock. A Cloud." *A Pocket Book of Modern American Short Stories* (Ed. Phillip Van Doren Stern). New York: Washington Sq. P, 1943.
Woolf, Virginia. *The Death of the Moth and Other Essays*. New York: Harcourt, Brace & World, 1942, 1970 by Marjorie T. Parsons, Executrix.
Woolf, Virginia. *To the Lighthouse*. New York: Harcourt, Brace & World, 1927, 1955 by Leonard Woolf.

Works Consulted

Freud, Anna. *The Ego and the Mechanisms of Defense (The Writings of Anna Freud, Vol. II)*. New York: International UP, 1966.
Freud, Sigmund. *New Introductory Lectures on Psychoanalysis* (Trans. James Strachey). New York: W.W. Norton, 1965, 1964 by James Strachey.

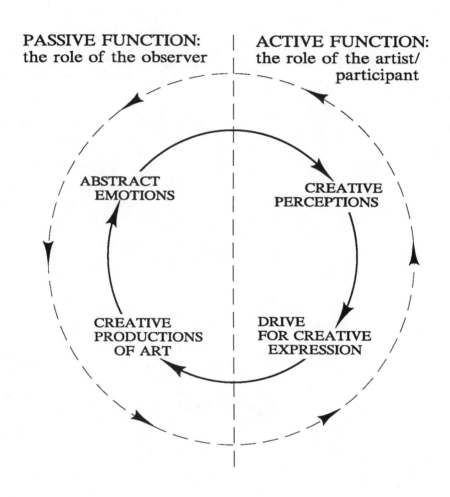

PASSIVE FUNCTION:
the role of the observer

ACTIVE FUNCTION:
the role of the artist/
participant

ABSTRACT
EMOTIONS

CREATIVE
PERCEPTIONS

CREATIVE
PRODUCTIONS
OF ART

DRIVE
FOR CREATIVE
EXPRESSION

Figure 3: THE WHEEL OF CREATIVE FUNCTIONS

Chapter Five
Why the Creative Lifestyle?

I know the bottom she says. I know
it with my great tap root:
It is what you fear.
I do not fear it: I have been there.

—*Sylvia Plath, "Elm"*

The personal life of the artist is non-essential to his art and this is why: his work propels his life, not his life his work. This is another substantial difference between the creative person "driven" to find some mode or medium of expression and others who are not. That his problems are intricately interwoven with the material of his art is a part of what this study of creative drive is addressing.

Beethoven's deafness, his penchant for young boys, or his insane biliousness tell us nothing about ourselves and why we respond to his music, so we must table them. When we gaze into the bright yellow colors of Van Gogh's "Cornfield Behind the Asylum at the Fall of the Day with a Reaper," we do not need to know that it was painted during a convalescence from a psychotic attack. Drinking, drugs, the psychological imbalances of whole generations of artists, recent and not so recent, should not really concern us.

The personal lives of artists may haunt, entertain, intrigue, or delight us, but they do not explain the artist or the work. The fact of the matter is that we ought not care about the physical or psychological problems of artists. What we need to care about is the confrontation of ourselves and our society in their work—the cathartic effect of the work on our psyches and the opportunities which the work provides for a new look at the transcendent truths that are not personally afflicted or culture-bound.

The world is replete with alcoholics, sex addicts, and all sorts of other disoriented, compulsive, or otherwise afflicted people, but only in those in whom we find a unique perception combined with an overriding drive to share the essence of the human experience do we find a potential workman of art or generative thinker. That the person with an overwhelming drive to create is more vulnerable externally than other people in society has already been discussed. Having cast aside the problems of conventional living and personal goals, he or she is captured by other more dangerous dilemmas.

To these environmental struggles is added still another more complex and internal factor which even if he could deny and avoid the consequences of the external milieu would still attack him because it is inherent in his physical and psychological make-up. From recent psychiatric and medical research and its implications, we find an interesting and compelling relationship between the mental balance and stability of the "driven" creative person and his or her actual productivity as measured in creative projects completed.

In the most real sense the creative work itself becomes the method through which the creative person attempts to find and maintain his inner psychological balance. Carl Jung explains in his autobiography how he discovered this process in himself. In *Memories, Dreams, Reflections*, Jung discusses a period in his life when as a successful psychiatrist nearing forty he became consumed by dreams and a psychic pressure which caused terrible disturbances in his emotional equilibrium. Finally, unable to find any memory or reason to explain the disturbing fantasies, he resigned himself to "simply do whatever occurs to me."

Strangely, he felt compelled to gather stones from the lakeside and shallow water of the shore he walked each day on the way to his office. With some relief he began to build cottages, a castle, and eventually a whole miniature village with these stones. He continued the project until everything was complete, but still his mind would not rest. Not knowing why, Jung felt that he must keep looking for stones. One day he happened upon a red stone which had been stream-polished, and instantly it occurred to him that this would be a perfect altar for the miniature church in his village. He hurried to his office and putting the "altar" in place, found his mind enormously relieved:

> This sort of thing has been consistent with me, and at any time in my later-life when I came up against a blank wall, I painted a picture or hewed stone. Each such experience proved to be a "rite d'entreé" for the ideas and works that followed hard upon it. Everything that I have written this year (1957) and last year, *The Undiscovered Self, Flying Saucers: A Modern Myth, A Psychological View of Conscience*, has grown out of the stone sculptures I did after my wife's death. The close of her life, the end, and what it made me realize, wrenched me violently out of myself. It cost me a great deal to regain my footing, and contact with stone helped me. (175)

From his own experience Jung began urging sculpture, painting, drawing, and even writing as a means by which a patient could objectify the troublesome contents of his own mind. At one point he defined the process as "a means of protecting the center of the personality from being drawn out and from being influenced from the outside" (175). In a similar way the creative person must sort through and select even if seemingly at random from the vast array of emotion-charged events in his or her life. The energy of the drive will be tapped to flow into constructive work while at the same time maintaining and protecting the creative person's center of being—a center of being which contrary to popular opinion may be fragile and vulnerable beyond any accessibly objective evaluation. It is usually a question of survival.

If this process of a creative outlet siphoning off energy from the emotional conflicts of the artist's life is interrupted or prevented, there is the very real and very great danger that he or she will merge with the rich production of the individual mind (subconscious) and be lost to reality completely. But this rarely happens, the mind struggles against it; the self strives for preservation and survival against all odds.

It is not the psyche of the artist or creative person that is fragile, but the delicate balance which is critical to his or her living and working in society. And to this we must add a final facet of the problem of his psychological inheritance. The emotional control essential to the well-balanced mind is tied to the sensitive maneuvering of the creative artist between work and fatigue. Like a complex system of checks and balances, the creative process guides the psyche. A program of rest, diet, and psychological support is in some instances not enough to help the artist escape the active functioning of his or her own imagination. When in desperation the creative person for release and escape turns to drugs or alcohol or suffers mental breakdown, he can expect no better than disgust, disdain, and rejection from the society which craves his or her successes. It is a grim picture indeed.

Given the obvious plight of the creative person in today's society, it is essential to explore through more intensive psychological, analytical, and medical as well as genetic research the implications of the drive to create. By examining recent innovations in medical and genetic research, which will be discussed in Chapters Nine, Thirteen, and Sixteen, and by reviewing several contemporary artists and the way their lives demonstrate the difficulties of the working artist and creative person in contemporary life, it may be possible to find new understanding of the creative process and the place, if there is one, we should give to the study of creative drive.

To both open and close the peculiar circle attempted in this discussion of the contemporary artist locked into a life and death struggle with the demands of his or her creative vision and the expectations of an insensate and cloyed society, I quote a paragraph from the closing pages of Virginia Woolf's novel *The Waves*. It is in a very real sense my dedication to the ideas included in this book. Here we have in a nutshell the plight of the contemporary workman in art as expressed by a superior artist:

> Better burn one's life out like Louis, desiring perfection; or like Rhoda leave us, flying past us, to the desert; or choose one out of millions and one only like Neville; better be like Susan and love and hate the heat of the sun or the frost-bitten grass; or be like Jinny, honest, an animal. All had their rapture; their common feeling with death; something that stood them in stead. Thus I visited each of my friends in turn, trying with fumbling fingers to prise open their locked caskets. I went from one to the other holding my sorrow—no, not my sorrow but the incomprehensible nature of this our life for their inspection. Some people go to priests; others to poetry; I to my friends, I to my own heart, I to seek among phrases and fragments something unbroken—I to whom there is not beauty enough in moon or yew tree; to whom the touch of one person with another is all, yet who cannot grasp even that, who am so imperfect, so weak, so unspeakably lonely. There I sat.(361)

Works Cited

Jung, C.G. *Memories, Dreams, Reflections* (Ed. Aniela Jaffé, Trans. Richard & Clara Winston). New York: Vintage Books, 1961, 1962, 1963 by Random House.

Plath, Sylvia. "Elm." *Ariel*. New York: Harper & Row, 1961.

Woolf, Virginia. *The Waves*. New York: Harcourt, Brace & World, 1931, 1959 by Leonard Woolf.

Works Consulted

Readings in Contemporary Psychology (Ed. Robert E. Lana, Ph.D., Ralph L. Rosnow, Ph.D.). New York: Holt, Rinehart and Winston, 1972.

PART II:
The Drive to Create—Vice and Virtue

Chapter Six
Historical Perspective on Mental Illness and Its Treatment

Volcanic passions raging with such destructive intolerance could not and cannot be the result of mere lack of knowledge. They indicate that some elemental force, some basic and blind human instinct must be touched by the very emergence of the problem of mental disease.

—Gregory Zilboorg, M.D.,
History of Medical Psychology

We are really not so different from our remote ancestors who hunted witches and attributed abnormal behavior or unusual events to demons. Much as in primeval days the act of suicide is still perceived as either an act of great courage or an act of cowardice. We cannot treat it in any way dispassionately. We still advise the neurotic or psychotic person to "pull himself together" as if his or her malady were a matter of his own volition. This irrational struggle against medical and psychiatric intervention has a long and tragic history. For the most part, it is a story of human carnage and destruction familiar to every student of modern psychology.

Probably the earliest form of treatment of the mentally ill person in primitive oriental cultures involved hypnotism. There is evidence that the shaman of certain Siberian, Chinese, and Malayan tribes used various forms of hypnotic suggestion to control insane people. However, in most parts of the ancient world sacrificial and ritual murder were more widely employed. The reasoning was simple: the gods in their rage designated the choice that would appease them by visiting a mental affliction on the person (Zilboorg 27-35).

For centuries the western world lived in an equally dark shadow which found its root in the Mosaic Law:

> A man also or a woman that hath a familiar spirit, or that is a wizard, shall surely be put to death; they shall stone them with stones; their blood shall be upon them. (Leviticus 20:27 KJV)

Under a liberal application of this law and an equally strict interpretation, hundreds of thousands of people were put to death. And one thing is certain—the mentally ill person rarely had an advocate who would plead his or her cause. Today the vestiges of fear and hostility linger on. In many political systems incarceration of "insane" dissidents is an unchallengeable and effective means of social control. And in many sectors of our own population the stigma which surrounds mental illness is as incapacitating as the presence of mental disease itself. An ancient Greek proverb expressed this rule of thumb: "If you want to kill a dog, call him mad."

The very euphemisms we use for mental illness—*madness*, *crazed*, or the slang term *crazy*—conjure up images of frothing mouths and delirious eyes. An icy chill creeps up the spine as we stare into empty and hollow sockets. And we continue adding euphemisms for mental illness to our repertoire of language and metaphor, hoping like our primitive ancestors to stave off the advance of disease by denying its true existence. We inaccurately but politely refer to someone's attack of "nerves" or their "nervous breakdown" or "collapse" or we say someone has gone "bananas."

As we expand our population on this earth and aggregate in more and more populated areas, our sensitivity to abnormality grows. The key to our thinking about mental problems is locked up in the box marked "control." We do not trust our reasonably sane and similar neighbors, much less the diverse or obviously abnormal. In fact, we do not even trust our own illogical whims.

Discussion groups, lecture series, books, and organizations have proliferated in the past few years to teach us the "art" of self-control, the technology of self-management. Around our modern consciousness in the United States today has grown up a veritable "self-help jungle." But there is still something about this problem of mental health which will not go away, which continues to knock at the back door of reason. At the same time we rush to pick up the latest book on the latest method of emotional self-help, we are furtively glancing over one shoulder fearful of arousing too much suspicion of our motives. We buy books about mental breakdowns, thumb the pages of magazines which feature the latest diet plan and some first-person account of mental disease, and we hand over millions of dollars a year to astrologers, cartomanciers, and other cosmic consultants hoping by the flurry of self-conscious activity to keep the wolf from the door. In the most real sense possible the dimly-lit cavern of the human mind—conscious and subconscious—has become the new frontier.

Taking the historical perspective we are able to see that the paradox of human consciousness is to fear and yet to be attracted to and fascinated by the unknown. What we attacked in terror just yesterday or fled from in disgust today, tomorrow will be placed under the microscope of empirical inquiry and dissected. The language which we first used superstitiously to control the invasion of mental illness becomes the point of divergence as we explore, experiment, and learn to understand.

The manic-depressive or bipolar disorder is the oldest- and best-known mental disorder in medical history. A critique of its history will broaden the foundation of our comprehension of this disorder. At the same time, a backward glance will help us look forward with more acute vision.

Early Greek physicians were responsible for the first empirical human observations and naturalistic explanations of mental illnesses, and their treatments of the mentally ill person, although physically inaccurate, were on the whole, sympathetic. Most Greek medical writings incorporate discussions of mental illness and its treatment with their expositions of other medical problems.

Hippocrates (460-377 B.C.), the Father of Modern Medicine, and Galen (A.D. 130-201), another well-known Greek physician, passed on to us in their writing only bare mention of their treatment of mental disease, but they did include accounts of these disorders. We suppose that their therapy centered on the "classical theory" of disease.

The "classical theory" maintained that the body was composed of four basic juices, the so-called "humors" or "vapors." These "humors" controlled body equilibrium. Blood, yellow bile, black bile, and phlegm corresponded to the four elementals, air, fire, earth, and water, with each humor balanced by two of four qualities: hot, moist, dry, cold. A tidy but somehow confusing system arose which limited medical thinking because of its incongruities until the eighteenth century. According to the classical theory of disease, one humor predominates in each of four temperaments: sanguine, choleric, melancholic, and phlegmatic. It doesn't take much of a student of language to comprehend what each of these terms represents regarding symptoms. All disease was supposed to result from an imbalance in the humors—the predominance of one, the failure of one, or an imperfect mixture.

The first analysis of melancholia, the earliest recorded mental affliction, was made on the basis of this theory. It was determined by Greek physicians that the disorder developed from an imbalance of black bile. To a certain extent the Greek diagnosis caught on, because today we still refer to an irascible, unpleasant person as bilious.

Obvious even to these early Greek physicians was the fact that their theory of disease simply did not cover all medical questions. Some time after 300 B.C., a number of factions and schools began to contest or enlarge upon the theory of humors. A newer concept attributed illness to changes in the solid components of the body. The most prominent school to come out of the change of thought was Methodism, which taught that all disease arose from abnormal constriction or relaxation of body tissues— "status strictus" or "status laxus."

From medical writing in the first centuries A.D., we have specific references to the treatment of melancholia and mania. It must be remembered that it was not until fairly recently that these two disorders have been seen as separate manifestations of the same disorder. In fact only a few people in medical history even saw them as causally linked. Certainly at the time of Greek and Roman medicine, the mainstream of professional thought was to treat mania as a completely different disease.

Around A.D. 30, Celsus, the Roman encyclopedist, contributed an entire chapter on mania and melancholia in his book *De Re Medica*. Later, around A.D. 100, Soranus of Ephesus, a methodist, wrote two volumes on acute and chronic disorders which included chapters on mania and on melancholia with descriptions of how each should be treated medically. Both of these works have survived in Latin, probably through the work of the translator and historian, Caelius Aurelianus (c. A.D. 500).

Soranus prescribed a serious attitude for the medical personnel dealing with an abnormally cheerful patient. He recommended a friendly, encouraging manner for use with the downcast. Soranus also referred to Plato's belief in two kinds of mania: one of divine origin and one from physical exertion. He blatantly dismissed the former cause as out of the realm of medical practice, but he defined the latter as "a disturbance of reason without fever" (Zilboorg 67-72).

Interestingly, Soranus reported that mania was most common in young men and rare in women and children. Dr. George Winokur of the University of Iowa College of Medicine wrote in a 1973 article for the *Journal of Nervous and Mental Diseases* that of the 6.8% of all people in the United States suffering from an affective disorder, women were represented almost twice as often as men. What social and cultural factors would promote an incidence of emotional and mental disorder in women double that figure in men? What social biases are operating today which were not in ancient Greece or how is it our society produces the opposite effect? Of course, some effect may be due to our methods of collecting the data, which differ a great deal from the methods of the early Greeks. The comparison problem is one which I recommend to my friends and colleagues in sociology (82-96).

Soranus thought that the primary causes of mania were overexertion, licentiousness, alcoholism, and a build-up of tensions produced in the absence of menstrual periods or in the case of males, bleeding from hemorrhoids. Other causes, the origins of which he could not discern, were simply noted as "latent." Perhaps this category of causality presaged the recent genetic studies of affective illness which seem to establish the presence of gene-specific factors.

For the treatment of mania Soranus recommended a moderately light, warm, airy room with high windows so that the patient could not jump out. If insufficient attendants was a problem, Soranus suggested the careful use of restraints to keep the patient as quiet as possible. Physical therapy for the manic person included oil poultices, blood-letting, leeches, and scarification. Passive exercises such as rocking or listening to dripping water were indicated for insomnia, along with massage and long walks. Soranus further urged strengthening the reasoning ability by asking questions or encouraging the reading of texts which contained false statements the patient was supposed to criticize.

Activities were recommended for recovering patients. For these people Soranus emphasized the importance of light reading, play acting in a drama contrary to the mental state suffered, and delivering speeches to friendly audiences. Intellectual pursuits which ranged from chess to travel were reserved for more educated patients. Soranus also sought reform in treatment methods used by some in that period by opposing any therapy which used confinement in darkness, starvation, continuous fettering, opium, excessive blood-letting, enemata, alcohol, whipping, music, or lovemaking.

We do not know what the recovery statistics were for Soranus's treatment methods, but on the whole he presented a total treatment approach that was humane, sympathetic, and reasonable. He apparently based his therapy on the assumption that mental illness was actually a physical disease and did so centuries before anyone would see connections between dietary deficiencies, genetic disorders, or metabolic disturbances with behavioral accompaniments. He identified mania as a disease of the head and melancholia as a disturbance of the esophagus. Although Soranus made no written references to prognosis, Aretaeus observed the frequency of relapses and the life-long course of the disease.

Celsus used many of the same treatments as Soranus and Aretaeus but was more ruthless in his use of cathartics, drugs, and blood-letting. He introduced a form of "psychotherapy," so-called for its shock quotient. Torture, whipping, sudden and brutal duckings were a few of the methods used to inflict pain on the person in the hope he would regain his senses (Zilboorg 72-78).

Primitive and unreliable but always empirical, the Greeks and Romans pursued their medicine in a rational and logical manner. But during the Middle Ages the light of medical science like most other knowledge flickered and all but went out. For over a thousand years mental illness was again identified with witchcraft, evil spirits, and the work of the devil. The medieval period produced whole psychic epidemics. What better example of mass psychoses do we have than the children's crusades, Jew-baiting, or the flagellationist movement.

In 1486 an infamous handbook appeared which would carry the barbarity of the sane through the next two and one-half centuries. The *Malleus Maleficarum* or "Witches' Hammer" was written by two Dominicans, Heinrich Kraemer and Johann Sprenger. This "textbook of the Inquisition" became the accepted philosophical authority of such noteworthy Renaissance physicians as Fernel, Paré, and Johannes Lange (Zilboorg 145-174).

The *Malleus Maleficarum* gave ecclesiastical and legal authority to the folklore of the Middle Ages; included within its pages are some of the actual cases brought before the councils for review. These recorded cases demonstrate that the number of mentally ill tried and convicted must have been enormous. The etiology of recognizable mental diseases is accurately presented, but the causes are ascribed to a sinister demonology. Women were the prime target of the investigations with the treatment of wizards and sorcerers brief by comparison. It was against women that the ascetic, medieval mind turned, seeing her as the source of all evil.

With a slight nod at the medical practitioners of the day, Kraemer and Sprenger assented to the possibility at least of natural diseases, but their criteria were vague and poorly defined. In the *Malleus* they referred to physical causes for bad humors in the blood or the stomach but summarily stated that if presence of these particular maladies were not discovered, then witchcraft was to be presumed the cause of whatever affliction was involved. If the disease was incurable, they claimed witchcraft; if a disease set in suddenly, witchcraft was certainly the agent; and any disease, fevered or not, accompanied by delusions or delirium was obviously a visitation of the devil and witchcraft was the suspected medium. Gregory Zilboorg in his history of this period quotes from the *Malleus Maleficarum* as to the origins of witchcraft:

> All witchcraft comes from carnal lust which is in women insatiable. See Proverbs XXX: "There are three things which are never satisfied, yea a fourth thing which says not, It is enough; that is, the mouth of the womb. Wherefore for the sake of fulfilling their lusts they consort even with devils."

> The devils have six ways of injuring humanity. And one is, to induce evil love in a man for a woman, or in a woman for a man. The second is to plant hatred or jealousy in anyone. The third is to bewitch them so that a man cannot perform the genital act with a woman, or conversely a woman with a man; or by various means to procure an abortion, as has been said before. The fourth is to cause some disease in any of the human organs. The fifth, to take away life. The sixth, to deprive them of reason. (159)

Parts of the *Malleus* are so full of sexual detail as to seem almost a handbook of sexual pathologies, according to Zilboorg's analysis. He recommends reading the *Malleus Maleficarum* as an instructive and enlightening book about social changes and cultural breakdowns. The book is anti-erotic and misogynous in the extreme, and Zilboorg calls it a "gruesome testimonial" to socially acceptable madness:

> The Old World seems to have risen against women. . . . Even after she had been tortured and broken in body and spirit, woman was not granted the privilege of facing the world in a direct way. The witch, stripped of her clothes, her wounds and marks of torture exposed, her head and genitals shaven so that no devil could conceal himself in her hair, would be led into court backwards so that her evil eyes might not rest on the judge and bewitch him.
>
> Never in the history of humanity was woman more systematically degraded. (161)

And here must be inserted one reassuring fact about humanity. Even out of such dark and terrible times as these days of the Inquisition represent, man seems to rise above himself, to gain some new foothold on civilization. The pendulum swings. A new era is born.

The horrors of the Inquisition were put to rest as the age of the individual moved onto the stage of history. In 1501 a man named Magnus Hundt coined the word "anthropologia" and wrote a book called *On the Nature of Man*. With the birth of rationalism, the search for natural causes for mental disease was renewed. The transition was not an easy one. A rationalistic search for causes did not immediately produce humane and sympathetic treatment for people who as a rule through the ages had been tortured and burned alive, but step by step, progress was made in providing for the needs of the mentally ill person.

In the mid-sixteenth century Paracelsus bravely published a book entitled *Diseases which Lead to a Loss of Reason*. Contrary to what clerics were still saying, he maintained that mental illnesses were not caused by evil spirits, but by natural diseases. And Paracelsus became the first physician to reorder and expand the original classical arrangement identified by the Greeks and Romans. He enlarged the three categories of mania, melancholia, and phrenitis to include four more specific disorders—epilepsy, "true insanity," St. Vitus dance, and suffocation intellectus (hysteria).

Paracelsus said that mania was a disturbance of reason and not of the senses. He described the disorder as consisting of excited and unreasonable behavior, agitation, and irritability. He recognized a tendency to relapse and said that the illness could be primary, occurring in otherwise healthy individuals, or it could be secondary to other diseases. A substance whose vapors rose to the brain from distillation near the diaphragm was the physical mechanism of the disease as Paracelsus saw it. He further advised that if a person's substance arose from the excreta, the patient would refuse food, would talk to himself, would be given to vomiting, and would ignore his surroundings. If, however, the substance were distilled in a patient's limbs, he would become cheerful, wild, excited. If the substance coagulated in the head, it might change to worms or the formation of ulcers. Paracelsus dramatically refuted the theory of four humors, seeing mania as a distortion of the "spiritus vitae" alone.

"Melancholici" was one of Paracelsus's five states of "true insanity," all five of which he described as permanent states related to the stars. He viewed the moon and stars as having influence over madness in ways similar to iron filings drawn from the earth by the sun. Although his concepts were a bit unusual, Paracelsus was adamant that natural causes, not the devil, were the source of mental illnesses.

Unfortunately Paracelsus did not maintain his adamancy consistently throughout his writing or over the entire period of his life. We are told that in a later book, *De Lunaticis*, he recommends that madness can be avoided by confession and that under certain circumstances burning the victim is warranted to avoid his being used by the devil. Paracelsus could not totally resist the social milieu or completely reject the psychological climate of his age. He did support the opponents of the *Malleus*, although later he confounded the cause-and-effect theory which he had so valorously proposed (Zilboorg 195-200).

Other sixteenth-century thinkers such as Montaigne, Francis Bacon, Erasmus, Levinus Lemnius, and others brought the individual more and more to the center of things. Emphasis shifted toward the social, political, and economic responsibilities of each person in the society. A rational and logical approach to man and his environment slowly but surely buried the Inquisitor and his ruthless court. The last witch was put to death in Germany in 1775 and the last witch killed in Europe died in Switzerland in 1782.

One of the greatest contributors to psychiatric progress was Johann Weyer. A man of methodical, scientific thought, at the age of seventeen he began studying under Cornelia Agrippa, the famous Renaissance physician, lawyer, and theologian. It was through Agrippa without doubt that he became dedicated to scholarship and humanitarian reform.

Weyer was very different in temperament from the fiery and irascible man who was his mentor for three years. But he became the epitome of a new sort of physician, the modest instigator of a revolution in medical thought. Weyer combined the best of empirical observation with the conscientious application of new methods to his medical practice.

It was Johann Weyer who contributed to medicine its first description of scurvy, quartan fever, and hydropsy, and invented the speculum for vaginal examination. But his most profound interest lay in the area of mental disease. From 1562 until his death in 1588, he wrote and published several monumental works on medico-psychological problems as well as several small treatises on disease. His books directly confronted the demonology of the Inquisition.

In one of his books, *De Praestigiis Daemonum*, Weyer uses his unique ability for keen logic and irrefutable scholarship to challenge the religious and ecclesiastical hierarchy, demanding that witches should be turned over to physicians for treatment and that only devilish criminals be punished. In a methodical, systematic way he reviewed all the historical references to witches and witchcraft, building his case toward one startling conclusion: witches are mentally sick and the monks who torture them are the real criminals.

After attacking the superstitions of the day, the book turns to a scholarly refutation of the *Malleus*, citing mistranslations and misinterpretations of the Bible with a dry humor. Weyer states, for example, that the Hebrew word *khasaph* does not mean sorcerer, but it is nearer the Greek *pharmakos* which is a person who uses medicaments or poisons unwisely or with criminal intent. He then proceeds to examine the widely-used drugs of the period which produced stupor or delirium. Carefully Weyer constructs a complete picture of drug after-effects, the influences of which resembled "the crimes and possessions" of people convicted by the Inquisition. Some of the drugs identified are familiar to us: belladonna (atropine), opium, hyoscyamus, and hashish.

Johann Weyer was the first practitioner of medicine to describe the role of the physician as psychotherapist, stressing the sanity of calling the physician rather than the executioner in cases of stupor or possession. One by one Weyer scrutinized clinical problems very similar to the problems seen by psychiatrists today. He included descriptions of schizo-affective disorders, obsessive-compulsive neurosis, paranoia, mania, and melancholia. Although Weyer left no comprehensive theory or dogma to explain his philosophy of treatment in mental illnesses, he did push the problems of psychopathology back squarely into the path of the medical practitioner, separating at least in his own mind the religious and legal questions from the basic medical need of the mentally ill person.

The stand taken by Johann Weyer was a revolutionary one, but with the exception of a handful of men with similar ideas, his writings were held in contempt for over a century. In fact, the practical problems of mental illness were for most of the seventeenth and eighteenth centuries simply removed from public concern and social intervention. The statement made by Inspector-General Jean Colombier in 1785 about conditions in French hospitals is typical of the kind of treatment provided during these two centuries:

> Thousands of lunatics are locked up in prisons without anyone even thinking of administering the slightest remedy. The half-mad are mingled with those who are totally deranged, those who rage with those who are quiet; some are in chains, while others are free in their prison. Finally, unless nature comes to their aid by curing them, the duration of their misery is life-long, for unfortunately the illness does not improve but only grows worse. (Zilboorg 316)

The pockets of advancement which did intersperse the latter part of this period hardly touched the mass of insane people. Shock therapy became the new method of medical intervention during the eighteenth century. Charles Darwin's grandfather, Erasmus Darwin, was a physician who invented the rotating chair which spun the insane person around until blood oozed from the mouth, ears and nose. Successful cures were for years attributed to this treatment as well as to a contemporary method of dunking the person in ice water. Castration and starvation were also used as well as drugs—datura, camphor, and digitalis. Textbooks of the period included sections on magnetic cures and the introduction of crude forms of electric shock.

Into this melee of medical confusion stepped several important innovators: Pussin, his student Pinel, and Pinel's student Esquirol. Pinel was already interested in the problems of insanity when he was made Professor of Hygiene and Internal Medicine at the new School of Medicine in Paris in 1794. In 1801 he published a treatise which was later hailed as the first textbook of modern psychiatry called *Traite Medico-Philosophique sur l'Alienation Mentale* or more simply *Traite de la Manie*.

Pinel's stated purpose for the book was to observe the facts of mental disease and bring order to the chaos of treatment methodologies. Taking up the matter of causation first, Pinel said that heredity was the primary cause and that harmful environmental factors in education and society provided secondary causes. He identified a tertiary cause as an irregular way of life; a fourth cause cited was the influence of spasmodic passions (fright, rage); fifth was the influence of enervating and oppressive passions (grief, hate, fear, remorse). As a sixth cause Pinel saw an inherent danger in happier passions which could lead to mania, as opposed to the melancholic constitution as a seventh cause. The eighth and last category of causality listed by Pinel was a catch-all placement for physiological factors such as alcoholism, amenorrhoea, non-bleeding hemorrhoids, fever, peurperium, and head injuries.

Pinel gave a thorough and careful description of the symptomology of mania, melancholia, dementia, idiocy, and hypochondriasis. In his analysis of head injuries he even noted the presence of conditions which today we know as aphasia and alexia. He felt that the basis of all mental illness was found primarily in the effect on the emotions. His concept of mania covered virtually all the agitated states of mind, but he identified the cause as a disturbance of the nervous ganglia in the abdominal cavity. This was a more or less updated version of Plato's concept that mania was somehow connected to stomach problems. Pinel did see mania as a self-limiting disorder. Most of the categories developed by Pinel are for the most part symptomatic states rather than a delineation of the disease. He lumped together schizophrenia and hypomania, including under "melancholia" all types of depressions, paranoia, neuroses, and general paresis. "Dementia" was the category Pinel used to include such disparate conditions as severe schizophrenic states and debilitating paresis as well as the phobic states seen in much milder neuroses.

The major importance of Pinel's work was his use of the hospital as a therapeutic tool. He proposed and enforced significant changes in hospital organization and administration, allowing the segregation of patients with various disorders. He added a convalescent section to the hospital for recovering patients in which there were workshops and more freedom for self-determination. Pinel was the first to abolish the use of chains, and his use of strait jackets and other restraints was restricted to short-term bases for criminally violent patients only.

Pinel's ideas were incredibly daring and innovative, especially in the light of public opinion in the early part of the nineteenth century. He felt that even the mental attitude of idiots would improve if they had something to do, so he introduced all sorts of crafts and handwork for them. Feeling much as the Greeks that too much emotional stimulation was not wise for the disturbed person, Pinel restricted religious services or observances which might tax his patients. He stressed the importance of physical exercise to relieve tension and moderate the insomnia of many illnesses. Some sort of mechanical work was provided for all patients. No one was starved and food was distributed fairly, not as reward for inaction. Probably the most startling discovery made by Pinel was that recovered patients made excellent nurses for the insane because they could treat the worst cases with firmness but with the sensitivity that comes from personal experience (Zilboorg 319-44).

Both Pinel and Esquirol believed in early separation of the patient from his family and friends in order to relieve all the pressure inherent in social situations and to better control the progress of the disease. They developed the method of gradually returning the patient to society in order to lessen the emotional crisis of readjustment and to prevent relapses. In sharp contrast to other nineteenth-century practitioners, Pinel and Esquirol advocated using drugs sparingly and for only short periods of time. Camphor and opium were preferred for their sedative effects on very agitated or violent patients.

How effective were the methods employed by Pinel? A serious statistician, Pinel spent long hours trying to evaluate his procedures and revise the less effective means of promoting mental health. He found that mania was found primarily between the ages of puberty and forty-five and that the onset of melancholia was usually seen in the years between twenty and forty. This is roughly what clinicians still observe today. As for the success ratio, Pinel claims that 51% of his cases of mania were cured compared to 62% of the melancholic, 19% of the dementia cases, and no cures recorded with idiots. Surprisingly, he states that the average hospital stay in mania was only five and a half months and only six and a half months for melancholia. Out of 444 cures, Pinel saw only 71 relapses.

Especially appropriate to this study of creative drive is the observation made by this brilliant and innovative psychiatrist that mania and melancholia seemed to be much more prevalent in such professions as the arts and the clergy. He also noted certain critical times in the lives of artists and clergymen when they seemed more prone to develop manic and melancholic symptoms. Pinel called for a moral and ethical evaluation to determine the extent of emotional strain in these professions so that new attention could be given to education and reform. Based on his information Pinel felt that society placed inordinate demands on its artists and clergy and then censured them when their health broke down.

Esquirol continued the work of Pinel, becoming an influential lecturer and researcher in the field of psychiatry. Ferrus, another noteworthy student of Pinel, continued the work of hospital reform and spent most of his life building the concepts of work therapy.

It should be recalled here that the nineteenth century saw the birth of psychology as a valid research science. Wundt and his associates in Leipzig, Germany and other laboratories and schools around Europe established cerebral localization for the senses and developed the concepts of measurement of sensory stimulation through their research. Researchers began to see a biological basis for behavior in human beings.

Unfortunately, as often happens in the enthusiastic climate of new discoveries, the pendulum went too far. A hopeless acceptance of inheritable degeneration was applied to any disorder for which a clearly physiological problem could not be discovered. Popularization of the Darwinian theory of evolution led to a misinterpretation of psychiatric disease. A "mini" Dark Age of medical treatment for the insane emerged from the philosophical turmoil.

Benedict Morel perfected this "new philosophy" and in 1857 published his long explanation in a book, *Traité des Degenerescences Physiques, Intelletuelles et Morales de l'Eespece Humaine*. In the simplest terms he claimed that any deviations, mental, emotional, or physical, from the normal human type were degenerations transmissible by heredity and deteriorating progressively until extinction. He stated his "law of progressivity": the first generation of a degenerate family would be "nervous"; the second generation would be neurotic; the third, psychotic; and, the fourth would be idiots who would die out.

A vogue ensued coincidentally with the degenerative theory of mental illness that ascribed a relationship close to insanity to any extremes of human behavior, especially genius or criminal. Some defined genius as a neurosis and others saw genius as merely a form of degeneration. The folklore popular since Aristotle's time was revived and elevated to scientific stature. Criminals were regarded as congenital degenerates with a clinically recognizable physical appearance and accompanying social stigmata. People of unusual talents or abilities were suspected of madness or criminal intent. Deviance of any sort was observed superstitiously.

At this point as history seemed about ready to repeat itself and the horrors of the Inquisition be reinstated under scientific aegis, two major reforming forces stepped into the chaos of psychiatric medicine—Sigmund Freud and Mendellian genetics.

Today there are two major areas of scientific research in psychiatry. One area deals with genetic data seeking to identify genetically linked characteristics which can produce the biochemical dysfunctions seen in many mental disorders. Research is revealing the basic biochemistry of the brain, nervous system, and endocrine system and the part these play in health and disease. The other primary area of research is in the area of treatment modalities, especially in recovery from mental illness, alcoholism, and co-dependency. A new "systems approach" is allowing therapists to intervene and promote on a more sensitive, cognitive basis the healthier interaction of family members, recognizing that all who make up part of the family system have been affected by the disease. The community and family have become the center of our mental health programs because enough data has been collected and analyzed to prove that although there are hereditary aspects to most diseases, the environment and stress place critical burdens on the biochemical processes of the human body and mind. The medical and genetic research will be discussed and reviewed in Chapter Nine, and Part Four will address various new treatments and education programs that promote recovery and mental health for all who are touched by the problems of mental disease. In the next two chapters the attention of this discussion focuses on the artist, scientist, or other creative workman who labors under an intensive drive to create.

Knowledge is the only effective antidote to ignorance and superstition.

Works Cited

Winokur, M.D., George. "Types of Affective Disorders." *The Journal of Nervous and Mental Disease.* Vol. 156, 1973.
Zilboorg, M.D., Gregory. *A History of Medical Psychology.* New York: W.W. Norton, 1941.

Works Consulted

Ackerknecht, Erwin H. *A Short History of Psychiatry.* New York: Hafner, 1968.
Alexander, M.D., Franz G. and Sheldon T. Selesnick, M.D., *The History of Psychiatry: An Evaluation of Psychiatric Thought and Practice From Prehistoric Times to the Present.* New York: Harper & Row, 1966.
Rosen, George. *Madness in Society.* Chicago: UP Chicago, 1968.

Chapter Seven
Mental Illness and Creative Drive

In science such a moment of apparent illumination is never an ultimate act of faith, as it might be for the theologian or for the poet and artist. It is rather the starting point for an investigation; but it supplies the investigator both with a beckoning goal and a "vis-a-tergo" without which nothing new is ever discovered.

—*Lawrence Kubie, M.D.*, Neurotic Distortion
of the Creative Process

Psychiatry has come a long way in the ten years since this book first appeared. There have been two new diagnostic manuals since I used the *DSM II* in 1977 to describe and discuss mental disorders and their treatment. *DSM III* (*Diagnostic and Statistical Manual of Mental Disorders*) was published in 1980. In 1987, *DSM III-R* was issued to make a few adjustments for the major changes which had occurred in the *DSM III*.

In this chapter I will review the new ways of classifying and coordinate this discussion of creative drive with those changes. Then, in Chapter Eight I will return to my discussion of the creative drive as it is expressed in the lives of artists, especially writers and other generative thinkers. Chapter Nine will deal with the new breakthroughs in medical and genetic science which not only affirm the reality of gene-mapping for the bipolar (manic-depressive) and other affective disorders, but which also disclose the future genetic manipulation. Cloning and other alterations of genetic material within human individuals may be attempted in order to eliminate or modify the inheritance of the bipolar disorder or any genetically linked factors that may be significant in the development of a specific mental illness in the individual.

I look on the new approaches as hopeful. The *DSM III* has standardized and simplified the old psychoanalytic extrapolations of mental disease by placing diagnosis along five major axes of clinical evaluation. The use of the multiaxial classification system for mental disorders grew out of the 1967 World Health Organization seminar in Paris, which addressed the mental disorders of children. The evaluation was to be noted on three axes—clinical syndrome, intellectual level, and etiological factors. Another seminar two years later in Washington yielded still another axis in order to deal with social and cultural factors in diagnosis. Most of the changes which led to the changes in the American Psychiatric Association's manual were made to coincide with the International Classification of Diseases, Clinical Modification, 9th edition, known as ICD-9-CM, of the World Health Organization (406-7).

> The International Classification of Diseases (ICD) is an essential tool for the collection and dissemination of comparable mortality and morbidity data throughout the world. Mental disorders have been assigned an increasingly prominent place in the ICD; and the proposals for their classification in the 9th Revision, which became effective as of 1 January 1979, have been formulated on the basis of an extensive WHO program involving a series of seminars and consultation with leading mental health experts in many countries. (408)

This is a great step forward in helping psychiatrists assist recovery and is, I believe, a major breakthrough along with the "systems approach" in family therapy, recovery groups specific to various disorders, and the 12-Step programs which have mushroomed from the 54 years of success by Alcoholics Anonymous in the treatment of the otherwise hopeless disorder of Alcoholism or Jellinek's disease. The multiaxial classification makes certain that diagnosis includes not only the traditional types of disorders which may have caused the individual to come for help or to be referred by some attending physician or agency, but it also surveys aspects of the person's environment and other areas of functioning that might have been overlooked in the past (23).

In psychiatry there is a basic dichotomy underlying any discussion of mental illness: a person may be said to be suffering from a neurotic disorder or a psychotic one. The neurotic person is out of focus intellectually and at odds with himself emotionally, but he is able to function in day to day living. He works, raises a family, attends political meetings, endures economic ups and downs, pursues hobbies, and follows whatever other interests he or she may have; but, for the most part, the neurotic person sees his or her life as basically unrewarding and sees himself as not fully able to cope with the daily pressures he must face at work, at home, or even at the bowling alley or on the tennis court with his friends. Every person is potentially neurotic depending upon the circumstances in which he or she finds himself or herself.

Behavior that is rewarding and acceptable for a member of an Australian aborigine tribe would be considered neurotic if displayed by a Manhattan businessman or woman. This fact is the basis of the well-known concept of "culture shock." "I" may be confident of who "I" am, but most of my behavior including my patterns of thought has been learned through a complex process of interaction with my environment. My relationships with other people, especially people I consider significant to me personally, have taught me ways of responding, reacting, and thinking which are characteristic more or less of my culture, however broad or narrow my concepts of that "culture" may be. In fact, the more tied I am to my culture and the more narrow my concept of that culture, the more likely it is that if I am placed in a community or in a situation very different from my accustomed milieu where my actions do not elicit familiar responses, I will appear neurotic. I could even become neurotic to the point that when I return to my own "home" environment, I will have trouble readjusting.

From this brief discussion you can see, I hope, that a neurotic disorder is a problem involving how we relate to our environment, a matter of personal and social maladjustment. However, if people with whom I have lived all my life and who love and respect me and for whom I reciprocate love and respect, see an abrupt change in my behavior; if I no longer respond as they are used to; if they find it impossible to communicate with me or do not understand my attempts to communicate with them; if my behavior is erratic and unpredictable or if I refuse to move or eat or respond; then I will be said to be "out of touch" with reality. A person who is psychotic is not in touch with the reality of who he or she is or where he or she is.

Neurotic people are painfully aware of their maladjustment, and the awareness itself, may become a matter of consternation. Neurotic people are able to communicate their discomfort and often do. Psychotic people, on the other hand, may or may not be aware of their maladjustment, but they insist on believing, even when presented proof to the contrary, in their own internal distortions of reality. Facts and logic do not coincide for people who are "out of touch" with reality. Their perception of the world around them is grossly distorted, but the crux of their illness is that they believe that the distortion is true. Because of this belief, all of thier actions will proceed from a logic which is based on false premises, and the behavior when viewed by those outside their internal system of thought will have no apparent reason or rationale.

The term *neurotic disorder* thus refers to a mental disorder in which the predominant disturbance is a symptom or group of symptoms that is distressing to the individual and is recognized by him or her as unacceptable and alien (ego-dystonic); reality testing is grossly intact; behavior does not actively violate gross social norms (although functioning may be markedly impaired); the dis-

> turbance is relatively enduring or recurrent without treatment and is not limited to a transitory reaction to stressors; and there is no demonstrable organic etiology or factor. (*DSM III* 9-10)

When psychiatrists, psychologists, social workers, nurses, and other mental health professionals discuss adult mental illness, they use the *DSM III* classifications to identify several major psychiatric disorders: organic, schizophrenic, affective, anxiety, somatoform, dissociative, psychosexual. Organic disorders include all forms of mental disorders in which there is actual damage to the physical systems of brain and/or nervous system, including substance-induced or substance abuse (addiction, alcoholism, cocaine, etc.). In earlier terminologies schizophrenic disorders were referred to under the general term, cognitive. This was because the major problems noted in the functioning of the individual had to do with the cognitive functions. With the new, better delineated symptomology, the cognitive dysfunction is only part of the diagnostic picture:

> Characteristic symptoms involving multiple psychological processes. Invariably there are characteristic disturbances in several of the following areas: content and form of thought, perception, affect, sense of self, volition, relationship to the external world, and psychomotor behavior. It should be noted that no single feature is invariably present or seen only in schizophrenia. (182)

Researchers are still trying to define and identify the biochemical processes associated with these disorders, but preliminary and follow-up programs of investigation have shown that the illnesses have in common some sort of brain chemistry imbalance or malfunction which affects the processing of stimuli to the point that resulting thought patterns and cognitive functions are impaired. Subsequently, after onset of the disease the person suffers deterioration from a previous level of functioning in such areas as work, social relations, and self-care. "Family and friends often observe that the person is 'not the same'" (181).

The age of onset of the schizophrenic disorders is usually childhood or early adulthood. For the most part it is life-long and although there may be periods of remission or improvement, the general level of functioning continues to deteriorate after each episode. Schizophrenia is not diagnosed unless symptoms have lasted at least six months (184-5).

Ordinary stimuli are somehow perceived differently by people suffering from schizophrenic disorders. There have been tremendous advances in metabolic research and the genetics of the schizophrenic disorders— family inheritance. But, the prognosis for most schizophrenias is still terribly poor. The wide range of variation in schizophrenic symptomology and the debilitating effect of a life-long battle with mental and conceptual distortion make these disorders difficult to diagnose and unbelievably hard to treat successfully. The clinical picture of a person exhibiting consistent patterns of schizophrenic behavior over a period of years is a person perpetually "out of step" at best and "out of touch" at worst with the environmental cues around him or her.

Stimulation from sound, sight, smell, taste, touch, and kinesthetic activity seems distorted sometimes even from very early childhood. The chemical processes in the brains of schizophrenic individuals are such, research seems to indicate, that perceptions of the world and other people are in flux and inconsistently changing. A terrible paranoid state often arises in conjunction with schizophrenic reactions because the person becomes convinced that a sinister plot is being waged against him by unknown people or forces who are manipulating the environmental cues. With intellectual elegance events and impressions may be linked in a cause-and-effect manner by the paranoid schizophrenic person in order to prove to others that the world is conspiring against him or her. These unpredictable mental alternations may push a person with a schizophrenic disorder to bizarre and often exotic behavior. For the most part the schizophrenic is harmless—almost defenseless in society. At times, however, as in any psychotic episode in which a person is out of touch with reality, a person suffering from a schizophrenic disorder may become violent. Often the origin of their violence comes from the paranoia or from some unknown fears. These are people who need extreme love, care, and protection for and from themselves.

At his or her most sane and healthy the schizophrenic person is typically seen by society as a peculiar person or as somewhat "defenseless"; often schizophrenics cannot seem to fit into any group in society. Many are exploited or taken advantage of. Most suffer from an awareness that their perceptions do not quite fit in with the world around them, but they are powerless to know what to do about it. Drugs are being used and some are being tried on experimental bases which help people suffering from these disorders to maintain enough ego strength and self-esteem to survive and function in society. Group therapy has helped, as well as self-help and family-help groups which continue to spring up in clinics and day hospitals across the country. New breakthroughs in diet therapy and other programs are helping promote better functioning among the sufferers of these disorders, but survival in society is still precarious. In fact, the life expectancy for schizophrenics is lower than for the general population.

Manifestations of schizophrenia usually appear early, by puberty or even during childhood or pre-school years. One major problem facing researchers dealing with metabolic descriptions of schizophrenic disorders is the carelessness in diagnosing these problems. With the new *DSM III-R* the criteria are more strict. Hospital admissions indicate that care and supportive therapy are in most cases a life-long proposition. In November 1973, the *Archives of General Psychiatry* published the report of a follow-up study of hospital admissions done by Drs. James Morrison, George Winokur, Raymond Crowe, and John Clancy, a group of psychiatrists whose original study had been dubbed "The Iowa 500."

From 1934 to 1944, these doctors, concerned about the random procedures for diagnosing admissions to the Iowa State Psychiatric Hospital, decided to apply scientific research methods in order to standardize criteria used for identifying schizophrenic or affective disorders. In the follow-up study twenty-five to thirty-five years later, they found out what had happened to the original 500 patients used for the study and how well their criteria seemed to apply on critical re-analysis. Based on their "very stringent research diagnostic criteria" which were discussed in a paper published in October 1972, in the *Archives*, the doctors diagnosed 200 schizophrenics and 325 affective disorders with 95% accuracy in chart agreement with attending physicians and 93% agreement with their original diagnosis in 1935. Thirty-five years later in 1970, "nearly all affective disorder patients appeared to recover." Only 8% of the schizophrenic patients had recovered (678-682).

For this reason a close examination of the schizophrenic disorders is not a part of this discussion. References to mental illness as it relates to the operation of a creative drive will refer almost exclusively to affective, anxiety, somatoform, dissociative, or other related disorders. by excluding them from this discussion, I am in no way implying that people afflicted with schizophrenic disorders are not creative or even that they do not have a drive for creative accomplishment. There is evidence to the contrary, especially where the visual arts are concerned. But the truth is that these disorders are socially very disabling and restrictive, and for people suffering from schizophrenic disease, existence in society is of primary importance and consumes most of their energy. They may be endowed with innate genius or inordinate creativity, but they are the world's truest victims being assailed in man's most sensitive and critical part—the patterns of thought. Hopefully modern research into brain chemistry and metabolism is near the brink of discovering advanced treatments for the schizophrenias which will release them to enjoy more independent functioning in society, but until more progress is made, on the whole, people suffering from these disorders have a tenuous grasp on the competencies of life.

Some clarification and explanation is necessary at this point concerning the metaphoric shifts from the *DSM III* to the *DSM III-R*, which is now the ruling manual for diagnostic criteria for mental health and related professionals. *DSM III* was widely acclaimed and even received well internationally because it increased validity and reliability of psychiatric diagnosis.

> In 1983 the American Psychiatric Association decided, for several reasons, to start work on revising *DSM III*. For one, data were emerging from new studies that were inconsistent with some of the diagnostic criteria. In addition, despite extensive field testing of the *DSM III* diagnostic criteria before their official adoption, experience with them since their publication had revealed, as expected, many instances in which the criteria were not entirely clear, were inconsistent across categories, or were even contradictory, plus the systematic descriptions of the various disorders needed to be reviewed for consistency, clarity, and conceptual accuracy, and revised when necessary.
>
> Also in 1983, the American Psychiatric Association was asked to contribute to the development of the mental disorders chapter of the tenth revision of the International Classification of Disease (ICD-10), which is expected to go into effect around 1992. (Introduction xvii)

The Introduction to *DSM III-R* goes on to say that publication of the revised DSM was originally planned to coincide with the publication of the ICD-10 in the early 90s, but because of the burgeoning literature from research (addressed in Chapter Nine of this book) and the new experience of handling the *DSM III*, still another revision, *DSM IV*, would be planned to coincide with the ICD-10.

Some of the major changes involve a shift in focus from etiological and pathological processes to a descriptive approach. Hopefully, this will allow greater freedom in research and at the same time more strict and careful use of specific criteria for diagnosis.

> *DSM-III-R* can be said to be "descriptive" in that the definitions of the disorders are generally limited to descriptions of the clinical features of the disorders. The characteristic features consist of easily identifiable behavioral signs or symptoms such as disorientation, mood disturbance, or psychomotor agitation, which requires a minimal amount of inference on the part of the observer. (xxiii)

Several diagnostic changes affect our study of creative drive and creativity as discussed in this book and must be noted here. The first is the exclusion in *DSM III-R* of the term *neurosis* or *neurotic disorder*. Instead *DSM III-R* breaks down the functioning of the person into evaluation and description: *mild, moderate, severe*. This seems an improvement over former classifications by introducing a more precise assessment of the level of impairment. It also eliminates the disagreements that arise from previously "fuzzy" or etiologically disparate approaches to non-psychotic states.

Another change is the deletion of the term *affective* in favor of the more appropriate and specific term *mood disorder*. Again, this change was designed to improve observation of the patient's behavior and to be more descriptive than anything else. Other disorders in which affect plays a major role are distinguished: anxiety disorders, somatoform disorders, dissociative disorders, sexual disorders.

DSM III-R also decries the use of labels, such as schizophrenic or manic-depressive or alcoholic, opting for the admittedly more cumbersome approach of "a person with Schizophrenia" or "a person with Alcohol Dependence." This is to ensure that two misconceptions about mental disorders are at least addressed and hopefully at some point eliminated:

> 1) that a classification of mental disorders classifies people, when actually what are being classified are disorders that people have.
> 2) that all people described as having the same mental disorder are alike in all important ways. (xxiii)

This is certainly a major step forward from the chains and abuse of the medieval-to-early twentieth-century asylums and most certainly from the psychosocial destruction of the human being by metaphoric ostracism and attack. How long it will take for this minuscule shift in distinction to take effect in actual social practice remains to be experienced. Certainly, hope is warranted. And for the artist, suffering under the extremes of social disapproval, perhaps this will relieve one of the strains on his or her creative drive and self-expression. Freedom is, when people are.

One setback which seems unfortunate but necessary in the wake of new research and broadening of psychosocial awareness of the courses of various syndromes and mental disorders is the disclaimer embedded in the *DSM III-R* that it is only descriptive and not authoritative (Cautionary Statement xxix).

Although descriptively comprehensive, *DSM III-R* is not a textbook, since it does not include information about theories of etiology, management, and treatment. It should also be noted that the *DSM III-R* classification of mental disorders does not attempt to classify disturbed dyadic, family, or other interpersonal relationships (xxv).

Now to discuss the social side of mental disease requires close attention to these changes in the *DSM III-R*, which in attempting to describe and define aberrant, pathological human disorders, does not set value judgments on dealing with those behaviors in society:

> It is to be understood that inclusion here, for clinical and research purposes, of a diagnostic category such as Pathological Gambling or Pedophilia (child sexual abuse) does not imply that the condition meets legal or other nonmedical criteria for what constitutes mental disease, mental disorder, or mental disability. The clinical and scientific considerations involved in categorization of these conditions as mental disorders may not be wholly relevant to legal judgments, for example, that take into account such issues as individual responsibility, disability determination, and competency. (Cautionary Statement xxv)

Sanity and insanity are purely legal terms used to indicate that a person is in such state of mind that he or she is or is not aware of the consequences of his or her actions. It involves the old question of knowledge of right and wrong. This is why there is so much disagreement between psychiatric testimony and the legal definitions used in court proceedings. Whatever our perspective or persuasion, it is evident that psychotic and disturbed people *are* either *out of touch* with the basic premises of their environment or painfully impaired or maladjusted.

Parenthetically it must be stated that regardless of the traditional connection between insanity and genius or between creativity and madness, the fact is psychotic people do not create works of art from their psychotic states. The two worlds—Art and Insanity—are mutually exclusive. They bear the same relationship to each other as sense and nonsense.

The range of disease which seems most prevalent among artists include those which were termed *affective* disorders and under the new classification are now called *mood* disorders. In these identifiable mental illnesses the mood or emotions, the emotional content of events, and the basic feeling functions of the psyche are disturbed. Included under this term are the depressive diseases and the bipolar disorders (manic-depressive disorders). What used to be described as *affective* disorders but which are now listed under the headings of anxiety, somatoform, sexual, or sleep disorders, include the phobic and obsessional states plus the various manifestations of those states, such as hysterical pain or conversion, sleep problems, sexual dysfunctions, and the various ways our minds attempt to process trauma and compensate or adjust to stress. All of these problems exhibit wide variation, fluctuation, or distortion in mood, emotional tone, and the processing of stimuli both inside and outside the body. Problems of erratic thought content or paranoid states involved with these disturbances are secondary to the primary problem of emotional responses which are out of kilter.

> Mood refers to a prolonged emotion that colors the whole psychic life; it generally involves either depression or elation. (*DSM III-R* 213)

In Chapter Thirteen in connection with the study of Virginia Woolf and her illness, there is a discussion in more detail about the manifestations of the depressive disorders and the etiology of the manic-depressive disorder, now designated bipolar disorder. Before describing in depth the findings of the research scientists, it will help to view the range of disorders included in this discussion. The most genetically pristine descriptions have been for the bipolar disorder, but other genetic effects and possible means of transmission have been described for many other psychiatric illnesses. There has even been research into the possibility of a genetic link in families where suicide is prevalent. The old *Nature vs. Nurture* debate is merging into a *Nature interacting with Nurture* systemic-correlations calculation problem.

Depression is the common cold of mental illnesses experienced by most people during their lifetimes at some time or another and to one degree or another. It is only considered a pathological condition when the course of the disorder seriously affects, interferes with, or disrupts a person's normal day to day functioning in society, or if its episodic nature seems more internally controlled than related to external factors such as death, divorce, or some other significant loss. If the internal factors seem more important or the person also has extreme highs or periods of elation which also interfere with normal living, then psychiatrists identify the illness as bipolar disorder (manic-depressive disorder). The experiences of mania are much more rare than any other mental illness and cannot be explained from any environmental frame of reference; the wild range of emotion must be seen as an outward display of some internal physiological disequilibrium.

Phobias are morbid fears associated with morbid anxiety. Obsessions are preoccupations of thought which can be traumatic past experiences or memories or evidence of certain repressed emotions. Obsessional states are fraught with all sorts of affective responses including the most persistent and observable behavior anxiety. Phobias, however, are specific to certain stimuli or more often, stimulus. The singular response is fear. We are all familiar with the more common phobias: agoraphobia, claustrophobia, acrophobia—fear of open spaces, closed spaces, high places. In each of these escape is seen as difficult or embarrassing and the perception of danger is intensified to alarm and panic. The behavior includes shortness of breath or smothering sensations, dizziness, unsteady feelings, or faintness, or choking, palpitations, accelerated heart rate, trembling, shaking, sweating, nausea or abdominal distress, numbness or hot flashes, or chills, chest pains or discomfort, fear of dying or going crazy or being out of control during the attack. The Panic Disorders including those associated with Agoraphobia or other phobias usually occur in association with depression. The *DSM III-R* uses the criteria for diagnosis that either four attacks have occurred within a four-week period or after one or more attacks, fear that another attack would occur persisted for at least a month (235-245).

Obsessions on the other hand pertain more to ideas or emotional impulses which may or may not be attached or attributable to any specific cause but which persist in the individual's mind and cannot be gotten rid of by any conscious process. Often *rituals* are used in order to subconsciously *control* the obsessive thoughts or emotions. These ritual actions are denoted compulsions which seem to relieve some of the anxiety of the obsessive state of mind. Usually the ritual or repetitive behavior is not connected in a realistic fashion with the dreaded event or obsessive thought that it is supposed to control. Often in the milder cases, the person recognizes the excessive or unreasonable effect of his or her actions, does not enjoy doing the compulsion, but does relieve some tension by the actions (hand-washing, counting, checking or touching) (245-7).

An example is given in psychiatric circles of Pascal's obsession that there was always an abyss which he could see at his left side. Speculation goes that this was the result of a traumatic experience he had had as a youngster when his coach was nearly thrown into the Seine River. Freud emphasized in volume one of his *Collected Papers:*

> We must distinguish: (a) obsessions proper; (b) phobias. The essential difference between them is the following:
> Two components are found in every obsession: (1) an idea that forces itself upon the patient; (2) an associated emotional state. Now in the group of phobias this emotional state is always one of "morbid anxiety," while in true obsessions other emotional states, such as doubt, remorse, anger, may occur in the same capacity as fear does in the phobias. (*Psychiatric Dictionary* 556)

Cyclothymia is a mood disorder which once was taken as a personality type. The person experiences milder fluctuations of mood of the manic-depressive sort which although much more intense do seem to follow the normal patterns of mood shifts which are common to most people. The term cyclothymia would be used to identify a person who regularly shifts to extremes of mood but rarely requires hospitalization as would a person suffering from the more severe and dramatic manic-depressive reactions. According to the *DSM III-R*, this diagnosis would be made only if the person had suffered chronic mood disturbance for at least two years with extremes from hypomania to depression. A clearly Manic Episode or Depressive Episode would change the diagnosis to Bipolar Disorder (226-8).

Even before this emotion-packed twentieth century, people throughout history have seen psychotics as "out of control" and have reinforced the concept that civilization requires the throttling of emotion. Freud and his associates may have riddled the idea of repressing emotional responses, but as societies go we have not conclusively decided the relative merits and demerits of acting out just how we feel. Control is still the primary message of our family and school pedagogy, intrinsically reinforcing three major rules: don't talk, don't trust, don't feel.

From culture to culture and from community to community within cultures there has always been and is today a range of behavior that each society considers acceptable, especially in the area of emotional display. For example, compare the emotional functioning of the Irish to that of the British, or contrast the modes of expression of southern Italians and northern Italians. And in the United States there is an implicit heterogeneity of acceptable emotional display based on background, family, class, race, national origins, or sexual preference.

However, a person obviously out of control of his or her emotions traditionally and in most social situations today is seen as insane or not rational. It is on this rationale that we judge King Lear mad and argue the instability of Hamlet. On this argument attorneys base their appeals for lenience citing extenuating circumstances and "temporary insanity."

And it was on this basis that virtually an entire nation deemed King George III of England a lunatic. Historians tell us that George III may have suffered from an hereditary disease called porphyria which exhibits manic-depressive symptoms with episodic attacks until neurological deterioration leads to death. Rejection by his peers and ridicule by his inferiors resulted from the insane and unreasonable emotional outbursts of the ill king.

Because of the unique ability of emotion to drive behavior, the first vague mental connections I hope are being made between creative drive and the intensive moods and often ingenious variety of emotion associated with the affective disorders. It is not because Art equals Emotions, but because it is through the emotions that Art intercepts our living and elicits our non-verbal responses. A response to something that happens to us if it is more than a reflex reaction inevitably will involve our emotions and necessarily will carry an emotional prod. Our outward expressions or internal repressions are essentially bound by the emotional cues we have learned to both receive from and give to those significant others around us. One of the recent focuses in the area of alcohol and addiction recovery where the family systems are concerned relates to denial. For years in our society the pervasive and persuasive concept has been that if we do not examine problems, especially within our family contexts, then the feelings, usually painful, will go away. This attitude leads us to deny that anything is wrong, and then we deny that we have the angry or painful feelings connected with what we have already denied is happening. This is crazy-making. The result is mental disease. Feelings do not just go away. They must be acknowledged and expressed in some way. This process was called catharsis by the ancient Greeks. It was a major impetus in the development of the Greek drama.

The word "creativity" itself has an emotional content separate and distinct from any rational definition of the term. We may not be able to agree on what creativity is or how it can be identified; we may not even agree on the primary emotional content of the word itself, but no one has ever been insulted by being told something he or she said or did or thought or expressed was "creative." Usually, the word fills us with feelings of increased self-esteem. Therefore, it is obvious that the word carries a positive emotional connotation which inspires positive emotion by its very use. The word is a metaphor for a behavior that we humans feel good about, admire, desire to have for ourselves, think about, talk about, write books about, take courses in, study, teach, and otherwise pursue.

In a similar way the word "drive" has an emotional quality and content. It conjures up images of tense extremes of deprivation and satiation or the frenzied activity between the extremes. The random emotions of our personal memories or experiences with hunger, thirst, desire, successes or failures mysteriously tangle inside us as we respond to this pseudo-scientific term. Accepting, if not the fact, at least the concept of psychological drive commits us to look for the underlying physiological components which control the conditions under which the drive operates.

Just as the ancients treated exotic humors that were fictitious and were later replaced by more sophisticated understanding of physiological determinants such as hormones, enzymes, and neural transmitters, perhaps in psychology as well we shall one day discard "drives" for more precise and descriptive biological terminology. But for now that word "drive" with all its attendant emotional quality will serve as the verbal peg on which to hang behavior. The word is quantitative and relates to a process energized on a spectrum from deprived state to satisfied state.

I have proposed a "drive to create" which is somehow responsible for the actual production of creative work whether in the arts or sciences, and which to some degree or another operates in every human being to promote mental recreation and psychological balance. I have stated that there is some sort of relationship between this "drive to create" and the mood disorders and other psychiatric disorders, including alcoholic and addictive diseases. I have chosen as a study an artist, a writer, who is well-known for both the quality and quantity of her creative output and who is equally associated with an unfortunate insanity known as manic-depressive psychosis.

Historically very productive creative people have had emotional breakdowns, and this has occurred in enough cases that a myth has been perpetuated linking Art and its production to insanity. This is the folk observation which has become part of our folklore about artists. All of us are affected by this misconception to one degree or another.

We may logically "know" that insane people do not create great works of art. We may even reject as preposterous the concept that crazy people invent things, write great literature, compose music, fill our stages with unique and riveting performances, and so on. But at the same time, we do know that innumerable artists seem to have suffered mental and emotional instability, living lives of repeated mental breakdowns or drug addiction, or alcoholism, or all of these. And the more we read, and the more we think about it, the more we begin to feel there may really be some connection. And then, into the flim-flam of our emotional absorption with the folklore, the news that yet another artist has committed suicide or overdosed on drugs or alcohol pushes us to reconsider the problem of Art and Insanity. And we wonder.

Coming back down to earth, we must realize that many people through history have suffered from insanity. Many have recovered from their illnesses to live useful, productive lives. All of these people, however, were not artists. In fact, if we could compare all the insane of all the ages, we would probably find that the greater proportion, recovered or not, did not write or paint or do whatever we think creative people ought to do. Therefore, there must be some other factor to be considered, another unit or piece of the puzzle to make the picture complete; there must be some other element which separates the victims of mental disease from the productive artists, scientists, and generative thinkers who also have mental breakdowns. That unit or element is what is identified as the "drive to create."

The drive to create exists to some degree in each of us and finds expression in the normal ebb and flow of our emotional responses to the events of living, but in the artist or highly generative person the drive to create is exploded through an increased affectivity and sensitivity to emotional stimulation into a total, unique, and individual expression of his or her experience of life.

The artist just like the rest of us becomes burdened with the affective build-up associated with any biological or psychological drive state. Creative self-expression is the only constructive means through which artists can reduce the tensions inherent in the drive state to any effective degree. Without a suitable outlet to ensure the constructive channeling of the emotional content collected from his or her reactions to the world, the artist will inevitably break down. The various defensive mechanisms seen in mental disorders as well as the self-destructive use of drugs and alcohol can be seen as the result of deflected energy from the drive state. The dangers of these attempts to moderate or control emotional intensity are obvious: restrictions, suicide, possibly death. The creative process is aborted and shut down.

The energy produced by any biological drive must be released or reduced by some positive means or the functioning of the organism will be impaired. This is fundamental. The degree of the impairment depends upon the strength of the drive in the individual, the availability of a means to achieve release, and the level of satisfaction attainable. For persons in which the drive to create operates at a very low level in their overall composite psychological and biological functioning, the failure to release the energy and the pressure of the drive may result in nothing more than ennui or a mild depression characterized by lowered self-esteem and sadness. But, in the artist who must deal with an inordinately strong drive to create which supersedes other more basic drives (in some instances even the more apparently physiological drives such as food, sex, or sleep), there are much more dramatic results when the drive is thwarted or frustrated.

In the case of the artist, if there is no opportunity to achieve release; or if access to the means by which the release may be obtained is blocked;

or if the completion of a project does not bring the relief sought because the artist's rudimentary level of satisfaction has not been attained, then the resulting impairment will most likely be emotional, and depending upon the genetic predisposition, the result could include any one of a range of psychophysical or mental disorders: bipolar disorder, depression, alcoholism, drug addiction, crippling phobias, obsessional states, ulcers, sleep disorders, sexual dysfunction. If frustration of the drive to create is prolonged without adequate therapy or intervention, suicide becomes the only means of release from the inner assault of the drive state and its resulting tensions. The suicide may be a deliberate act or the result of an accident or terminal disease. This is a very sad state when a person endowed with an intense perception of the world and an equally intense drive to express that perception turns radically from the processes of life-affirming and life-sustaining activity into dissolution and disease.

The burden to create or not to create is further complicated by the genetic quality of this factor in human behavior which seems characteristic of the drive to create. That the drive is the result of the genetic expression of a basic biological unit (perhaps a single gene or a combination of other biochemically specific genes) which is associated with or genetically linked to the genetic transmission of the emotion-laden mental disorders seems to be strongly indicated by medical studies. At this time researchers have theorized that the stresses of living interact in some undetermined way with a genetically determined predisposition toward these disorders to produce the biochemical changes which bring on breakdown. As in the studies of cancer and other biologically disruptive diseases, the environmental components are multiple and poorly understood (Miner 117-118).

Dr. Kay Jamison, Associate Professor of Psychiatry at UCLA School of Medicine and Director of the UCLA Affective Disorders Clinic, wrote in an article for *The Harvard Medical School Mental Health Letter*:

> How might a major mental disorder such as bipolar illness be linked to creativity? First, the illness itself may influence creativity by its cyclical nature and the long-term changes in mood and behavior it causes. Second, the experience of having bipolar illness may make a person sensitive to a wider range of emotions and perceptions. (4)

Jamison goes on to discuss the studies since the 70s related to creativity and affective disorders. Quoting from several studies, especially one by Nancy Andreason in which 10 of 15 writers suffered from major affective disorder, compared with only 2 of 10 in a control group matched for age, education, and sex. Also the affective disorders were more highly represented in the families of the writers than in the relatives of the control group. Jamison refers to still other research which indicates that children with bipolar disorder have high incidences of special abilities such as unusual reading capacity or exceptional artistic or mathematical talent. In a study Jamison herself conducted with 47 British writers and visual artists who had attained distinction for their work (Royal Academicians or associates of the Royal Academy), she found 38% had been treated for an affective disorder and 50% of the poets had required medical intervention in the form of lithium maintenance, anti-depressants, or hospitalization (5).

Jamison closed her article by quoting one of the artists in her study:

> People can be talented, hard-working and masters of their craft—but it takes a kink in someone's personality to make them like a genius. This 'kink' can be a bitter childhood or just a demon of frustrated energies that if not channeled into work becomes self-destructive. Mood, upbringing, or whatever passion chases talent out of someone, is irrelevant, because if someone has genius they don't need moods to heighten their work; it pours out of them. (6)

There is other evidence which will be examined more closely and which supports the presence of a biochemical imbalance in the brains of clinically ill people and which predicates that the resulting dysfunction occurs when a genetic component is transmitted via the x-chromosome and interacts with environmental stresses to bring about its crippling effect on brain metabolism. Evidence for the genetic transmission and the x-linkage (meaning the component is carried by the female sex chromosome) has been compiled from numerous studies and follow-up studies are in progress. Correlations have been done with color-blind studies which are sex-specific and with the x-linked blood groups, and a statistically significant relationship has been found. The incidence of manic-depressive illness in first-degree relatives ranges from 20% to 40% with population studies of patients and their relatives showing no male to male distribution of the disease. On the other hand, it is statistically significant that the illness is passed from father to daughter or through the mother to sons and daughters (Cadoret and Winokur 21-25).

Considering the psychiatric disorder of Virginia Woolf, it is probable that Sir Leslie Stephen contributed more to the presence of manic-depressive illness in his younger daughter than just the environmental influence of his wild moods and emotionally demanding personality.

Applying the methods of the psychohistorian as well as the good medical researcher, we are able to trace the genetic transmission based on this experimental evidence. Virginia was the only child of the four children who were born of the union of Leslie Stephen and Julia Jackson Duckworth who manifested the psychiatric illness. Mrs. Stephen's three children from her marriage to Herbert Duckworth were all apparently normal, mentally healthy individuals. But, Laura, the only child of Sir Leslie's marriage to Harriet Marian Thackeray was, we are told by biographer Quentin Bell, hopelessly insane, and Bell alleges that the unfortunate child had the same malady as her poor mad grandmother Thackeray, the wife of William Makepeace Thackeray .

Biographers of William Makepeace Thackeray in chronicling the afflictions of the famous author have included descriptions of the melancholia which appeared after the birth of Isabella's third child, Harriet Marian, and from which she suffered for the rest of her life. Piecing together the story, it isn't difficult to recognize the clinical symptoms of manic-depressive illness from the biographical data. Considering the significance of the x-linkage, Laura must have inherited her "hopeless insanity" via x-chromosomes from both her parents, Sir Leslie Stephen and Harriet Thackeray Stephen. In the cases of Virginia and Vanessa Stephen, we assume that the x-linked illness was dominant or fully expressed only in Virginia and that the inheritance was paternal.

Martin E.P. Seligman in his book *Helplessness* describes how normal life events may bring stress factors to bear on an individual who may carry the genetic predisposition to a psychiatric illness:

> Many laymen believe in a pyramid of the sciences—physics explains chemistry, which explains biology, and on up to economics or politics. A parallel of this in psychology is the belief that physiology causes behavioral and cognitive states, but that cognition and behavior don't cause physiological changes. But the arrow of causation goes both ways. On the one hand, the physiological changes caused by lower blood sugar can cause feelings of fatigue and faintness. On the other hand, if I tell you your house in on fire this cognitive information will cause adrenalin flow, sweating and dryness of mouth. (73)

But, the skeptic may ask, can behavior be controlled by a single genetic factor which transmits a single biochemical dysfunction? Yes. Today scientists have established that many biochemical abnormalities that are genetically determined have behavioral manifestations. One of the more common examples of this is the Lesch-Nyan Syndrome. This abnormality is the result of a genetic disorder which involves the absence or deficiency of one of over 6,000 enzymes in the body. When there is a gross deficiency or absence of the enzyme hypoxanthine guanine phophoribosyl transferase (HGPRT), children suffering from the disorder become severe self-mutilators. The specific behavior, self-mutilation, was traced to a biochemical deficiency transmitted by a single gene (Mars 944-955; Seegmiller, et al., 1682-1684).

The range of individual metabolism and the effect of the biochemical impairment involved in psychiatric disease is still to be discovered. The knowledge of brain chemistry and the critical relationships that lie within body metabolism are frontiers now being explored. For the artist working under the additional stress imposed on him or her by artistic vision, the work of the medical researchers is even more critical and more essential to mental health and creative productivity. And who knows, we may actually be standing on the perimeter of a new Renaissance, a revolution in the arts and sciences, because mentally healthy creative people can be more productive than mentally ill artists, scientists, thinkers. The energy inherent in the genetic drive for creative accomplishment may help push mankind away from destructive systems and toward cooperation and accomplishment if it is released from the squalor and spectacle of mental disorders.

Works Cited

Andreason, N.C. "Creativity and Mental Illness: Prevalence Rate in Writers and Their First-Degree Relatives." *American Journal of Psychiatry*. Oct. 1987;144(10):1288-92.

Bell, Quentin. *Virginia Woolf: A Biography*. Vol. 1. New York: Harcourt Brace Jovanovich, 1972.

Benet, Laura. *Thackeray: Of the Great Heart and Humorous Pen*. New York: Dodd, Mead, 1947.

Cadoret, M.D., Remi J. and George Winokur, M.D., "X-Linkage in Manic-Depressive Illness." *Annual Review of Medicine*. 1975; 26:21-5.

Diagnostic and Statistical Manual of Mental Disorders-III. Washington, D.C.: American Psychiatric, 1980.

Diagnostic and Statistical Manual of Mental Disease-III-R. Washington, D.C.: American Psychiatric, 1987.

Freud, Sigmund. *Collected Papers*. Vol.1 (Trans. J. Riviere; pub. Leonard and Virginia Woolf). London: Hogarth, The Institute of Psychoanalysis. 1924, 1925.

Jamison, M.D., Kay. "Creativity and Mood Disorders." *The Harvard Medical School Mental Health Letter*. June 1985; 1(12):4-6. Kubie, M.D., Lawrence S. *Neurotic Distortion of the Creative Process*. Lawrence, KS: Kansas UP, 1958, 1961.

Mars, Robert. "Genetic Studies of HG-PRT Deficiency and the Lesch-Nyan Syndrome with Cultured Human Cells." *Federation Proceedings*. May-June 1971; 30(3):944-955.

Miner, Gary D. "The Evidence for Genetic Components in the Neuroses." *Archives of General Psychiatry.* 1973; 29:111-118.

Morrison, James, John Clancy, Raymond Crowe, George Winokur. "The Iowa 500: Diagnostic Validity in Mania, Depression, and Schizophrenia." *Archives of General Psychiatry.* 1972; 27:457-61.

Morrison, James, George Winokur, Raymond Crowe, John Clancy. "The Iowa 500: The First Follow-Up." *Archives of General Psychiatry.* 1973;29:678-82.

Ray, F.R.S.L., Gordon N. *The Buried Life: A Study of the Relation Between Thackeray's Fiction and His Personal History.* Cambridge, Mass.: Harvard UP, 1952.

Seegmiller, J. Edwin, Frederick M. Rosenbloom, William N. Kelley. "Enzyme Defect Associated with a Sex-Linked Human Neurological Disorder and Excessive Purine Synthesis." *Science.* 1967 May-June; 155:1682-4.

Seligman, Martin E.P. *Helplessness:On Depression, Development, and Death.* San Francisco: W.H. Freeman, 1975.

Chapter Eight
The Drama of Drive

*The artist's life cannot be otherwise than full of conflicts, for
two forces are at war within him—on the one hand the common human longing for happiness, satisfaction and security in
life, and on the other a ruthless passion for creation which may
go so far as to override every personal desire. . . . There are
hardly any exceptions to the rule that a person must pay dearly
for the divine gift of creative fire.*

—*Carl G. Jung,* Modern Man in Search of a Soul

And now down to the nitty-gritty of the drive to create. The person
who accomplishes his creative goals and excels as an artist is distinguished
from equally or more creative peers by the primary attribute, drive. It is
the inner force of this psychological compulsion not to fame, nor to wealth,
but to the compelling images of one's own mind which sets a person apart
as an artist. To succeed where so many try and fail, the creative person must
have not only sensitivity, talent, training, and all the thousand other things
we more or less think contribute to artistic accomplishment, but in addi-
tion, he must deal with the demands of an internal pressure which constantly drives him or her toward acts of creation.

The basic premise of this study of creative drive is that the innate tension in the personality of the artist comes naturally, transmitted genetically,
and is somehow linked or associated with the genetic inheritance of the
mood or other affective psychiatric disorders. Creativity as a quality or
source should be carefully distinguished from the quantifying and empow-
ering force of the creative drive. They are two separate things entirely.

The drive to create is a biological and psychological force, the existence and operation of which can be isolated and observed in all human
functioning to one degree or another. It is, however, the intimate association we see between the mood and other affective disorders and the creative productivity of working artists which demonstrates the more specific
and unique role the drive to create plays in creative and artistic accomplishment. That the effects of the drive are enhanced and intensified by a genetic
relationship to various mental disorders makes study and analysis of its
operation essential to both the mental health and creative output of our
artists and generative thinkers, as well as to the well-being of any persons

interested in maximizing their innate creative drive either in work or in recreation.

Since the data suggesting x-linkage and other means of genetic transmission of the bipolar disorder have been demonstrated in research studies (see Chapter Nine), it is reasonable in the light of our present knowledge of behavioral genetics to believe that the same biochemical factor which produces the increased emotionality and mood disturbances apparent in the mood disorders is the same factor responsible for an intense internal drive toward creative expression. At the very least, the correlation we see between the driven artist and the presence of affective states suggests that a close genetic linkage is involved in the inheritance of both. Central to this hypothesis is the distinction between creativity per se and the drive to create. Just as creativity alone does not guarantee creative enterprise, the drive to create does not function without qualification.

It is not difficult to recognize the presence of a drive which seems to promote the artist's productive state of mind and which even at times pushes the creatively endowed person to overcome incredible odds. However, it is much more important to understand how and why the drive is an essential part of creative functioning and what problems are encountered when the functions of the drive are distorted in disease or through circumstances which render creative accomplishment virtually impossible. Also, the satisfaction and quality of the work will not be the same when external reward or approval is given priority to the internal freedom and satiation through work of the drive state. This, if it be true, has important application to the "teaching" of the talented and gifted students in our schools and deserves the time and attention of close scrutiny and testing in research settings as well as the classroom.

As Jung so aptly put it, this "ruthless passion for creation which may go so far as to override every personal desire" is the reason some people achieve outstanding success while other, perhaps more talented individuals hang back and allow their talents to fade or be sublimated into other activity. With the knowledge gained through medical research in the past twenty years, we are able for the first time in history to understand the nature of the drive's genetic inheritance and to discover the psychological principles which govern its operation in the human psyche.

AXIOM I: Creative production is the result of a drive to create.

COROLLARY I: All humans are by design creative and procreative, but all humans are not dominated by the psychological drive to express their innate creativity.

We have already observed with our other psychological drives that they are not equally distributed or equally strong in all individuals no matter how basic they may seem. During the Nazi death camp experiences and in other extreme instances where food deprivation became a critical factor in survival, there were those who refused to cannibalize others, denying the biological aspects of the drive for food by certain psychological override. The integrity of a belief system took precedence over survival on the animal level.

This interplay between purely biological aspects and the psychological life of the soul is what makes the functioning of the human organism so much more difficult to monitor and to study. It is apparent from human history that even though we are animal organisms with all the basic physiological drives and attributes of animals, we are also a complex psychologically functioning organism, and what is even more maddening, when one seeks to break down human behavior into its component parts for experimentation or discussion purposes, is the fact that there is a delicate balance and play within the biological and psychological aspects of each individual human being at any given moment on any given day. And so, in our research, when we set up systems to aid our thinking about human behavior, we make models of behavior which like the rules of the old Latin-English grammar are made to be broken and yet are proven by exceptions.

Given this difficulty in generalizing about human psychological drives, it is conceivable the dubious and the curious will immediately think of exceptions and jump to demand answers to specific cases. Still, I believe the basic principles presented here do hold for a wide range of creative drive and can provide useful means for promoting the mental health and physical well-being of artists and other creative people while increasing the wealth and quality of their creative production.

Why then do certain driven people fall short of creative accomplishment, and why do some apparently gifted artists and other talented people seem to fail even in the wake of great effort? The answer to both of these questions is bound to the dangerous and critical connection which exists genetically and biochemically between the drive to create and the mood and other affective disorders.

Dr. Lawrence Kubie deals with this problem in his book *Neurotic Distortion of the Creative Process*. He points out one major factor which inhibits creative production:

> In early days the importance of the unconscious in the derivation and shaping of the neurotic process was still a fresh and astonishing discovery. There-

fore it was natural to assume that it must also be the source of the creative drive and of the great inspiration in human life. It is out of this natural but fallacious deduction that many erroneous cliches have been drawn: such as the notion that a man produces only from his unconscious, that to be creative a man must be sick, and that consequently the artist, scientist, or writer had better guard and protect his neurosis from the therapeutic intervention of the psychiatrist. (47)

There are two basic factors working against those gifted and driven people who do not achieve their potential. As Kubie has pointed out, some artists seek to embrace their neurotic and psychotic tendencies rather than receive healing and growth away from them. Considering the probable genetic relationship between the drive to create and the predisposition to mood or other affective and addictive disease, this is a serious misstep. Mental illness can never be viewed as an artistic advantage, but only as a hindrance to creative productivity. An artist may achieve in spite of his psychiatric illness, but he or she never achieves because of a neurosis or psychosis.

The other primary cause of failure is the presence of drive without the native ability or without any access to materials or opportunity. It is true that many driven artists throughout history have overcome incredible obstacles, but there are circumstances in which no matter how driven a person may be, he or she lacks any of the things which would equip him or her for creative pursuits. I suspect that in these instances the people drift toward the mental illness or addictions and merely swell psychiatric statistics. If a person simply lacks the physical ability to perform in a chosen area, he will fail. Or if he lacks any means to his end, he will not measure up to the requirements of his drive. Here is the problem of craft which must intercept at some critical point the drive to create and the production of art or genius. If Virginia Woolf had been born into the lower working classes of late Victorian London rather than into an upper class literary family, the nuances of language and particularly the written language which became her artistic medium would have been entirely "out of reach." If she had not been a member of the privileged classes, it is certain she would have not escaped institutionalization which would also have served to end any prospect of artistic development.

AXIOM II: The amount of creative output of the individual artist or thinker is proportional to the control it is possible to maintain over his or her neurotic or psychotic tendencies.

COROLLARY II: If the artist or generative thinker is prevented from working in the area of his or her drive, then illness is inevitable.

Creation requires hard work and a synchronizing of perceptions, thinking, and creative energy. A mentally healthy mind can utilize the emotions and the experiences of life while both coordinating the energizing effect of the drive and sustaining the physical force necessary to complete the creative cycle. Whenever it occurs, illness breaks up the process.

Kubie's important book on creativity outlines other areas which operate in creative enterprise, but I have synthesized the basic elements in these short axioms and corollaries. From his experience as a psychiatrist, Kubie elaborated on the influence of painful emotions on all levels of psychological processing whether conscious or unconscious or preconscious, and he emphasized the significant role that painful memories or experiences play in gaining freedom for the creative person to operate. A similar effect was noted by Carl Jung in his psychiatric practice which led him to formulate the concept that a painful or disturbing tension of opposites in the psyche builds the drive which pushes creative people to perform.

Paradoxically, the act of creation is the release of disparate elements from the subconscious (I use the subconscious to include both preconscious or hypnagogic material and what would be considered purely unconscious material) which form the most painful and central core of the artist's personality. The drive to create, however, is the force by which the conscious mind and ego, threatened by assault from this retinue of subconscious suffering, consolidates and reinforces itself against the overwhelming influence of those painful emotions or repressed experiences. In the most real sense possible the drive to create is both a unique asset and a burden to the creative mind.

The proper channeling of its force and the enhancing of its operation will actually ensure the mental health rather than afflict it. While stirring the boiling pot of subconscious reflections, observations, experiences, memories, and their attendant painful emotion, the drive builds the pressure of that internal state forcing the artist or creative person to project those subconscious elements into a more objective form with which the conscious mind can safely deal and over which the assailed self can gain some enlightenment and relief. This is why the tools and knowledge of the craft and the subsequent acquired skill are such an integral part of the formation of a work of art.

The drive to create serves as a psychological homeostatic device through which the conscious mind can deal with distressing and repressed materials and still maintain its equilibrium and by means of which the personality can defend itself against pathological invasion. It is the heightened emotional response and acute sensitivity which accompanies the genetic predisposition to the mood, affective, and addictive disorders which constantly feeds the subconscious mind with material which must be handled if psychiatric illness is to be prevented.

Essential to any understanding of the physiological and genetic facets of the drive to create is a recognition of the interrelationship and interdependence of psychological states and physiological functioning and brain metabolism. There is a tandem effect between emotional responding and the biochemical reactions to those responses. Because the artist draws on the wealth of his sensitivity to emotional stimuli, greater strains and actual demands are placed on his basic metabolic resources. The stress is further magnified by the artist's intense need to insure both the creative operation of his drive and the psychological balance necessary to maintain the force of his artistic production. It is this extension of mental and emotional powers which places the inordinate drain on the physiological systems. Because of the genetic relationship between the drive to create and the sensitive metabolic processes which can trigger a psychiatric disease, the consolidation of the psyche is not enough. The more biological physical resources still may be so taxed in the process that neurotic, psychotic reactions or even a physical breakdown will exact a toll. The unique vulnerability of the artist is no simple matter, but a more complete comprehension of the forces interacting on the artist at work can provide the means of safeguarding and supporting his psychological and physical functioning.

On 23 June 1929, Virginia Woolf made this entry in her diary:

> I am horrified at my own looseness. This is partly that I don't think things out first; partly that I stretch my style to take in crumbs of meaning . . . and so I pitched into my great lake of melancholy. Lord, how deep it is! What a born melancholic I am! The only way I keep afloat is by working. . . . directly I stop working I feel that I am sinking down, down. (139-140)

With these basic premises in mind let's re-examine the circumstances of Virginia Woolf's breakdowns. It is possible in this way to trace the emergence of her creative drive and artistic development as a writer. Her first breakdown came during her thirteenth summer, in 1895 after her mother's death. The trauma of losing the strong mother around whom the events of 22 Hyde Park Gate revolved was the precipitating factor which catapulted Virginia into this first psychotic attack.

After Virginia recovered from this early illness, there were only minor setbacks to her health until her father's death in 1904. This time her breakdown lasted almost two years. Later when writing about this period, she recalled that she had tried desperately to prove that there was nothing wrong with her although she knew that there was. It was during this attack that Virginia first attempted suicide, throwing herself out a second-story window.

Thin and shaken by this bout of illness, she commenced what was to become a life-long pattern: she was impatient to be writing again. In effect the story of her slow and painful recovery is the story of her search for her own creative outlet and unique style. The medium she chose—language and writing—was the one which for years she had used to psychological advantage. Even as a very young child she had carved her niche in life by nightly entertaining her brothers and sister in the nursery with her storytelling. Later she had thought up, designed, and run the tiny family journal. After her father's death, recovering from her psychotic state, with equal determination she tentatively wrote reviews for *The Guardian* and helped with Maitland's *Life of Sir Leslie Stephen*. She busied herself with her diary entries and began writing her first novel. As she did, her health improved and her mental stability returned.

Creative talent as a writer and the interaction with a severe mental illness held Virginia Woolf in a precarious balance. There was the constant assertive care of a Leonard Woolf to draw her back from too much emotional stimulation by parties, friends, or physical exertion; but her work itself, although helping maintain her psychological equilibrium, made its immeasurable demands on her concentration and physical reserves. Given her creative work as a reservoir for all her subconscious turmoil and the monitoring of her health by a meticulous Leonard Woolf, it is extremely noteworthy that the last thirty years of her life produced only two more major breakdowns. For a person with such dramatic, early breakdowns and such a critical balance of physical and mental stability in adulthood, the fact that for almost thirty years she suffered only two more primary attacks is remarkable.

It seems certain, as Leonard Woolf tells us, that the danger of a mental breakdown was closely connected with her work. Aside from the terrible strain and intensity that writing produced in her, Virginia also suffered from a neurotic fear of criticism and an almost irrational drive for literary perfection. She became the victim as well as the anointed subject of her intense drive to create. Tied to that drive was the inherent danger of her mental disorder. Neither came first, chicken-and-egg style; they developed simultaneously and in some ways proportionately to each other like an intricate physio-psychological checks and balances system.

The drive for writing held at bay the psychiatric illness, but at the same time the basic physical and emotional demands of her writing made a careful regimen of rest and diet essential to her health and productivity as a creative artist. These same principles to one degree or another can be applied to all working artists and people in creatively demanding occupations. The actual dangers involved in overlooking or violating these basic premises cannot be exaggerated.

In early 1913 Virginia learned that Gerald Duckworth, on the advice of his readers, intended to publish her first novel. With publication assured, Virginia's neurotic fear of criticism and her requirement for perfection kindled the subconscious fires of insecurity and painful childhood memories. These stressful psychological elements combined with the physical strain of her late summer wedding to Leonard Woolf and their two months abroad (August to November, 1912) brought on her third major breakdown, the first of her married life.

An overdose of barbiturates almost ended her life in suicide at the age of 32 with only one of her nine novels nearing publication. There was a very real possibility that she would be institutionalized and her writing career would end, but the brilliant and responsible young man who had fallen in love with her retrenched his own aims and ambitions and resolved that Virginia Woolf would survive mental illness. Leonard Woolf could not consciously have understood how right his actions were for her health and artistic productivity even though he could observe first-hand the positive results. Only today in the retrospective light of the past ten to fifteen years of metabolic research can his care of her be fully appreciated as revolutionary. The drive to create, an inherited mental illness, a love affair with life, and a dance with death—this is the story of Virginia Stephen Woolf.

In *Beginning Again* Leonard observes the interrelationship of her writing and mental health:

> the connection between her madness and her writing was close and complicated, and it is significant that, whenever she finished a book, she was in a state of mental exhaustion and for weeks in danger of a breakdown. In 1936 she only

> just escaped a breakdown when finishing *The Years*; in 1941 she wrote the last
> words of *Between the Acts* on February 26, and 23 days later on March 21 she
> committed suicide. (81)

Her life ended during the strain of completing a novel and preparing it for public scrutiny. There was a constant threat of death from the war that was pounding England in the spring of 1941. She was 59 years old. Why did this final breakdown which led to her death occur?

Everything seemed to indicate, Leonard Woolf tells us, she was doing much better than ever before. Virginia leaves in her notes to Leonard and Vanessa the abnegation of her ability to withstand the mental assault of another breakdown. She says she cannot pull them down into that abyss, feeling as she did that she did not have strength enough to recover. But, what was the ultimate key to this last struggle between her art and mental disease?

Returning to Kubie and his analysis of creative functioning, we can outline the kinds of circumstances under which the drive to create demands such flexibility of mind and personality that psychiatric and even physical illness is almost inevitable. It was into one of these predicaments that Virginia Woolf was finally led in the spring of 1941. They include:

1. Some people are driven toward creative accomplishment for its own sake, as a means of solidifying their own identity or of securing a more psychologically comforting niche in the world. Their drive can cloud the issues of deeper psychological problems which otherwise might be amenable to treatment and preventive therapy.

Irvin D. Yalom and Marilyn Yalom in an article prepared for the *Archives of General Psychiatry* identify Ernest Hemingway as this sort of artist:

> Just as there is no doubt that he was an extremely gifted writer, there is also
> no doubt that he was an extremely troubled man, relentlessly driven all his life,
> who in a paranoid depressive psychosis killed himself at the age of 62. . . .
>
> The mechanisms employed to ward off dysphoria (self-belittlement and
> self-abasement)—alcohol, writing, intense physical feats—all the frenetic attempts to perpetuate the image he created, interlocked to form only a partially
> effective dam against an inexorable tide of anguish. . . .
>
> Grandiosity does not occur de novo, it arises in response to an inner
> central identity experienced as worthless and bad. (486)

Hemingway's drive to create was connected with a deep psychological need to shield himself from his own emotional and physical vulnerability at the mercy of painful elements in his subconscious mind. The fact that Hemingway gave us unique insight into a human mind is evidence that the drive to create can push someone to a level beyond his or her own pathological or otherwise restricted capacities (86-91).

In Hemingway's *The Old Man and the Sea* we have a story of such depth and humanity that it attains the level of myth. It is the inimitable story of one man's struggle with the products of his own mind and the will to survive. In the story the old man triumphs over his adversary, the sea— long-accepted symbol of the unconscious—but comes up empty-handed; and so it seems Hemingway could not feel affirmed by the results of his creative drive. Worn down from the life-long battle, suffering the delusions and despair of alcohol abuse, he took his own life.

2. Many people, because they fear public challenge, choose life-size problems as the object of their drive and are inevitably swamped by their own attempts at mastery. These people are locked in, trapped into a self-contained system which an outsider can never penetrate. The fear of an open confrontation and failure is so intense that eventual withdrawal into insanity or suicide often occurs without apparent warning. In fact, their emotional responses may seem cruel or eccentric to others who have no access to their subconscious source of frustration (80).

3. Other driven and creative individuals choose easy, quickly-realized goals because emotionally they require the immediate reinforcement of praise and approval in order to relieve their anxiety and ratify the sense of worth they project onto a narrow, self-effacing image. They live a life of constant emotional repression with occasional outbursts of anger which seem especially idiosyncratic to their usual demeanor of hilarity or unadulterated enthusiasm (78).

These people are otherwise enthusiasts or human "doings" always designing, organizing, writing histories for their clubs, helping with church or civic "projects" like cookbooks, jokebooks, or bazaars. They find thousands of everyday outlets for their creative drive. There is nothing wrong with any of these activities as long as they do not reflect a neurotic attempt to solve the frustration of creative drive that is being misdirected and misapplied. If, however, they run out of projects or if praise is withheld or if they are criticized for their domineering or overzealous manner, they are likely to eschew former triumphs and withdraw into a state which can lead toward suicide, depending upon the manner and degree of the neurotic distortions.

4. Some highly creative people pursue endlessly the figure of a father, starting and dropping career after promising career when the point

of independent self-reliant work is about to be achieved and the aid of the father figure is no longer required (79).

I think Sylvia Plath is a good example of the destructive turn this combination of drive to create and sinister pathology can take. With the success of her poetry, novel, and radio dramas, she turned on the figure within her and in the poem "Daddy" declared:

> Daddy, I have had to kill you.
> You died before I had time—

It is probable that destroying herself was a token destruction of the father image which still haunted her, entangled dangerously as it was with her drive to create. In his prologue to *The Savage God*, A. Alvarez gives us his opinion as a friend and fellow poet:

> Why then, did she kill herself? In part, I suppose it was a "cry for help" which fatally misfired. . . . First, when she and her husband separated, however mutual the arrangement, she again went through the same piercing grief and bereavement she had felt as a child when her father by his death, seemed to abandon her. Second, I believe she thought her car crash the previous summer had set her free; she had paid her dues, qualified as a survivor and could now write about it. But as I have written elsewhere, for the artist himself art is not necessarily therapeutic. . . . (36)

Perhaps her "car crash" had been a subconscious attempt to "kill" the father image which had not achieved its purpose. All we know is that she seemed unable to put to rest the image and the abandonment she felt. She was filled with an ever intensifying drive for artistic production. Losing control over these painful emotions, Sylvia Plath took her own life. That her pathology gained the energy and force of her drive seems conclusive. With primeval fury she throws herself on her father's grave figuratively trying to rid herself of her own disease. Unfortunately for us who must judge her art before its prime, she did not emerge from the psychic storm:

> Daddy, you can lie back now.
>
> There's a stake in your fat black heart
> And the villagers never liked you.
> They are dancing and stamping on you.
> They always knew it was you.
> Daddy, daddy, you bastard, I'm through.

5. Another anxiety-driven creative person may live his life on an artistic or scientific treadmill fearing at the completion of one piece of work that he may never create another. Pathetically, he or she cannot let paint dry on one canvas before starting another. Artistic perfection is not the goal, nor success, but rather a compulsive outpouring of the subconscious. Kubie observes this distortion in some of his scientist colleagues:

> There is the anxiety-driven scientist who lives on a treadmill, who can never finish one piece of work without immediately being seized with terror that he never will be able to complete another. He can never lie fallow, never rest, never accept a moment's peace; because without work he is in a torment of anxiety. . . . As he plunges from one task to the next, he is brother to the artist who cannot let paint dry on one canvas before he starts the next, for fear that he never will be able to paint again; or to the writer who is in the same predicament; or to the millionaire who can never stop accumulating. (80)

Kubie goes on to say that these do not break down from overwork, although they do work long and hard, but from the fact that "success" always cheats them. This person lives in a half-life between efforts with little regard for individual welfare or success. In spite of his constant dredging of the subconscious, his self-awareness decreases almost like a psychological law of diminishing returns which raises the anxiety and pushes him farther away from the goals of art. And indeed success when it comes is only another burden to take him away from the work he or she seems to need to do. This neurotic distortion is more related to ritual, obsessive handwashing than to the creative process energized by the healthy expression of creative drive.

Erskine Caldwell may be an example of this kind of writer. I hesitate to categorize such a great writer this way or give very many examples for this category of others who may qualify. Erskine Caldwell gave us some of the most astoundingly powerful novels in contemporary American literature, but he also wrote scores of little-known, second-rate works which should never have been published. Much of Caldwell's life was spent in a continual stream of half-baked melodramas that could not even touch the creative level of such classics as *God's Little Acre* or *Tobacco Road*. He simply could not control the steady flow of compulsive writing. Not to write, it seems, was synonymous with psychic death. The quality of the production was to him evidently irrelevant or at least not a cause for conscious concern. He found his existence in the shadows of his subconscious reflections with little creative drive available to mold or shape them into creative design.

This list of possible deflections of creative energy is hardly exhaustive. I have selected the ones which seem to me most dangerous for the creative or generative mind. I also have demurred from becoming either a witch-hunt investigator—dredging up mile after mile of depressing examples from the lives of great writers, artists, thinkers—or a gossip columnist. This book is to beat a path toward the healthy use of creative drive. It is enough, I think, to mention the major pitfalls, illustrate from the life of Virginia Woolf, and let the reader apply the information to those cases which may be particularly troublesome to him or her, if that seems desirable.

To recapitulate before taking a closer look at Virginia Woolf and the possible distortion which plagued her to the point of suicide, there are several ways in which neurotic or psychotic tendencies, whether genetically inherent and pristine or linked to painful repressions in the subconscious, can deflect or sidetrack the healthy creative expression of the individual workman of art, business, science, or research. It can be seen in these cases that energy which would in healthier circumstances find its way into rewarding and relieving or satiating activity "catches" on the ragged edges of unresolved conflict or submerged painful and threatening memories and becomes the energy of self-destructive activity. The ones already discussed include:

1. The distortion that occurs when a personal neurosis such as Hemingway's chronic low self-esteem becomes the end-product of the drive rather than the creative work itself bringing reward and healing to the soul.

2. The distortion that occurs when a person chooses a life-size, challenging problem to work on that does not bring satisfaction or reward. Such people so fear personal scrutiny or criticism that they submerge their creative drive in projects so large they actually prevent creative functioning.

3. The distortion that occurs when easy, quick goals are accomplished out of the desire for rewards and praise. This leads a person to seek the applause more than the work itself. Applause doesn't last very long. And the person is never satisfied because the only one being cheated, he or she knows at some level, is himself or herself.

4. A common distortion of creative drive is illustrated by Sylvia Plath's tragic death and her absorption with the painful memories attached to her father's death when she was a child and the abandonment feelings she could not escape. In a society like ours today, without stability of homes or likely therapeutic intervention to assist in recovery of this sort, many are in danger of losing the creative self through disordered attempts to avoid

abandonment. Through the mushrooming of 12-Step Programs taken from the original steps worked out in Alcoholics Anonymous fifty-four years ago, there are signs that this problem of unhealthy loss of creative energy can be resolved in most cases. Those artists or other creative people who identify with this problem of familial alcoholism or childhood trauma could probably benefit from the Al-Anon ACA 12-Step Program (Adult Children of Alcoholics or Other Dysfunctional Families). A healthy artist is a productive, generative artist.

5. Many creative and highly charged individuals like Erskine Caldwell rarely rise above their psychopathology because they choose a treadmill of production to hold at bay the overwhelming anxiety of their emotional disorder. Doing is substituted for being and the creative process becomes compulsive rather than natural and healthy.

The destructive force of Virginia Woolf's drive falls into still another category. Some artists are so obsessed with certain specific past associations and painful personal conflicts that when these pressures are finally subdued in the subconscious through their creative efforts, they find themselves set adrift emotionally without further elements in their personality on which to draw for new creative projects. The drive to create, however, continues to build. If new internal resources, for whatever reasons, cannot be mustered, then the energy of the drive will be distorted into destructive and pathological activity (Kubie 90-97).

Virginia Woolf's drive was welded to subconscious residues of repressed childhood pain and conflict. Her sensitivity and shyness as a child darkened her initial joy of storytelling until the forces which drove her toward literary accomplishment were the same forces which drove her to put to rest those distorted and demeaning memories. Virginia recognized some of this in herself, referring to her parents in her diary entry of 28 November 1927:

> I used to think of him and mother daily; but writing the *Lighthouse* laid them in my mind. And now he comes back sometimes, but differently (I believe this to be true—that I was obsessed by them both, unhealthily; and writing of them was a necessary act).

She had somehow managed to put to rest the worst of those pains and problems from the past—even the overpowering emotional extremes of her father and the indomitable will of her mother. But with the completion of *Between the Acts* and the daily threat of the bombings, Virginia Woolf may have been pushed into the realization at some level of her personality that she had written out that part of her mind and was standing on the virgin soil of her own unique self.

The adversary death was conveniently at hand as the drive to create began to turn her toward self-destruction, the physical expression of a psychological completion she may have already felt. Near the end of December 1940 she makes this observation in her diary:

> I actually opened Matthew Arnold and copied these lines. While doing so, the idea came to me that why I dislike, and like, so many things idiosyncratically now, is because of my growing detachment from the hierarchy, the patriarchy. When Desmond praises *East Coker*, and I am jealous, I walk over the marsh saying, I am I: and must follow that furrow, not copy another. That is the only justification for my writing, living. (332)

As the new year 1941 grew a little older, Virginia Woolf began to lose more of the thread which tied her to her past. In mid-January she visited a bombed-out London, the breaking of another tie:

> A complete jam of traffic; for the streets were being blown up. So by Tube to the Temple; and there wandered in the desolate ruins of my old squares: gashed; dismantled; the old red bricks all white powder, something like a builder's yard. Grey dirt and broken windows. Sightseers; all that completeness ravished and demolished. (334)

Slowly the thread grows to the size of a rope, and Virginia Woolf seems unable to find a place for herself in a new era with a new future not hung on the pegs of the past. Leonard Woolf has told us her mind seemed stable and her spirits high as she finished her last novel. That her suicide came unexpectedly is certain: his vigilance was down. He was caught off-guard without perceiving that dangerous state of her mind. Why? Because it was different from past days when, having completed a novel, the old monsters from her painful and timid childhood would not be put aside but would continue to raise their ugly heads. The plague of self-consciousness was gone; the certainty of future harassment from the old griefs was over, done with.

Virginia Woolf hesitated; perched at the edge of a broad new savannah, she made a few false steps, then turned and plunged back into her own past. As terrifyingly unreal and disturbing as the haunts of the past had been, in its own way, the blank page of the future was equally threatening. The suicide of Virginia Woolf was the rational choice of an artist who could not have an existence apart from the painful personal absorption with the things of her past.

Late in January she added in her diary:

> This trough of despair shall not, I swear, engulf me. The solitude is great.
> Rodmell life is very small beer. The house is damp. The house is untidy. But
> there is no alternative. Also days will lengthen. What I need is the old spurt.
> "Your life, like mine, is in ideas," Desmond said to me once. But one must
> remember one can't pump ideas. I begin to dislike introspection: sleep and
> slackness; musing; reading; cooking; cycling: oh and a good hard rather rocky
> book. . . . (335)

What a different Virginia Woolf is beginning to emerge from the
person who only ten years before had "reeled" across the last ten pages of
The Waves in a delirious state of mind, her ideas throbbing the pen with
their force! The change is as arresting to us as it was unnoticed by Leonard.
It never had occurred to him that he had to protect her from outgrowing
her own mind. In the 8 March 1941, entry, the last of her published diary,
we see a frail reflection of the former Virginia Stephen Woolf. She talks
of occupying herself and in the beginning of the end sees life with barely
a few historical connections to her personal past:

> I mark Henry James' sentence: observe perpetually. Observe the oncome of
> age. Observe greed. Observe my own despondency. By that means it becomes
> serviceable. . . . I will go down with my colours flying. This, I see, verges on
> introspection; but doesn't quite fall in. Suppose I selected one dominant fig-
> ure in every age and wrote round and about. Occupation is essential. And now
> with some pleasure I find that it's seven; and must cook dinner. Haddock and
> sausage meat. I think it is true that one gains a certain hold on sausage and had-
> dock by writing them down. (336)

Perhaps the "one dominant figure in every age" would have included
her father and the *National Dictionary of Biography* he wrote. But, as she
states, and through the pages of her diary and novels, we have come to
believe, she had put to rest her childhood—the painful memories of her
father's wild moods and the tedious hours he spent at his writing, her
autocratic mother's early death, and her own timidity and emotional
vulnerability to the hypocritical attitudes of oversolicitous and histrionic
relatives. In this little reflection before dinner, we see her look over her
shoulder and consider the work of biography which had consumed her
father. Is she folding herself psychologically back into those pages which
interspersed her traumatic childhood? We can only guess because on 28
March 1941, Virginia Woolf drowned in the River Ouse.

Works Cited

Alvarez, A. *The Savage God: Study of Suicide*. New York: Random House, 1972.

Jung, C.G. *Modern Man in Search of a Soul*. New York: Harcourt, Brace & World, 1933.

Kubie, M.D., Lawrence. *Neurotic Distortion of the Creative Process*. Lawrence, KS: U of Kansas P, 1958.

Plath, Sylvia. "Daddy." *Ariel*. New York: Harper & Row, 1961.

Woolf, Virginia. *A Writer's Diary* (Ed. Leonard Woolf, The New American Library). New York: Harcourt, Brace & World, 1953, 1954 by Leonard Woolf, 1968 by The New American Library.

Yalom, Irvin D. and Marilyn Yalom. "Ernest Hemingway: A Psychiatric View." *Archives of General Psychiatry*. 1971; 24(6):485-94.

Chapter Nine
Psychiatric Update

*A creative moment is part of a longer creative process, which
in its turn is part of a creative life. How are such lives lived?
How can I express this peculiar idea that such an individual
must be a self-generating system? Not a system that comes to
rest when it has done good work, but one that urges itself on-
ward. And yet, not a run-away system that accelerates its
activity to the point where it burns itself out in one great flash.
The system regulates the activity and the creative acts regen-
erate the system. The creative life happens in a being who can
continue to work.*

—*Howard E. Gruber*, Towards a Theory
of Psychological Development

Scientific research continues to construct a body of evidence for the
genetic transmission of various psychiatric disorders, especially the bipolar disorder. Already genetic markers are being discovered which help
identify genetic carriers and their place on the human chromosome. There
is cloning of cells, and it is hoped in the near future genetic intervention
in human development may be a reality. This is the age of Aldous Hux-
ley's "brave, new world."

The excitement of genetic discovery should be tempered by the moral
and ethical issues raised by genetic intervention. My mind is haunted by
the memories of photographs in the Holocaust Museum at Ein Karem,
Israel, of Nazi human experiments. In Chapter Sixteen I will discuss some
of the issues other than medical and psychiatric raised by the new advances
in genetics. For this section of the study of creative drive and its possible
genetic relationship to the affective disorders, I hope to present as clearly
and concisely as a lay person can the evidence for genetic transmission of
these disorders.

At the end of Chapter Seven I mentioned "the squalor and spectacle
of mental disorders." In this chapter I will attempt to describe both squalor
and spectacle. When *DSM III-R* emerged in 1987, it produced a wave of
backlash in psychiatric circles. A number of dissenting and ridiculing
voices were raised. It was even seen by some critics as an ill-advised and
ill-assembled departure from the well-received *DSM III*. Books were
written that moral and social codes were being undermined; articles decried alleged politicization of the new edition. Diagnostic reliability was

challenged. Since research accuracy relates directly to the validity, consistency, and reliability of diagnostic criteria, this controversy over the *DSM III* and the *DSM III-R* and the subsequently hoped-for *DSM IV* (scheduled for 1993 publication) illuminates the fact that we are a long way from resolving major difficulties in diagnosis. There is enormous hope, however, in the kind of research results being obtained in the biochemical and genetic fields. This is the face of psychiatric therapeutic intervention today—the squalor of diagnostic integrity, the spectacle of advanced genetic and biochemical studies.

In this chapter I want to introduce the basic concept of the catecholamine hypothesis of elation and depression which has been around since the sixties. Next, I will review the biochemical and genetic search for markers and gene-specific transmission of the affective disorders, especially the bipolar disorder. Finally, I will include the efficacy of therapeutic intervention today both by chemical management and psychotherapy. In Chapter Seventeen I will discuss other extra-psychiatric approaches to management of some of these disorders through psychological self-help groups and problem-specific 12-Step programs inspired by the success of Alcoholics Anonymous in recovery for alcoholics and drug addicts.

According to a 1972 lecture by Dr. William E. Bunney, Jr. of the National Institute of Mental Health (NIMH), the most useful hypothesis we have to explain the biochemical dysfunction apparent in the affective disease manic-depressive psychosis is the catecholamine-indoleamine theory of elation and depression. A catecholamine—epinephrine, norepinephrine, serotonin, dopamine, adrenaline, noradrenaline—is an adrenergic substance in the brain known as a neurotransmitter, a chemical by which a neuron fires another neuron in the central nervous system (CNS). The CNS includes not only the brain, but all the peripheral nerves in the body which report directly to the brain.

In the brain we find a large tract of neurons (nerve cells) which are referred to as the median forebrain bundle (MFB). It is thought by researchers that stimulation of this set of neurons produces sensations of pleasure and reward in the brain. For this reason it is theoretically considered the physiological center for the pleasurable emotions. Norepinephrine is the primary transmitter substance for this area of the brain. In the septum, a neighboring structure in the brain, scientists have found a cholinergic substance, reserpine, which has the ability to inhibit or "shut down" the MFB. In manic states it is believed there is an excess of norepinephrine or a reduction of reserpine or both which allows the brain to become overstimulated and to attack the systems of the body with hyperactivity.

There is an increase in emotional excitement and elation combined with frenetic motor activity and exorbitant thought content as neurons in the brain are chemically stimulated without respite. This is one way that these catecholamines are thought to interact (Bunney #5).

On the other hand, in depression scientists see the opposite reactions taking place with other neural-related substances affecting the rate of norepinephrine production and actually producing a biochemical or metabolic malfunction in the brain. Animal studies have shown reduced amounts of norepinephrine in the brains of clinically depressed animals. Autopsy reports from depressed patients who have committed suicide also show reduced levels of norepinephrine in the brain and spinal fluid (Ibid.).

Dr. Bunney qualifies the evidence as not entirely satisfactory on an empirical basis, but he says that the hypothesis is a useful research tool which can be subjected to major modifications as new information about brain metabolism is collected. The actual "trigger mechanism" which sets off the biochemically altered events in the chain of metabolic functioning is still unknown, but environmental factors which may be stress-related, such as emotional trauma, fatigue, or dietary habits, may have a great deal of influence on the development of the disease state (Ibid.).

An October 1985 issue of the *Journal of Clinical Psychiatry* carried an article proposing that a spectrum exists from change, to crisis, to turmoil, and, at times, to illness at watersheds in the life cycle of a person who is vulnerable to bipolar or other affective disorder. Affective experiences were seen to be both mobilizing as the emotional catalyst in human growth experience or if certain life events and genetic predisposition become operational, then the same experiences can become a devastating psychotic mood disturbance. The paper went on to discuss the dynamics of biologic systems, chronobiology, and developmental experience as prime factors in the sequence of affective cycles. All of these are related to life events in a critical fashion (Addario 46-56).

A 1985 article in the *Journal of Clinical Psychopharmacology* presented a case of mania produced in a nonbipolar patient when L-dopa, a drug that stimulates catecholamine production and has been tested for use with depressed patients and certain schizophrenic disorders, was given in large doses on a long-term basis. This demonstrated that classic manic syndrome could be induced by catecholamine augmentation (Harsch, Miller, Young 338-39).

In the *Journal of Clinical Psychiatry* in 1986 another article examined the case of an individual in which the "on-off" phenomena of manic-depressive mood shifts was clearly demonstrated involving the neurotransmitter dopamine, thereby supporting the biochemical theory of elation and depression (Keshavan, David, Narayanen, Satish 93-4).

The primary difficulty in testing the catecholamine hypothesis is the inability to test effects in animal studies. Animals do become clinically depressed, as has already been noted, and studies of depression can be done by using experimental drugs injected into rats and other animals in which depression has been induced. Whether the animal depression truly duplicates human depression is unknown. However, no mania has been observed naturally occurring or has been induced in animals, and, therefore, animal research models cannot be used. The use of human subjects is strictly voluntary and must be carefully monitored. In a 1986 study using human subjects, dextroamphetamines were given in single 20 mg. dosages as a model for mania since there are close similarities to manic states that can be observed. Subjective experience, physiological and endocrine changes, and responses to other drugs can be noted. This sort of experimentation is helping aid the pharmacological studies in mania (Jacobs, Silverstone 323-29).

In an letter about a preliminary study using reserpine published in 1986 in the *American Journal of Psychiatry*, several doctors expressed confidence in the continued use of the catecholamine hypothesis and its implications for drug therapy in the reduction of mania:

> Numerous alternative drug treatments have been offered in the past to ameliorate the symptoms associated with the manic phase of manic-depressive disorder. These methods generally involve manipulation through serotonin-ergic, adrenergic, dopaminergic, and GABA-ergic systems. . . . In the early 1960s, reserpine, which has serotonin- and catecholamine-depleting properties, was shown to have some value in the treatment of mania and excited states. . . . Because of the positive results with reserpine reported here, we will be assessing the value of this agent in manic population using an appropriately controlled design. (Telmer, Lapierre, Horn, Browne 1058)

In July 1987 an NIMH (National Institute of Mental Health) report appeared in *Hospital and Community Psychiatry*. Written by Marilyn Sargent of NIMH and titled "The Gene Hunt," it gave a rousing shout that the race to find the offending genes in mental illness was on! The strides forward that Sargent heralded included:

1) the identification of "chromosomal markers—pieces of genetic code—that seem to be inherited along with psychiatric disorders" (718);

2) a proposed gene bank at the Alcohol, Drug Abuse, and Mental Health Administration (ADAMHA) which would "serve as a repository

for blood cells collected from families with psychiatric disorders and alcoholism, from which genetic researchers could draw" (718).

Sargent wrote that it would take 3-5 years after approval for the gene bank to become operational. In the rest of her article, she outlined the progress made in genetic mapping of chromosomes and the distinguishing of markers that identify the direct inheritance of the predisposition to the disease. Most of the work to the present has been accomplished in the genetics of affective diseases, especially manic-depressive psychosis. Three markers were discussed by Sargent and researchers are continuing to test for these in the general population and for other markers in more isolated populations (718-19).

A ten-year study was done on the Old Order Amish population of Pennsylvania that yielded the first real evidence of a specific gene that could be linked to manic-depressive illness and its inheritance. In an article published in the British journal *Nature* in February 1987, the work of Janet Egeland, Ph.D., of the University of Miami and her colleagues from Miami's School of Medicine, the Yale University School of Medicine, and the Massachusetts Institute of Technology was reviewed:

> These findings point to a gene on chromosome 11, in the region of the insulin and Harvey-*ras*-1 marker genes, that predisposes members of this Amish family to manic-depressive illness. (Sargent 718)

Miranda Robertson in her "News and Views" article for another issue of *Nature* in March 1987 described the research this way:

> Genetic analysis of such a disease faces obvious difficulties. First, the diagnosis of the disorder necessarily requires subjective assessment; second, if more than one gene is involved, genetic evidence from different families cannot necessarily be pooled; and third, incomplete penetrance may make it very difficult to establish a clear link between the inheritance of a given gene and the inheritance of the disease. (Robertson 755)

Robertson's article explains one problem with this kind of genetic research is finding a large and inbred population among Europeans and North Americans. The Amish population was ideal because they marry within their own group, keep genealogical records, and do not use alcohol or drugs, so that the diagnosis of affective mental disease is not complicated by other factors. By cloning genes the researchers used the markers to trace the inheritance of the variants of the gene region and of the incidence of affective disorder in the families. They found that the two genes—one an insulin gene and the other a cancer-disposing gene—lying close together on the short arm of chromosome 11, were frequently inherited together with affective disorders. There were several problems though. The Amish are no more prone to manic-depression than the general population. Even in those individuals in which the identifiable inheritance pattern was found, not all developed tumors (Harvey-*ras*-1 gene marker) or other insulin-related problems or affective disorders (Ibid.).

In a March 1988, article for *Pharmacopsychiatry*, Janet Egeland published more results from her work. After a detailed description of her research, she summarized that it was important to ask why certain people "at risk" remain well while others develop the diseases. A question was raised also about testing to see if the affective disorders are part of the same genetic spectrum. Dr. Egeland urged that the Amish study maintain a research strategy of interface between psychiatry and other scientific disciplines (Egeland 74-5).

Other genetic markers being studied by various research teams include two genes on the X chromosome—one for color blindness and the other for a deficiency of glucose-6-phosphate dehydrogenase (G6PD), an enzyme that helps metabolize glucose. This study was published in the March 19, 1987, issue of *Nature* by a team of New York doctors in cooperation with Yale University School of Medicine and the Jerusalem Mental Health Center, Hebrew University-Hadassah Medical School in Jerusalem, Israel. Their results confirmed that a major affective disease can be caused by a single genetic defect. The doctors saw their work as a first step in characterizing the primary genetic abnormality that can hopefully lead to improved understanding of etiology, nosology, pathophysiology, and even prevention or treatment tools for bipolar affective disorder (Baron, Risch, Hamburger, Mandel, Kushner, Newman, Drumer, Belmaker 289-92).

Still another issue of *Nature* (March 1987) reported a study of several other North American populations—an Icelandic family and three non-Amish North American families. These failed to produce the same findings as the Amish study. This led the research community to decide that no single common gene can be found for all populations. Manic-depressive disorder is a heterogenous disease caused by different genes in different populations (Detera-Wadleigh, Berettini, Goldin, Boorman, Anderson, Gershon 806-08).

A separate article in that same issue gave results supporting genetic heterogeneity in manic-depression, citing that families with multiple cases of manic-depression have been described with both autosomal dominant (as in the Amish studies) and X-linked (as in the Israel studies) modes of genetic transmission. The authors also discussed the relevance of genetic mutations (spontaneous alterations in the genetic code) involving the tyrosine hydroxylase (TH) gene which encodes the rate-limiting enzyme for the synthesis of the three neurotransmitters (catecholamines) thought responsible for the manic-depressive behavior (Hodgkinson, Sherrington, Gurling, Marchbanks, Reeders, Mallet, McInnis, Petursson, Brynjolfsson 805-06).

Egeland and her colleagues discussed their search for a gene that predisposes individuals to bipolar disorder in a 1987 *Journal of Psychiatric Research* article. They sought to clarify the role of genetics in the study of affective disease, saying that it was necessary to have correct diagnoses and large homogenous populations to examine for genetic transmission. In order to find and identify a marker linked to the disease, two other factors were very important, according to the team of researchers:

1) a correct model for genetic transmission;

2) highly polymorphic (having more than one form) DNA markers.

Also the team reported that two approaches to establishing a linked marker, then identifying the susceptibility gene, included the prediction of candidate genes and/or the determination of a physical map of the genetic region under study (Gerhard, Egeland, Pauls, Housman 569-75).

A 1987 *Science* article reviewed the research of the same Amish-study team, commenting on its relevance to the ongoing work of biochemical and genetic research:

> Even before this research (the tyrosine hydroxylase investigations) begins, the marker for manic-depression is expected to have social consequences. By showing that this psychiatric disorder is genetic in nature, the investigators hope they have removed the stigma of manic-depression. They have shown, says Egeland, that "these swings in mood and energy are not necessarily things that people can control." (Kolata 1140)

Much more research could be quoted here, and I append additional references for the more scientifically minded in the Works Consulted list at the end of this chapter. But I would like to complete this discussion of the genetic report with a quotation from a 1987 *Science* editorial by Daniel Koshland, Jr. In his sweeping essay, Koshland hails the breakthroughs in molecular genetics and biochemical research as opening scientific inquiry up to broad social and political ramifications. Citing the genetic and biochemical nature of the bipolar disease, as Koshland sees it, is not really so surprising since the brain is an organ like the liver or heart or kidneys or pancreas. What is more critical now in light of this new knowledge of biological significance is to remember that we human beings are given free will. The old debate of nature versus nurture is not resolved by brain metabolism any more than discovering new drug therapies will eliminate disease. I am personally very grateful for Koshland's drive for honesty and his expressed awareness of who we are as human beings:

> This picture may seem obvious to a scientist, but our judges, journalists, leg-islators, and philosophers have been slow to learn this lesson. When children do not behave, parents or schools must be at fault. If prisoners are not reha-bilitated, prison programs must be inadequate. If suicides are not prevented, stress must be excessive. Equally simplistic is the contention that there is no crime, only disease; no guilt, only a bad combination of genes. The truth is that we are dealing with a very complex problem in which the structure of soci-ety and chemical therapy will play roles. Better schools, a better environment, better counseling, and better rehabilitation will help some individuals, but not all. Better drugs and genetic engineering will help others, but not all. It is not going to be easy for those without scientific training to cope with these complicated relationships even when all the factors are well understood. It will be even harder while the scientific research is still unfolding. However, the debate on nature and nurture in regard to behavior is basically over. Both are involved, and we are going to have to live with that complexity to make our society more humane for the individual and more civilized for the body poli-tic. (Koshland 1445)

With this summary of genetic and biochemical research, I turn toward the treatment modalities presently being used to help those suffering from the affective disorders. There is ongoing research in this area to promote more consistent diagnosis and better coordination of therapeutic interven-tion for the patient and his or her family. Diagnostic tests have been developed and standardized which help identify and confirm the clinical impression of an experienced therapist. One of these that has been devel-oped is a fixed format for interviewing called the Schizophrenia and Affective Disorders Scale (SADS). Severity of depressions can often be determined using a rating scale—the Beck Scale is filled out by the pa-tient; the Hamilton Scale is completed by the interviewer. Two other tests used to determine the accuracy of diagnosis are the Minnesota Multipha-sic Personality Inventory (MMPI) and the projective personality test, the Thematic Apperception Test (TAT).

It should be remembered that with mood disorder or affective illness as with many other physical disorders, there may be periods of relatively good health interspersed with periods of ill health. The purpose of treatment is the restoration of good health and functioning as soon as possible or the maintenance of remission. Today there are antimanic and antidepressive drugs and a variety of approaches to therapy.

In *The Harvard Medical School Mental Health Letter*, September to November 1988, a series of articles were published outlining the various approaches to the treatment of mood disorder. In general, treatment for these and other affective diseases uses a combination of therapeutic methods, the most common of which is some form of psychotherapy combined with drug treatment. The most revolutionary breakthrough in treatment for mania has been the use of lithium carbonate.

Treatment of mania and depression with lithium is an innovative therapy which is supported by ongoing research and clinical evidence for its effectiveness. Introduced in the 1950s, the monitored use of lithium proved effective in a large percentage of the patient population. Several hundred thousand people are taking lithium regularly for a national savings of $65 billion in medical costs in the last 15 years, according to the National Institute of Mental Health (NIMH) (Sept. 1988, 2).

Lithium treatment was based on a concept of replacement therapy because functional deficits of this mineral compound had been found in manic-depressive patients. In two more recent studies, one published in *Neuropsychobiology* in 1985 and the other published in the *Journal of Clinical Psychiatry* in 1986, two different calcium channel blocker drugs were tested with some very positive results. This opens the field of inquiry into the biochemical relationship between lithium and calcium metabolism as it relates specifically to the manic state (Caillard 23-6; Brotman, Farhadi, Gelenberg 136-38).

The lithium treatment is particularly used in mania but can also be an effective therapy for the depressive phase of bipolar disorder. Usually continued for at least six months after recovery, it reduces recurrence of mania within a year by 50%. Long-term maintenance is used in cases where there have been several episodes of manic or manic and depressive psychosis. The success rate is around 70% with 20% of patients remaining symptom-free. Maintenance is implemented in cases in which symptoms come on abruptly, are severe, or in those cases in which the patient himself or herself may not be aware of early signs of relapse. Lithium is a mineral salt that can become toxic in the high dosages usually administered for bipolar disease. Regular checks must be made on blood levels to be certain the person does not receive too much. If there is too high a level, the person's life is threatened, and if the dosage is too low, the treatment will be ineffective and the mood cycling will break through. There can be adverse side effects (weight gain, hand tremors, excessive thirst or urination) and adverse changes in the heart, kidneys, or thyroid gland (Sept. 1988, 2).

Other drugs commonly used in the treatment of these disorders include the antidepressants—tricyclics, tetracyclics, and the monoamine oxidase (MAO) inhibitors. The MAO inhibitors block the action of an enzyme that breaks down norepinephrine and serotonin in the body. Some anxious patients are given major tranquilizers. In some cases anticonvulsant drugs are used for patients who have unusually rapid mood swings. Often a combination of drug therapies can help patients in particularly severe illnesses. For example, lithium may be combined with an anticonvulsant. Occasionally stimulants are used in the early stages of severe depression until the tricyclic drugs can become effective. Also, L-tryptophan, found in health food stores, can be helpful, especially if the patient is taking antidepressant drugs, because of its action along the serotonin pathways (Sept. 1988, 3).

Electroconvulsive therapy is becoming popular again after a decline in the 70s because political controversy questioned its usefulness. ECT, as it is called, produces a generalized grand mal seizure when an electric current is passed through the brain. The usual course of treatment is 8-10 sessions over two or three weeks. ECT is often the quickest way to get results in cases of extreme mania or extreme depression, and if done correctly, there are few side effects. It is the only safe treatment for pregnant women when drugs cannot be prescribed. No one knows why ECT works so dramatically. Some have speculated that the electric shock increases the permeability of the brain cells, improving the balance of catecholamines. ECT is the first choice for patients who are suicidal, aggressive, wildly hallucinating, starving, or in a stupor (October 1988, 1).

Several somatic therapies recommended for various depressions are reminiscent of the old Greek treatments. According to *The Harvard Medical School Mental Health Letter*, 60% of depressed patients improve if they are kept awake for one entire night or if they are awakened for the second half of the night. Some improve if they go to sleep several hours earlier than usual for several months. Cases in which these are successful lend credence to the old theory that circadian rhythms are disturbed in depressive states. The *DSM III-R* identifies a long-acknowledged depression called "seasonal affective disorder" in which certain people who consistently get depressed in winter and slightly manic or hypomanic in late summer seem to be affected by the amount of light they are receiving. Symptoms can be relieved by exposure to bright light for several hours a day in the winter and by controlling exposure in late summer (October 1988 1-2).

The most difficult to assess or regulate scientifically, but considered a very essential part of most therapies, are the various psychotherapies—psychodynamic therapy, interpersonal therapy, behavior therapy, cognitive therapy, group therapy, dyadic couples therapy, family therapy. Each of these methods revolves around the patient-therapist model—there are actually hundreds of approaches being used today—in which both enter into a therapeutic alliance in order to resolve as intensively as possible the painful or maladaptive elements in behavior or development which may be contributing to the psychiatric disorder.

Psychodynamic therapy has its theoretical foundation in Freud's work, although the modern practice resembles the Freudian model but little. Usually the therapy addresses painful elements in the psyche which may be aggravating the depressive or elevated emotional states. Still emphasized are the Freudian constructs of childhood experiences, defense mechanisms, and transference. However, the therapy is not designed to go on indefinitely but is planned for 5 to 7 months of intensive work. Often the modern Freudian descendant forces confrontations with painful material or evokes strong feelings with difficult questioning or statements used to bring out childhood repressions. Present conscious thoughts and feelings are more the focus today than the subconscious or unconscious. Some experts do not think this is an effective therapy for depression (October 1988, 2).

Interpersonal therapy borrows from psychodynamic therapy and others to form a basis specifically for treating depressions. It is not a new therapy, but a combination of older approaches. The chief goals are restoring self-esteem and improving communication. The theoretical background comes from the work of John Bowlby's attachment theory and Harry Stack Sullivan's therapy. The time interval is 3-4 months of weekly sessions. Therapists see their patients as having one of four primary problems which need therapeutic attention:

1) Grief as the result of the death or loss of a loved one or other significant loss. The therapist helps the patient explore his or her feelings, especially anger and guilt.

2) Needed clarification of interpersonal roles. Help is given to resolve social duties and expectations in daily lives.

3) Divorce, job change, or other social transition. This area centers on the need for help in adjusting to a difficult situation or re-shaping life goals.

4) Isolation and loneliness. These patients need help in social skills which may include some exploration and interpretation of the past (October 1988, 3).

Behavior therapy came about from the work of B.F. Skinner and is based on changing troublesome behavior through modification based on rewards (positive reinforcement). The depressed patient is taught how to change his or her behavior to receive greater rewards and satisfactions from life, to develop a "behavioral repertoire" that protects him from depression. Learning relaxation is another part of this approach (Ibid.).

Cognitive therapy works on the problem of altering the mood by changing the thought patterns. This treatment grew out of behavior therapy and focuses on the way in which feelings and thoughts are maintained by positive reinforcement. The patient learns to question assumptions that for a long time have been unacknowledged, for example, meanings of experiences established in childhood which quickly bring into play disappointment, loss, or rejection. Self-defeating thoughts are dealt with as symptoms that can be changed, thereby relieving the depression. Cognitive therapy requires 3-4 months of weekly sessions and has been very successful in certain cases. It is usually followed up with another 6-12 months of sessions to maintain the positive changes in thought processes.

Group therapy is often less anxiety-provoking and more effective for some patients. A social network can be formed and a support system initiated. This is also a positive part of the 12-step programs in recovery. The person becomes less isolated and less self-preoccupied and more hopeful as he sees others recovering. Family therapy has taken a real leap forward in recent years due primarily to the advance in "systems" theory that approaches the individual as part of a system rather than simply an isolated patient. Involvement of the family is a very health-promoting and dynamic way in which to insure future well-being of the patient and reduce recidivism. In one study, for example, more than half the husbands and wives of patients with bipolar disorder said that they probably would not have married them if they had known of the disease (November 1988, 1-2).

Discussing the results of a study on the comparative effectiveness of various therapies done by NIMH, *The Harvard Medical School Mental Health Letter* summarized:

Mood disorders apparently respond to both biological and psychotherapeutic treatment. From one point of view, each type of therapy is aimed at a different group of symptoms: cognitive therapy for pessimism and self-doubt; drugs or ECT for vegetative or physical symptoms; interpersonal therapy for social isolation and disturbed personal relationships; family or couples therapy for domestic problems; psychodynamic therapy for guilt, anger and internal emotional conflict. The treatments can also be seen as directed at different causes of depression: neurochemical imbalances, early upbringing, a bad family situation, social isolation and awkwardness. But in practice, all therapies ultimately affect all symptoms, and the causes of mood change exert so much mutual influence that none of them must be regarded as more fundamental than the others. (November 1988, 4)

Works Cited

Addario, D. "Developmental Considerations in the Concept of Affective Illness." *Journal of Clinical Psychiatry*. 1985 Oct.; 46(10 Pt 2): 46-56.

Baron, M., N. Risch, R. Hamburger, B. Mandel, S. Kushner, M. Newman, D. Drumer, R. H. Belmaker. "Genetic Linkage Between X-Chromosome Markers and Bipolar Affective Illness." *Nature*. 1987 Mar 19-25; 326(6110): 289-92.

Brotman, A.W., A. M. Farhadi,vA. J. Gelenberg. "Verapamil Treatment of Acute Mania." *Journal of Clinical Psychiatry*. 1986 Mar; 47(3): 136-38.

Bunney, W.E., D.L. Dunner, R.R. Fieve, M.M. Katz, J. Mendlewicz, G. Winokur. (Ed. Ronald Fieve). Lecture and Discussion. The Council for Interdisciplinary Communication in Medicine, Ltd. Psychiatric Recorder #5. Smith, Kline & French Laboratories, 1972.

Caillard, V. "Treatment of Mania Using a Calcium Antagonist—Preliminary Trial." *Neuropsychobiology*. 1985; 14(1): 23-6.

Detera-Wadleigh, S.D., W.H. Berettini, L.R. Goldin, D. Boorman, S. Anderson, E.S. Gershon. "Close Linkage of c-Harvey-ras-1 and the Insulin Gene to Affective Disorder Is Ruled Out in Three North American Pedigrees." *Nature*. 1987 Feb. 26; 325: 806-08.

Egeland, J.A., D.S. Gerhard, D.L. Pauls, J.N. Sussex, K.K. Kidd, C.R. Allen, A.M. Hostetter, D.E. Housman. "Bipolar Affective Disorder Linked to DNA Markers on Chromosome 11." *Nature*. 1987 Feb. 26-Mar 4; 325(6107): 783-87.

Egeland, J.A. "A Genetic Study of Manic-Depressive Disorder Among the Old Order Amish of Pennsylvania." *Pharmacopsychiatry*. 1988 Mar; 21(2): 74-5.

Gerhard, D.S., J.A. Egeland, D.L. Pauls, D.E. Housman. "Search for a Gene that Predisposes Individuals to BPI Disorder." *Journal of Psychiatric Research*. 1987; 21(4): 569-75.

Gruber, Howard E. "The Evolving Systems Approach to Creativity." *Towards a Theory of Psychological Development* (Ed. Sohan & Celia Modgil). Windsor, Eng: NFER, 1980.

Harsch, H.H., M. Miller, L.D. Young. "Induction of Mania by L-Dopa in a Nonbipolar Patient." *Journal of Clinical Psychopharmacology*. 1985 Dec; 5(6): 338-9.

Hodgkinson, S., R. Sherrington H. Gurling, R. Marchbanks, S. Reeders, J. Mallet, M. McInnis, H. Petursson, J. Brynjolfsson. "Molecular Genetic Evidence for Heterogeneity in Manic Depression." *Nature*. 1987 Feb. 26-Mar 4;325(6107):805-06.

Jacobs, D., T. Silverstone. "Dextroamphetamine-induced Arousal in Human Subjects as a Model for Mania." *Psychological Medicine*. 1986 May; 16(2): 323-29.

Keshavan, M.S., A.S. David, H.S. Narayanen, P. Satish. "'On-Off' Phenomena and Manic-Depressive Mood Shifts: Case Report." *Journal of Clinical Psychiatry*. 1986 Feb.; 47(2): 93-4.

Kolata, G. "Manic-Depression Gene Tied to Chromosome 11." *Science*. 1987 Mar 6; 235(4793): 1139-40.

Koshland, Jr., D.E. "Nature, Nurture, and Behavior." *Science*. 1987 Mar 20; 235(4795): 1445.

Robertson, M. "Molecular Genetics of the Mind." *Nature*. 1987 Feb. 26-Mar 4; 325(6107): 755.

Sargent, M. NIMH Report. "The Gene Hunt." *Hospital & Community Psychiatry*. 1987 Jul; 38(7): 718-9.

The Harvard Medical School Mental Health Letter (Ed. Lester Grinspoon, M.D.). 1988 Sept; 5(3):1-3.

The Harvard Medical School Mental Health Letter (Ed. Lester Grinspoon, M.D.). 1988 Oct; 5(4): 1-3.

The Harvard Medical School Mental Health Letter (Ed. Lester Grinspoon, M.D.). 1988 Nov; 5(5):1-4.

Textbook of Psychiatry(Ed.John A. Talbot M.D., Robert E. Hales M.D., C. Stuart Yudofsky M.S.). Washington, D.C.: American Psychiatric, 1988.

Telner, J.I., Y.D. Lapierre, E. Horn, M. Browne. "Rapid Reduction of Mania by Means of Reserpine Therapy." *American Journal of Psychiatry*. 1986 Aug.; 143(8): 1058.

Works Consulted

Balgir, R.S. "Serological Markers in Unipolar and Bipolar Affective Disorders." *Human Heredity*. 1986; 36(4): 250-3.

Blehar, M.C., M.M. Weissman, E.S. Gershon, R.M. Hirschfeld. "Family and Genetic Studies of Affective Disorders." *Archives of General Psychiatry*. 1988 Mar; 45(3): 289-92.

Cookson, J.C. "Drug Treatment of Bipolar Depression and Mania." *British Journal of Hospital Medicine*. 1985 Sept; 34(3): 172-75.

Cox, N.J., B.K. Suarez. "Linkage Analysis for Psychiatric Disorders." *Psychiatric Developments*. 1985 Winter; 3(4): 369-82.

Faraone, S.V., M.J. Lyons, M.T. Tsuang. "Sex Differences in Affective Disorder: Genetic Transmission." *Genetic Epidemiology*. 1987; 4(5): 331-43.

Gurling, H. "Candidate Genes and Favored Loci: Strategies for Molecular Genetic Research into Schizophrenia, Manic Depression, Autism, Alcoholism and Alzheimer's Disease." *Psychiatric Developments*. 1986 Winter; 4(4): 289-309.

Hodgkinson, S., H.M. Gurling, R.H. Marchbanks M. McInnis, H. Petursson. "Minisatellite Mapping in Manic Depression." *Journal of Psychiatric Research*. 1987; 21(4): 589-96.

Kidd, J.R., J.A. Egeland, A.J. Pakstis, C.M. Castiglione, B.A. Pletcher, L.A. Morton, K.K. Kidd. "Searching for a Major Genetic Locus for Affective Disorder in the Old Order Amish." *Journal of Psychiatric Research.* 1987; 21(4): 577-80.

Lewis, D.A. H.A. Nasrallah. "Mania Associated with Electroconvulsive Therapy." *Journal of Clinical Psychiatry.* 1986 Jul; 47(7): 366-7.

Loosen, P.T. "The TRH-induced TSH Response in Psychiatric Patients: A Possible Neuroendocrine Marker." *Psychoneuroendocrinology.* 1985; 10(3): 237-60.

Lykouras, L., D. Vassilopoulos, A. Voulgari, C. Stefanis, D. Malliaras. "Delusional Depression: Further Evidence for Genetic Contribution." *Psychiatry Research.* 1987 Jul; 21(3): 277-83.

Mallet, J., C. Boni, S. Dumas, M. Darmon, N. Faucon Biguet, B. Grima, P. Horellou, A. Lamouroux. "Molecular Genetics of Catecholamine as an Approach to the Biochemistry of Manic-Depression." *Journal of Psychiatric Research.* 1987; 21(4): 559-68.

Mendlewicz, J., P. Simon, S. Sevy, F. Charon, H. Brocas, S. Legros, G. Vassart. "Polymorphic DNA Marker on X Chromosome and Manic Depression." *Lancet.* 1987 May 30; 1(8544): 1230-32.

Mester, R. "The Psychotherapy of Mania." *British Journal of Medical Psychology.* 1986 Mar; 59(Pt1): 13-19.

Owen, M.J., S.A. Whatley. "Polymorphic DNA Markers and Mental Disease." *Psychological Medicine.* 1988 Aug; 18(3): 529-33.

Rice, J., T. Reich, N.C. Andreason, J. Endicott, M. Van Eerdewegh, R. Fishman, R.M. Hirschfeld, G.L. Klerman. "The Familial Transmission of Bipolar Illness." *Archives of General Psychiatry.* 1987 May; 44(5): 441-7.

Risch, N.; Baron, M.; Mendlewicz, J. "Assessing the Role of X-Linked Inheritance in Bipolar-related Major Affective Disorder." *Journal of Psychiatric Research.* 1986; 20(4): 275-88.

Suarez, B.K., C.L. Hampe, A.F. Wright. "Linkage Analysis in Manic-Depressive Illness." *Lancet.* 1987 Aug 8; 2(8554): 345-46.

Swann, A.C., S.K. Secunda, M.M. Katz, S.H. Koslow, J.W. Maas, S. Chang, E. Robins. "Lithium Treatment of Mania: Clinical Characteristics, Specificity of Symptom Change, and Outcome." *Psychiatry Research.* 1986 Jun; 18(2): 127-41.

Waters, B., D. Sengar, I. Marchenko, G. Rock, Y. LaPierre, C.J. Forster-Gibson, N.E. Simpson. "A Linkage Study of Primary Affective Disorder." *British Journal of Psychiatry.* 1988 Apr; 152: 560-62.

Winokur, G., R. Crowe, A. Kadrmas. "Genetic Approach to Heterogeneity in Psychoses:Relationship of a Family History of Mania or Depression to Course in Bipolar Illness." *Psychopathology.* 1986; 19(1-2): 80-84.

Winokur, G. "Family (Genetic) Studies in Neurotic Depression."*Journal of Psychiatric Research.* 1987; 21(4): 357-63.

Zuckerman, M. "Sensation Seeking, Mania, and Monoamines." *Neuropsychobiology.* 1985; 13(3): 121-28.

PART III:
Virginia Woolf—A Case In Point

Chapter Ten
Family History and Etiology of Virginia's Disease

I could not write and all the devils came out—hairy black ones.
To be 29 and unmarried—to be a failure—Childless—insane,
too, no writer.

—*Virginia Stephen Woolf,* A Writer's Diary

The early onset of Virginia Woolf's mental disorder and her parallel development as a creative writer can be carefully documented through Quentin Bell's authoritative biography of his famous aunt and by Leonard Woolf's volumes of autobiography which deal with the years of their marriage. In a very real sense it is to the constancy and devotion of Leonard Woolf that we owe the legacy of Virginia's writing. A creative and productive person himself, he dedicated his life to the battle to preserve and maintain her sanity. He placed himself against the mainstream of medical opinion and aborted efforts to order her assigned to a British asylum for custodial care. The token of his efforts remains unique and difficult to assess: the literary genius of Virginia Woolf.

In *Beginning Again* Leonard Woolf describes Virginia's first breakdown after their marriage in 1912 during which she was violently insane and almost succumbed to an overdose of barbiturates. From this experience until her death in 1941 by suicide, his vigilance never wavered. About her illness, he wrote:

> I do not know what the present state of knowledge with regard to nervous and mental diseases is in the year 1963; in 1913 it was desperately meager. . . .
> The course of Virginia's illness vitally affected the course of our lives, and therefore from the autobiographical point of view I feel I should deal with it in detail. . . . There was one remarkable fact about the two insane stages which throws light upon the primitive and chaotic condition of medical knowledge about insanity in 1913. There was at that time apparently a type of insanity scientifically known as manic-depressive. People suffering from it had alternating attacks of violent excitement (manic) and acute depression (depressive). When I cross-examined Virginia's doctors, they said she was suffering from neurasthenia, not from manic-depressive insanity. But as far as symptoms were concerned, Virginia was suffering from manic-depressive illness. (159)

Quentin Bell recorded Virginia Stephen Woolf's childhood and described the early history of her affective disorder. He tells us that at a very young age there were signs of her psychological fragility, her artistic sensitivity. She was in the truest sense the daughter of Sir Leslie Stephen, a brilliant but melancholic man who was responsible for the *Dictionary of National Biography*.

A scholar and an introvert, Sir Leslie was first married to Harriet Thackeray, the younger daughter of William Makepeace Thackeray, who left him a widower at 43 with a seriously afflicted child. Recovering from this tragic course of events, Sir Leslie married Julia Jackson Duckworth, a widow who had been a close friend of his first wife. Both were stationed in British society with impressive literary and social connections. Mrs. Duckworth brought three children to the marriage, and considering the hopelessly insane child of Leslie's first marriage, the new couple certainly had their share of problems. In swift succession four more children were added. Vanessa was born in 1879, followed by Thoby in 1880, Adeline Virginia in 1882, and Adrian in 1883.

The tumble of the Stephen nursery was the first dominating influence in Virginia's life. She was very slow learning to talk; according to Bell, she was almost three before indulging in language, but even then words, although hard-won, became her medium for expression. Her young childhood was typified as turbulent. She was seen as accident-prone and tempestuous with a considerable amount of what psychiatrists call "affect" or emotion. Her siblings dubbed her "the goat," a nickname which she carried into adulthood.

However, she was the uncontested family storyteller, nightly entertaining her brothers and sister in the nursery of their home at 22 Hyde Park Gate. After a bout of whooping cough at age six, Virginia became more reflective and thoughtful, declaring to Vanessa that she loved her father more than her mother. This loyalty was to prove an emotional burden which would haunt her and seriously afflict the pattern of her living until very late in her writing career.

Evidence of the magnitude of his influence on her is found in a diary entry made in November 1928 when Virginia was 46 years old:

> Father's birthday. He would have been 96, 96, yes today; and could have been 96, like other people one has known: but mercifully was not. His life would have entirely ended mine. What would have happened? No writing, no books— inconceivable.
>
> I used to think of him and mother daily; but writing the Lighthouse laid them in my mind. . . . (135)

And from this passage of *To the Lighthouse*, we catch a part of that devotion to her father that would have destroyed her, prevented her writing. Here we see the author building a defense for the unfavorable characteristics of the book's antagonist, Mr. Ramsey:

> Finally, who shall blame the leader of the doomed expedition, if having adventured to the uttermost, and used his strength wholly to the last ounce and fallen asleep not much caring if he wakes or not, he now perceives by some pricking in his toes that he lives, and does not on the whole object to live, but requires sympathy, and whiskey, and someone to tell the story of his suffering to at once? (57)

In 1891 Virginia organized the production of a weekly family journal called the *Hyde Park Gate News* to which the four young Stephens contributed. These newspapers contained Virginia's first attempts at writing fiction. Sister Vanessa ably furnished the illustrations, and the boys added news items from the household, ranging from the servants in the kitchen to guests to secret intrigues among their many relatives. And again, we are able to see the seeds of life-long problems. As Virginia wrote and edited this childhood venture, she was plagued by the most severe sensitivity to criticism. Leonard Woolf would later record that after publication of each novel she was driven almost to complete distraction by her fear of what would be said of her work. It was in the light of this inordinate dread of criticism that Virginia Woolf wrote and re-wrote everything, sometimes writing an entire novel over from beginning to end as many as seven or eight times.

Julia and Leslie were responsible for most of their children's early education. Although the boys were later sent off to school, the girls were kept at home. Because of this, Virginia Woolf would always refer to herself as "uneducated" even though, in fact, she learned Latin and Greek from her father and brothers and was well-versed in the classics and other texts which formed the basis of the best British education of the time. Feeling discriminated against by the educational establishment of her youth and its tradition of male-oriented education, she would become in adult life a staunch advocate of liberal education for women.

In the volume of his autobiography *The Journey not the Arrival Matters*, Leonard Woolf relates an incident which he claimed illustrated in an amusing way Virginia's "immaculate feminism," particularly where the question of education was involved:

> Morgan Forster asked her whether he might propose her for the London Library Committee. But years ago Morgan himself in the London Library itself, meeting Virginia and talking about its organization or administration, had "sniffed about women on the Committee." Virginia at the time made no

comment, but she said to herself: "One of these days I shall refuse." So now on Thursday, November 7, 1940, she had some quiet satisfaction in saying No. "I don't want to be a sop—face-saver," she wrote in her diary. (75)

Sir Leslie Stephen endured a wide range of mood swings, at times charming and enchanting with his children, at other times in despair over his literary work. He suffered from insomnia, anxiety attacks, nightmares, and an incessant need for reassurance and comfort. At least three severe depressive attacks followed each other in close succession in 1888, 1890, and 1891. His problems were compounded and Virginia's began when on May 5, 1895, Julia Stephen died from complications of influenza. "Her death," said Virginia, "was the greatest disaster that could happen" (Bell 40).

Sir Leslie, then 63, was consumed by his grief for his beautiful and devoted wife whom he fully had expected to precede in death. He "sac-rificed" his mornings to teach the lessons to his daughters which his wife had begun. He was cheerless, irascible, miserable, and bewildered. His children were covered by a pall of darkness and what Virginia would later refer to as an "oriental gloom" settled over the house.

Julia Stephen's death was the beginning of Virginia's emotional in-stability. The sensitive child was at the mercy of histrionic relatives who seemingly enjoyed magnifying Sir Leslie's grief and the tragedy of Julia's untimely death. Julia's daughter, Stella Duckworth, bravely took charge of the household as a model daughter, assisted by the practical and obsti-nate Vanessa who was fifteen by this time. But, Virginia, 13, suffered her first breakdown. She heard voices, became painfully excited, nervous, and then intolerably depressed. She was terrified of people, confused and tormented by the commotions of her mind. Her illness had all the earmarks of a severe depressive reaction: a somatic over-concern, an acute sensitiv-ity to criticism, and an extreme self-hate and self-ridicule. Her hyper-acute self-consciousness led to such severe anxiety about leaving the house that her fears bordered on paranoid distortions (agoraphobia).

The family doctor ordered all lessons stopped and enforced bed rest, diet, and a constant vigilance over Virginia's deteriorating condition. These were the very same precautionary measures which would be required for the rest of Virginia's life. They were the only available means to control the incapacitating specter of manic-depressive psychosis.

Parenthetically, I note that Quentin Bell insists that during this period Virginia and her sister Vanessa were at the mercy of their twenty-eight-year-old half-brother George Duckworth. It has been alleged that his sexual advances toward the young teen-aged girls were a nightly persecution that went undetected by the rest of the family. Others cite undeniably affectionate letters and references to George, by Virginia, as evidence that this was not true or only partially true.

Whatever the truth may be, and however far George Duckworth extended his role as educator and protector of the young girls, it is certain that from this period the disturbed, critically-shy Virginia suffered from a morbid sexual panic that was never to be resolved. Her posture of frozen terror set the defensive mode of sexual response from which she would never emerge. Although her relationship to Leonard Woolf was one of mutual respect and a confessed depth of love, she admitted openly to Vanessa not long after her marriage that she seemed hopelessly frigid. Even human sexuality would not be allowed to follow its naturally warm, comforting course in her development.

In the spring of 1897 Stella Duckworth was married to Jack Hills and moved across the street to 24 Hyde Park Gate. Although the loss of her step-sister and surrogate mother was painful, the convalescing Virginia was cheered by the sight of Stella's new happiness. Once again there was something in and about 22 Hyde Park Gate that was happy and alive with joy. Even Sir Leslie's morbid attitude warmed and lightened with Stella's wedding and marriage. Virginia was allowed to return to her lessons which had been deferred for over a year, and her father wrote to a relative: "I hope, though I still hope with trembling that she (Virginia) is a bit better" (50).

Virginia was now a rather thin, tall girl of fifteen reading voraciously and writing constantly. Her diary during this period reveals a sober and conscientious scholar who found comfort in the work of writing. The artist had begun to bud, but there would elapse almost eighteen years before the first fruit would appear. Through those intervening years she would write little essays, make money through teaching and journalism, and help with a major biography of her father. *The Voyage Out*, her first novel, would not surface for publication until March 1915, almost three years after her marriage to Leonard Woolf.

Stella and Jack Hills returned to London on 28 April 1897, after a honeymoon to Italy and the European continent. Stella suffered chills, and the doctor put her to bed diagnosing peritonitis. The family was stunned, but Stella passed the crisis and seemed to be improving. During this period Virginia's health seemed inseparably tied to Stella's. She was afraid Stella would die. There was a slow but steady recovery, but then it was discovered that Stella was pregnant. Her health began to deteriorate. Virginia's anxieties increased. The physical manifestations of her psychiatric illness returned. Stella maintained an optimistic, comforting demeanor, sitting by Virginia's bed and stroking her until she was calm; but on July 18, surgical intervention was required, and on July 19, Stella died.

Again the Stephen household was a mournful disaster area invaded by the wailful chorus of relatives that re-inhabited 22 Hyde Park Gate. Sir Leslie plunged once more into the pit of depression. Virginia's health, though, miraculously improved. The probable reason for this is that now the strong-willed, self-assertive Vanessa took charge of the house. She refused to in any way sympathize with her father or indulge his fits of grief.

Fortified by her intelligence and secure in the force of her personality, Vanessa determined to bring order into the traumatized chaos of the Stephen household. Under her direction lessons were resumed. Thoby was off to Cambridge and the new friends he brought home added a new life and vitality to Virginia's milieu. There was the witty genius, Lytton Strachey, who was to become a friend for life. Saxon Sydney-Turner was a fascinating young man who read all night and slept all day. And there was Clive Bell, the handsome poet, who was also an excellent horseman. And Leonard Woolf.

Contact with these young and generative minds led Virginia and Vanessa to a more liberal philosophy which as time passed came to be viewed by their conservative relatives as outrageous. They drifted farther and farther from the conventions of dress and social mores that the Victorian society of their parents had invested in them. Their father, who had himself been an iconoclast in younger days, sympathized with this new-found intellectual excitement. Virginia, however, without knowing it was living on the edge of another shadow. Within five years doctors would diagnose the presence of cancer in Sir Leslie. For two years Virginia would nurse her father, and seeing the tyrant released from the bondage of tyranny, she would feel sorry for him. The tie between them would become even stronger.

In February, 1904, Sir Leslie Stephen died. After the long illness and the years of his melancholic outrage, it was a pleasant release for the four Stephen children who were now entering young adulthood. But the melodramatic scenes during their father's final months which were played out by the burgeoning horde of solicitous relatives had placed an enormous burden on their emotional resources. To make matters worse, these same relatives concocted a laborious trip through Europe to "relieve" the grief of the orphaned young people. Virginia became very ill.

Emotionally exhausted and then physically worn out from the long "vacation," Virginia was filled with inordinate guilt. Unlike Vanessa who was glad to be free from her father's despotic temper, Virginia was convinced that he had wanted to live, that his relationship with his children was only beginning, that she had never done enough for him, that he had been the most perfect human being who had ever lived, and that he had suffered from her appearance of indifference. She forgot all Sir Leslie's disagreeable qualities in the magnification of her own self-hate and despair. Suffering intolerably from headaches, palpitations, and severe anxiety, Virginia sank into a depressive psychosis. By the early summer of 1904 her mental health was completely broken for the second time.

The "horrible voices" returned, and she switched to a driving mania which urged her to insane acts. Vanessa realized that Virginia hardly knew what she was doing and employed three nurses to stay with her. A close family friend, Violet Dickinson, came to their aid, and Virginia was removed to her house at Birnam Wood. In spite of all their vigilance, Virginia attempted suicide by throwing herself from a second-story window. She was not seriously harmed but lay in bed most of the summer hearing the birds singing in Greek and believing her hallucinations that King Edward VII was hiding in the azaleas spouting foul language.

By September her symptoms abated. Virginia was very weak but was very nearly herself again. She began to play a little tennis, studied Latin with Thoby, and lunged back into her writing. Having been invited by the British historian Maitland to help with the editing of a biography of her father, she agreed and went to Cambridge. She approved letters, corrected details, and even wrote a few pages of her own about Sir Leslie's relationship with his children. This was the first of her writing to find its way into print. However, after only two weeks Virginia became restless at Cambridge. She quarreled with Vanessa but in the end agreed to take her suggestion to go live in Yorkshire at Giggleswick School where their cousin Will Vaughn was Headmaster. Vanessa wrote a letter to Will and his wife Madge commending Virginia's health: "She is really quite well now—except that she does not sleep very well and is inclined to do too much in some ways . . ." (Bell 92).

Interestingly, Vanessa also describes Virginia's writing regimen, a routine she would follow roughly for the rest of her life as her health permitted. In the morning after breakfast she walked alone for about half an hour. Later she and Leonard Woolf would enjoy these walks together. Then writing would consume the morning until lunch. Afterward, she took another walk of a half hour and wrote again until tea (about five o'clock) or rested if she were not feeling well. She always went to bed early although attacks of insomnia would find her reading and editing in the middle of the night.

At Yorkshire she visited Haworth Parsonage and wrote an account of it for *The Guardian*, a London clerical weekly. This outlet became a regular source of income for Virginia's journalistic contributions and was the first step into the career for which she had been preparing most of her life. It was the fall of 1904 and Virginia was 22 years old.

Being well-educated herself and having the advantage of being the daughter of a prominent literary family, Virginia was throughout her life regularly employed as a writer of short articles and book reviews. And she eagerly accepted any writing assignment. She would try almost anything in order to practice her skill at the craft of language.

Early in 1905 the doctors proclaimed Virginia "cured." She was now able to join the stimulating household set up by her sister and brothers at 46 Gordon Square, Bloomsbury, London. This move had been made to escape the horrible ghosts of the past which would forever inhabit 22 Hyde Park Gate. It was also an announcement to their family and friends that they were breaking formally with the traditional society of a still-Victorian London. And so, the "Bloomsbury Society" was born.

Actually, there was very little formality observed. The house on Gordon Square became by today's standards a modest home where intellectual young people could gather to exchange ideas about art, religion, politics, literature, and whatever was newsworthy about the new generation of Englishmen living in a new century. At a time when "proper" young ladies and gentlemen never addressed each other by their first names, the Bloomsbury group scandalously dropped their titles for the casual first-name basis of Vanessa, Clive, Virginia, Thoby, or just Stephen or Strachey or Bell.

We are told that Virginia at this time for all her reading could not suppose any of her acquaintances being unchaste. Realizing as well her incredible sexual shyness, it seems logical that nothing especially licentious was going on at Bloomsbury in 1905. But there were parties and each Thursday there were late-hour discussions that often lasted until two or three o'clock in the morning. That "young ladies" should be "entertained" in their homes unchaperoned at such hours was unthinkable to their family and friends in society. Their behavior was considered not only outlandish but intolerable. Even Henry James, a dear family friend, is supposed to have groaned at their "plague of manner."

Who were these "deplorable" young men of Cambridge? For the most part they were the close friends of Thoby and Adrian Stephen. Most of them sat at the feet of the famous Cambridge lecturer G.E. Moore—Saxon Sidney-Turner, Leonard Woolf, Lytton Strachey, Clive Bell, Walter Lamb, Jackson Pollock, Roger Fry. They were the core of intellect and character which would shape the course of twentieth-century Britain.

Vanessa was by this time deeply involved in her study of painting. There were trips by the Stephen brothers to Paris and other parts of Europe which included their friends and their sisters as well. A sense of challenge and enthusiasm permeated the group; they were at the head of exciting changes which were sweeping Europe and Great Britain. After a memorable excursion to Paris to study art with Vanessa, Clive Bell hung a copy of a Degas in his room at Cambridge—a first for the stodgy institution.

About this time (1906) Virginia began writing for *The Times Literary Supplement*, a connection which she maintained with regular contributions of writing until her death. During this period, work was begun on her first creative endeavor, the novel which later became *The Voyage Out*. Also she began teaching a course in English literature at night for Morley College, an evening institute set up to "instruct and enlighten" the men and women of the working classes. Virginia struggled with this assignment until 1907, but little is known about how her eager efforts were rewarded. She did learn an immense amount about discussing intellectual concepts with her inferiors. These discoveries paved the way for her later work in the woman's labor movement after World War I.

Into this cheerful new environment, in soap-opera fashion another tragedy was tossed. Thoby Stephen, only 26 years old, died in October 1906 of typhoid fever which doctors had mistakenly diagnosed as malaria. Two days later Vanessa in despair over Thoby's death turned to Clive Bell, and they were married. Virginia suffered another battle with depression— to lose her favorite brother, to see her sister married, and to have to leave Gordon Square where she had found her life's only happiness. But this time, illness did not intervene. Instead, she pushed her grief into her work.

Before the Bells returned from their honeymoon, Virginia and Adrian were ensconced in a new residence at 29 Fitzroy Square which had once been the home of George Bernard Shaw. Bloomsbury had gained a second center just far enough from the first to make strolling back and forth a pleasant interlude on long extended evenings. One problem remained. The job of "looking after Virginia" was now out of Vanessa's capable hands and insecurely settling into Adrian's less dependable ones. Adrian was very bright but not at all the most responsible member of the Stephen clan. In the opinion of all, Virginia must marry, but whom?

Virginia, unworried by their harried concern for her future, spent her evenings teaching at Morley College and her days writing. She wrote literary criticism and essays and completed, then burned at least four of the six or seven versions of *The Voyage Out*. Her literary shyness was acute. For a period of three years she lived a very closed life in this tight circle of teaching, work, and cordial, casual evenings with the Bloomsbury intellectual elite.

Lytton Strachey became her dearest male companion and was voted by Bloomsbury the man most likely to marry her. However, Lytton's creative genius was turned almost as dark as Virginia's. He was, in short, a misfit, a brilliant and socially perfect man who was nonetheless not heterosexual. Fortunately for both of them, his proposal of marriage was rejected. They were both relieved and their close, respectful friendship was happily salvaged.

Writing and re-writing her novel, Virginia suffered occasional lapses of somatic symptoms—headaches, neuralgia, insomnia. But 1911 saw the return of a former member of Bloomsbury. Leonard Woolf returned to England on leave from his civil post with the government of Ceylon. He was welcomed by all his old friends—Clive and Vanessa Bell, Adrian Stephen, Maynard Keynes, Morgan Forster, Roger Fry, Duncan Grant, Lytton Strachey, and of course, the beautiful and shy Virginia Stephen. A courtship was subtly but definitely undertaken. Their friendship grew, and as it did, Virginia's shyness was relieved to the point that on 29 May 1912, she could tell Leonard Woolf that she loved him and would marry him. As Quentin Bell insists: "It was the wisest decision of her life" (87).

Works Cited

Bell, Quentin. *Virginia Woolf: A Biography*. Vol. I. New York: Harcourt Brace Jovanovich, 1972.

Woolf, Leonard. *Beginning Again*. New York: Harcourt, Brace & World, 1963, 1964.

Woolf, Leonard. *The Journey not the Arrival Matters*. New York: Harcourt, Brace & World, 1969.

Woolf, Virginia. *A Writer's Diary* (Ed. Leonard Woolf, The New American Library). New York: Harcourt, Brace & World, 1953, 1954 by Leonard Woolf, 1968 by The New American Library.

Woolf, Virginia. *To the Lighthouse*. New York: Harcourt, Brace & World, 1927, 1955 by Leonard Woolf.

Chapter Eleven
More History

Virginia is the only person I have known intimately who had the quality which one had to call genius.

—*Leonard Woolf*

In the volumes of his autobiography Leonard Woolf describes the yearly, daily, and almost hourly struggle Virginia and he had with the mental illness which threatened time and again to overwhelm her and their life together:

> During the time I lived in the same house as Virginia in Brunswick Square, and particularly in the months before we married, I became for the first time aware of the menace of nervous or mental breakdown under which she always lived. I had had no experience at all of nervous or mental illness and it was some time before I realized the nature and meaning of it in Virginia. It played a large part in her life and our lives and it was the cause of her death. (*Beginning Again* 75)

Of his incredibly long and difficult experience with Virginia's disorder, Leonard Woolf would simply write, in his most pragmatic tone: "The course of Virginia's illness vitally affected the course of our lives . . . (*Beginning Again* 160).

It seems impossible to separate the two most outstanding elements in the life of Virginia Woolf—her superlative talent for writing and her recurrent problems with manic-depressive illness. These two facts intermingle until as good moderns and students of psychology, we seem to detect a connection. And if there is no way to establish a cause-and-effect relationship, we are at least perturbed by the way in which her creativity and her madness seem to intertwine. We begin almost without consciously thinking about it or realizing that we are doing it, to analyze comments about her creativity, hoping to get some handle on the problem of Virginia Woolf's mental disease and her creative productivity. Leonard Woolf recalls in his memoirs:

> But at any moment in a general conversation with five or six people or when we were alone together, she might suddenly "leave the ground" and give some fantastic, entrancing, amusing, dreamlike, almost lyrical description of an event, a place, or a person. It always made me think of the breaking and gushing out

of the springs in autumn after the first rains. The ordinary mental processes stopped, and in their place the waters of creativeness and imagination welled up and, almost undirected, carried her and her listeners into another world. . . . (*Beginning Again* 30-31)

We catch another glimpse of that creativity "gushing out" as Virginia Woolf scribbled in her diary the completion of her novel, *The Waves*:

Saturday, February 7th, 1931

Here in the few minutes that remain, I must record, heaven be praised, the end of *The Waves*. I wrote the words O death fifteen minutes ago with some moments of such intensity and intoxication that I seemed only to stumble after my own voice or, almost after some sort of speaker (as when I was mad); I was almost afraid, remembering the voices that used to fly ahead. (161)

These two mirrors, creativity and mental illness, remarkably reflect Virginia Woolf. The reality of her artistic production, however, is the reflection of Leonard Woolf. Without his stabilizing influence, his patience, and the painstaking care he was wiling to give her, Virginia Stephen Woolf might well have spent her life in a British asylum. The turning point came soon after their marriage when they returned from their extended honeymoon in late 1912.

Virginia was working on one of the numerous drafts of *The Voyage Out*, and as her mind attacked the revision with a tortured intensity, the tell-tale symptoms of stress reappeared. She began experiencing headaches and insomnia. Near the end of the year, Leonard Woolf grew increasingly alarmed. He began to take notes on her condition using a cryptic script of his own invention. The purpose of these notes which he alone could decipher was to carefully monitor the variations in Virginia's mental and physical health. It was a practice which never outgrew its usefulness.

At the end of January 1913, the Woolfs consulted a number of doctors. One of their primary concerns was the advisability of having children. Although the doctors did not agree among themselves—some seeing childbirth as a panacea for almost anything—there was consensus that it could be "dangerous" for a person with Virginia's delicate balance of health that they decided against having a family. At times this imposed childlessness was a source of great grief to Virginia, but the events that were to follow that very same year sealed the immense wisdom of that decision.

By summer Virginia had entered an ever-downward spiral of headaches, insomnia, depression, and weight-loss. The anxieties and failing appetite were distressing, but the insomnia and depression were unbearable. And so we find written into the final pages of *The Voyage Out* this desperate reference:

> After waiting for a moment they both disappeared, and having turned on her pillow Rachel woke to find herself in the midst of one of those interminable nights which do not end at twelve, but go on into the double figures—thirteen, fourteen; and so on until they reach the twenties, and then the thirties, and then the forties. She realized that there is nothing to prevent nights from doing this if they choose. (330)

Something happened which should have been a cause of relief and satisfaction, but which pushed Virginia once more to the brink of the abyss she had already experienced in 1895, 1904, and for a shorter period in 1910. A publishing house owned by her half-brother George Duckworth accepted *The Voyage Out* for publication. Her literary shyness and the intense fear she felt of public scrutiny and criticism swirled about her as she edited and proofread the final copy. Her state of mind became increasingly precarious.

In July Dr. George Savage advised Virginia to return to Jean Thomas's rest home at Twickenham where she had recuperated before from similar crises. The visit was planned as a three-week stay with the promise of a holiday to Somerset with Leonard if she obeyed the doctor's orders. For both the Woolfs the separation was miserable. Desperately each seemed to cling to the thread of hope that this "rest" would somehow "cure" Virginia's disorder, and she would be restored to total health. It was an illusion which was soon to be dispelled once and for all.

Separated from her husband's strength and encouragement, isolated from the work of writing which she needed to be doing, Virginia grew more unstable and despondent. She seemed more and more like a child who had been scolded and put to bed. Thoughts of suicide hung in her mind. Reality blurred as she stepped nearer the edge, but she followed the doctor's orders and in three weeks was reunited with Leonard.

The promised trip to Somerset turned into a disaster. In the first place it was an exhausting excursion for the already weak Virginia. In the second place the progress of her illness continued unabated, and to compound matters they were away from home and the doctors and friends who could have helped them. Leonard concluded after reviewing several days' notes in his private code that Virginia's condition was very serious. With a sense of alarm, he sent for Ka Cox to come to Somerset. By now it was early September.

Ka Cox was one of Virginia's dearest friends, a warm, sensible person who was familiar with her past breakdowns. She came as soon as Leonard notified her about Virginia's state of mind. Her arrival relieved some of the strain, but there was very little she could do under the circumstances. She persuaded Leonard that they had to take Virginia back to London in order to get help. The return trip by train during which Leonard Woolf was constantly on the alert fearing that his wife might at any moment throw herself to her death was only the beginning of a long series of events he would never forget:

> The journey had that terrible quality of the most real of real life and at the same time of a horrible dream, a nightmare. Virginia was in the blackest despair. . . . (*Beginning Again* 156)

When they reached London, they went directly to the office of the psychiatrist, Henry Head. Dr. Head requested a consultation with Dr. Savage before deciding where Virginia should be placed, so the entourage tracked over to Brunswick Square where Vanessa and Clive were living. Leaving Virginia in a more cheerful mood chatting with Vanessa and Ka, Leonard started back to meet with Dr. Savage and discuss what had taken place at Somerset. While he was with Dr. Savage, the telephone rang. It was Ka Cox; Virginia had again attempted suicide. Somehow she had found a box of veronal tablets in Leonard's luggage which he usually kept locked, and she had taken the whole box. A mad scramble ensued:

> I telephoned to Head and he came, bringing a nurse. Luckily Geoffrey Keynes, Maynard's brother, now Sir Geoffrey, then a young surgeon, was staying in the house. He and I got into his car and drove off as fast as we could to his hospital to get a stomach pump. The drive, like everything else during those days, had the nightmare feeling about it. It was a beautiful sunny day; we drove full speed through the traffic, Geoffrey shouting to policemen that he was a surgeon "urgent, urgent!" and they passed us through as if we were a fire engine. I do not know what time it was when we got back to Brunswick Square, but Head, Geoffrey, and the nurse were hard at work until nearly 1 o'clock in the morning. Head returned at 9 the next morning (Wednesday) and said that Virginia was practically out of danger. She did not recover consciousness until the Thursday morning. (*Beginning* 156-7)

The return to consciousness did not see Leonard or Virginia safely to the end of this "nightmare." It was quite evident she was far from well. Besides this fact, the British government required all suicidal patients to be certified by a magistrate and placed in an asylum or authorized nursing home. Weighted with the heavy burden of deciding her care, Leonard Woolf toured several of the qualified institutions at the request of the authorities. He found them "dreadful, large gloomy buildings enclosed by high walls, dismal trees and despair." Unable to commit Virginia to a life behind those walls isolated from her work, her friends and family, and his love, Leonard quietly told the doctors he was "prepared to do anything required by them if they would agree to her not being certified." The doctors acquiesced on the promise that Virginia would live in the country with a minimum of two full-time nurses until she recovered.

Their modest home at Asham could not possibly accommodate two nurses, much less the four nurses who were actually needed to care for Virginia at this time, so Leonard was relieved when George Duckworth offered them the use of his country home at Dalingridge Place, complete with its staff of servants. The next two months extended the nightmare into mid-November. Virginia alternated violently between wild mania and deep depression. She was almost impossible to manage. She refused to eat and would have starved if Leonard had not patiently fed her. She attacked the nurses and would hardly speak to anyone except her husband. The insanity would continue into 1914, and after a respite of about six months, an intense manic swing early the next year would produce the opposite effect—a profound hostility to Leonard.

At this point the future of the Woolfs and the literary future of Virginia Woolf seemed especially dim. Clive Bell was prompted by sympathy to write to a family friend:

> Woolf bicycled over to lunch yesterday, looking ill and very much tired, I thought, and in very low spirits. Virginia seems to have been even worse since the veronal affair. . . . One begins to wonder whether she will ever get really sound again. (Bell II 17)

Under the circumstances a less mature, a more selfish person could have easily given up without incurring anything but extreme sympathy and sincere condolences from friends and relatives. The situation seemed less than hopeless, but Leonard Woolf was not one to give in to self-pity. Determined not to commit Virginia to an asylum life from which she might never emerge, he merely set his course and the course of their life together toward the promotion and maintenance of Virginia's well-being. Referring to the extent of his commitment, Quentin Bell comments:

> As it was he learnt the hard way and one can only wonder, seeing how hard it was, and that he had for so long to endure the constant threat of her suicide,

> to exert constant vigilance, to exercise endless persuasive tact at mealtimes
> and to suffer the perpetual alternations of hope and disappointment, that he too
> did not go mad. (Bell II 18)

After leaving Dalinridge Place they enjoyed six months of steady improvement at Asham. There were short trips to London and even a resumption of Virginia's writing. Then, one morning in February 1915, at breakfast she suddenly began talking to her dead mother. Her speech was wild and incoherent. After a two-day respite, Virginia once more slipped into an extreme mania. Nurses were called again, and they moved to Hogarth House where, unlikely as it seemed at this time, the Woolfs were to make British publishing and literary history. Violent and screaming, Virginia invaded their new home with a frantic hostility to life and toward Leonard. For almost two months he hardly saw her, but slowly she began to improve.

For two years the cycle of mania and depression had taken a tremendous toll on her personality, but she did recover. Perched on a precipice, her mind tired from the strain of mental illness and her physical health seriously impaired, Virginia Woolf now saw not one world but two. There is little hint in her creative writing of the price her illness evoked, and yet we know that her art was accomplished in the healthy interludes, bitten in large chunks from her sane hours. Leonard Woolf is there, modestly behind every page she wrote. He made her writing possible.

How did the Woolfs manage through those years? Quentin Bell summarizes their relationship in this manner:

> Never again were they to travel so far or for so long; but certainly they were
> in comparison with most of their friends, monogamous. In two months of
> wandering (on their honeymoon) they had discovered that their personalities
> were complementary, their sympathies extraordinarily close. Their love and
> admiration for each other, based as it was upon a real understanding of the good
> qualities in each, was strong enough to withstand the major and minor punishments of fortune, the common vexations of matrimony, and presently, the
> horrors of madness. It is proof of their deep and unvarying affection that it was
> not dependent upon the intenser joys of physical love. Even before her marriage, they must have suspected that Virginia would not be physically responsive, but probably they hoped that Leonard, whose passionate nature was never
> in question, could effect a change. A letter written from Saragossa to Ka Cox
> shows that clearly enough, if this hope was entertained, it was also disappointed.
> (Bell II 5)

A passionate monogamy and a confessed frigidity seem an unlikely combination to support almost thirty years of marriage and such an unusual depth of commitment. But the deep love and trust of a dynamic, working relationship between two people of high intellectual caliber should never be underestimated. In the Woolfs' case it was among other things a very productive relationship. Their Hogarth Press published writers who otherwise might never have been read and widely accepted in England—James Joyce, Sigmund Freud, T.S. Eliot. These among others who were innovative and progressive found the Woolfs not only sympathetic but instrumental in their careers.

Leonard Woolf literally exhausted the medical resources of his time to find help for Virginia, but the sobering knowledge he gained from conference after conference was worse than useless. The information he did collect made him vow inwardly to fight all the odds and meet all the costs of preventing Virginia's certification and probable commitment to an asylum. Why?

The answer lies in the facts of British psychiatry in the early 1900s. Accepted forms of treatment centered on physical therapy with hardly a hint of the mental and emotional support which forms the backbone of today's psychiatric philosophy. There were still vestiges of medieval treatments hanging on. The range of effective therapy included three basic means of handling psychiatric problems, the same methods which applied to most health problems at the end of the 19th century: purging, emetics, and bleeding (Howells 168-206).

A certain "sophistication" had set in with the Industrial Revolution, and various mechanical devices were added to physical therapy in order to restrain and "tranquilize" manic patients. Leather straps, canvas jackets, and cloth ropes were used to immobilize the arms and legs. Various methods of shock therapy were employed which were actually hazardous. Whirling chairs and rotating beds utilized the pressure of centrifugal force until the patient's nose began to bleed or he lost consciousness. A number of fatal injuries occurred from these "treatments" because people occasionally lapsed into comas and never regained consciousness. For this reason, they were finally abandoned (Howells 168-206).

Other crude forms of shock included the use of icy douches for women and putting patients into a padded hollow wheel for exercise. An innovation in therapy occurred when someone suggested dropping water on the patient's head from varying heights. Whether intentional or not, most of the methods retained if not the intent, then at least the effect, of punishment for patients who were usually already weakened by their disorders (Howells 168-206).

Life in the asylums of Great Britain during the first part of this century was not all misguided therapy, however. There were asylum bands which played for inmate parties and hospital functions. Progressive asylums used patient help for their administrative duties and certain janitorial chores, and some asylums even had their own journals which were written and edited by the patients themselves. Is it possible to picture Virginia Woolf writing and editing in isolation from the rest of England? Would her work have been found, tucked away in the pages of an asylum journal? Would her writing have penetrated that wall of silence which isolates the mentally ill from society?

Isolation was a key factor in the British psychiatric practice of that time. Inmates benefited in many cases from the country settings of most institutions with their spacious grounds and reduced contact with censorious community attitudes. But it is difficult to believe that a Virginia Woolf could have flourished under any circumstances which removed her from the intellectual society of family and close friends, separating her from their concern.

By 1900 at least 70% of Britain's mentally ill were certified and committed. Operating under the Lunacy Act of 1890, which remained effective until the Mental Health Act of 1959, most of these required commitments were based on suicide attempts and were made on a long-term basis. A person who attempted suicide or was suspected of having attempted suicide was required to be certified by this law and admission of certified persons to an asylum was considered mandatory. Not until the Mental Treatment Act of 1930 were voluntary commitments even permitted.

Most British psychiatrists of this period were little more than the medical officer of a particular psychiatric establishment, and their primary duties related more to the physical care of patients with very little attention given to what we would consider psychiatric treatment. As a consequence British psychiatrists with the exception of neurologists were not regarded with as much respect as their colleagues in other branches of medicine (Howells 168-206).

Until 1959 even the power of administration and discharge lay solely in the hands of the Medical Superintendent of an institution rather than in the hands of any attending psychiatrist. If Virginia Woolf had been certified and admitted to an asylum in the hopeless condition in which we find her in 1912, it is possible she could have been lost on the back wards and even her private physicians would not have been able to legally obtain her release.

But this did not happen. Leonard Woolf prevented it. He reviewed the facts and then made his decision. Because he did, we are able to review in depth the distinctive relationship between an inherited mental illness and an inherent drive toward creative accomplishment.

Works Cited

Bell, Quentin. *Virginia Woolf: A Biography*, Vol. II. New York: Harcourt Brace Jovanovich, 1972.

Howells, John G. and M. Olivia Osborn. "Great Britain" in *World History of Psychiatry* (Ed. John G. Howells, M.D., F.R.C.P., D.P.M.) New York: Bruner/Mazel, 1975.

Woolf, Leonard. *Beginning Again*. New York: Harcourt, Brace & World, 1963, 1964.

Woolf, Virginia. *A Writer's Diary* (Ed. Leonard Woolf). New York: Harcourt, Brace & World, 1953, 1954 by Leonard Woolf and 1968 by The New American Library.

Woolf, Virginia. *The Voyage Out*. New York:Harcourt, Brace & World, 1920, 1948 by Leonard Woolf.

Chapter Twelve
The Creative Process in Virginia Woolf

*And in me too the wave rises. It swells; it arches its back. I am
aware once more of a new desire, something rising beneath
me like the proud horse whose rider first spurs and then pulls
him back. What enemy do we now perceive advancing against
us, you whom I ride now, as we stand pawing this stretch of
pavement? It is death. Death is the enemy.*

—*Virginia Woolf,* The Waves

Virginia Woolf was the victim of a mental disorder which we now
identify as bipolar disorder or formerly manic-depressive psychosis. From
her diary and from Leonard Woolf's writing it is possible to piece together
the way in which this recurrent, episodic illness affected her life and her
creative work. It is almost axiomatic that her literary productivity could
not have been possible if she had been forced to endure an isolated confinement in a British asylum.

In earlier chapters we have discussed the problem of mental illness
in the artist in detail and described the way it is related to the presence and
operation of the creative drive. Virginia Woolf is a very pointed example
that institutional care is not necessarily the only or most compassionate
way to handle the mental breakdown of an artist. A new level of understanding and a new comprehension of the significance of the recent breakthroughs in medical and psychiatric research can relieve the anguish and
humiliation of institutionalization for artists facing health problems now
or in the future.

The mind of the artist is a delicately balanced and intricately tuned
instrument. When an exceptionally fine electronic device needs repair, we
do not throw it on the shelf and forget about it; neither do we turn it over
to someone who has no idea of its value or usefulness. Instead we search
out the most capable craftsman to work on it, and we bar no expense to
see it restored.

If we have learned to take such care of our expensive and sensitive
technological devices, and yet are unwilling or unable to consider the needs
and requirements of our artists and creative people, what kind of society
are we? Are we culturally so far from any empathetic or human view of
our mutual sufferings that material objects are worth more than people?
Have we ventured so far into the denial of our feelings, dissociated so

entirely from our authentic selves that we are more concerned with the quantity of things in our lives than the quality of that life? Where is the life of the soul today; and in a whisper we dare to question, where, the life of the spirit?

In his 1989 Inaugural Address President George Bush mentioned several times that a "new breeze is blowing" and that he believed we were becoming a "gentler, kinder nation." Those are very nice words, and much in our world begins with words. Still, we must also make the choices represented by the words. Metaphor is descriptive, not directive. Human behavior is not determined or programmed, even though we have much in common with the other living things on this planet. If the great experiment of democracy has proven anything in the past two hundred years it is that human beings can learn to be, to make choices—enlightened choices, humanitarian choices, creative choices. In this day more than ever before, perhaps, not to choose is the saddest choice. It is time to consider what some of the alternatives may be.

In 1939 Carl Jung, the famous but controversial psychiatrist, was invited to lecture at the Tavistock Clinic in London. During one of the question-and-answer periods, someone asked Dr. Jung to distinguish between a "pathological invasion" (psychiatric disturbance, especially psychosis) and "artistic inspiration." His reply is a challenge to us to find other avenues of therapy and support for our creative and generative people who from time to time because of their sensitivity, exhaustion, or frustration, lose their creative powers or are overtaken by illness:

> Between an artistic inspiration and an invasion there is absolutely no difference. It is exactly the same, therefore, I avoid the word "pathological.". . . To be "crazy" is a social concept; we use social restrictions and definitions in order to distinguish mental disturbances. . . . It is not an absolute increase in insanity that makes our asylums swell like monsters, it is the fact that we cannot stand abnormal people any more, so there are apparently very many more crazy people than formerly. (37)

Jung is an example of a person who had to find some creative outlet for his intensely personal view of the world. Even a cursory study of his work or a review of his books and memoirs reveals a personality with such an over-powering drive for creative expression that at times he himself experienced mental breakdowns. Like his psychiatric progenitor, Sigmund Freud, he was his own patient and his own analyst. Preferring to sort through and arrange his own perceptions and mental processes, he recorded as he did both the method and the madness.

And this is one of the most useful functions of the drive to create: to push subconscious shadows into conscious products with which the ego or personality can deal directly and impersonally using the internal energy of the drive to obtain the most objective subjectivity possible for the psyche. As the sensitive and painful elements of the artist's perception of life take more concrete shape and more pragmatic form, the artist then, as a person, is able to exert a kind of control over them that promotes his own sense of well-being and psychic solidarity. This kind of control and integration of the mind is never possible for the artist as long as these images remain solely as ephemeral haunts to consciousness. This process of loose associations integral to the creative process was discussed in Chapter Two.

Whether the images range from painful memories to doubts, fears, or morbid fascinations, raptures, elevations of spirit, the artist can use the energy they produce within the build-up of physical tensions to "create" the actual projects of his area of expression. The "media of expression" is the vehicle which transfers the force of his over-abundance of powerful sensory input into manageable form so that he or she can avoid being mentally, consciously swamped or emotionally drained.

The poem, the story, the dance movement, the dramatic interpretation, the painting, the sculpture, the musical performance, the composition or whatever other form chosen for this purpose reduces and channels the ghosts or preoccupations or exhilarations of the artist's mind. The drive to create, according to this model, proves to be the psychic force or energy within the personality which allows the mind to maintain equilibrium. It is the homeostatic device of the mind. It is in this way a psychologically functioning homeostatic device which if thwarted creates, instead of aesthetically pleasing projects of art or technology, of beauty and design, an uncontrollable build-up of raging tensions and stresses which serve to trigger the biochemical mechanisms of mental breakdown, addictive behavior, and even psychosomatic or stress-related diseases.

Leonard Woolf in his memoirs described the close relationship that existed between Virginia's insanity and her creativity:

> Some pages back I referred to the ancient belief that genius is near allied to madness. I am quite sure that Virginia's genius was closely connected with what manifested itself as mental instability and insanity. The creative imagination in her novels, her ability to "leave the ground" in conversation, and the voluble delusions of the breakdowns all came from the same place in her mind— she "stumbled after her own voice" and followed "the voices that fly ahead." And that in itself was the crux of her life, the tragedy of genius. (*Beginning Again* 80)

If we ask ourselves the question, curiously scratching the back of the head, which comes first—the creative mind or the mental instability—the answer is likely to seem paradoxical: neither and both. Any discussion of art is an exercise in the metaphor of the unique, and equally, any discussion of an artist involves his particular uniqueness as well as we can observe it. This is what makes the creative theories so complex and confusing: the disparate elements. The process and the product.

Virginia Woolf attained her creative level of art because she (to borrow a line from Thoreau) "marched to the beat of a different drummer." Her affective disease and many-faceted mind combined with a sensitive psychological structure to give her a wide-range view of life which provoked considerable internal turmoil by its wealth and diversity of sensory input. But the equation does not stop there.

Many people have had equally intelligent minds and equally unstable mental processes and yet they have lived obscure lives as odd-balls or eccentrics without even so much as a token of creative output. The actual monument to the creative expression of Virginia Woolf is impressive: nine novels, two biographies, seven books of literary criticism, over 500,000 words of diary, volumes of letters and lectures, some still unpublished. The enormity of her creative production is admirable even without the perspective of her disabling mental disorder and her poor physical health.

We would never have had the literary legacy of Virginia Woolf's writing in spite of her husband's meticulous care, if she had not inherited an internal drive to create. It was the drive which prodded her to gain control over the "voices" and visions which consistently threatened her rational mind. It was the drive for creative expression which pushed her to overcome all obstacles, challenge every impediment which prevented her from pursuing her art, writing. And the existence of her work proves that all discussions of art and all analyses of creative projects are incomplete without the central reference point of the presence and functioning of the drive to create.

Specifically, how did the drive to create function in the life of Virginia Woolf? First, it made creative expression not a goal or an afterthought or a series of entertaining mental interludes but a requirement for emotional functioning, equilibrium, mental stability. It brought structure out of the chaos of life.

Thinking of all those rats that have run through their mazes because hunger elevated their drive for food conjures a similar picture of the artist's mind which endures periods of fallow productivity until the pressure of internal motifs drives them to dig for new channels of expression. In excerpts from her diary, we are able to see clearly this process at work in the mind of Virginia Woolf:

> Talk of planning a book or waiting for an idea! Then one came in a rush; I said to pacify myself, being bored and stale with criticism and faced with that intolerable dull fiction [She was at this time writing literary reviews for the *The Tribune*.], "You shall write a page of a story for a treat; you shall stop sharply at 11:30 and then go on with the Romantics." I had very little idea what the story was to be about. But the relief of turning my mind that way was such that I felt happier than for months; as if put in the sun or laid on a cushion; and after two days entirely gave up my time chart and abandoned myself to the pure delight of this force; which I enjoy as much as I've ever enjoyed anything; and have written myself into half a headache and had to come to a halt like a tired horse and take a little sleeping draught last night; which made our breakfast fiery. I did not finish my egg. I am writing. . . . (117)

"The pure delight of this force" is surely the drive for creative expression. Writing was the medium Virginia Woolf chose. It suited her temperament and her brilliant mind. She had a vast gift for verbal description to which Leonard Woolf so often referred in his autobiography. Her unique talent for language, as we know, was demonstrated at a very young age in the nursery at 22 Hyde Park Gate.

Another aspect of the drive to create is that it adapts to the talents and intellect of each individual artist in proportion to the compelling degree to which it is inherent in his or her psychological make-up. We have discussed in Chapter Nine the mechanisms of genetic transmission of the psychiatric disorders most likely associated with the genetic inheritance of the drive to create. The significant element that seems to link the drive to create with these disorders is the fact that mood or emotion is affected. Even in the alcoholic or addictive diseases, it is the effective mood alteration that is sought after even before the actual physical addiction or craving sets in. Some "using" artists and creative people refer to their chemical addictions as "attitude adjustments." When we examine the question of the artist's emotional involvement with his work the relationship between the drive and the psychiatric disturbance becomes apparent.

Vincent Van Gogh's affectivity, for example, is well-documented. He painted life with such a painful sensibility that every kind of emotion is evoked in studying his work. His feverish attempts to relate to people and his final breakdown into madness after ten years of painting demonstrate the emotional extremes which assail the artist at work. He also drank heavily periodically and was taking the drug digitalis at the time of his death.

On the other hand, Georgia O'Keefe lived a long and productive life as an artist of intense work and did not suicide. Her circumstances were perhaps not as emotionally traumatic as Van Gogh's, even though she certainly had her own problems to cope with. I remember seeing a public broadcasting interview with O'Keefe when she was around 90. In response to a question from her interviewer about the huge 30-foot paintings of flowers, she explained simply that she had gone out into her garden in early spring and had been overwhelmed by the "experience" of the morning, the flowers, the dew, the light, etc. As she returned to her studio she wanted to capture the rapture on canvas. She told the interviewer that she knew if she painted them life-size that no one would ever "see" them as she had seen them that spring morning. So, she chose to paint them as giants for the "emotional effect."

Beethoven did not commit suicide, but we are told that his relentless egotism and volatile nature drove his favorite nephew to his suicide. Devoted disciples reported incidents when their "maestro" wandered the woods near his home in a manic "raptus" from which he would emerge to write his music. Dostoyevsky is supposed to have left his wife and children starving while he debated philosophy and wrote in a nearby cafe, and Tolstoy, noted for his wild episodes and emotional outbursts, barely survived a depression in middle age which drove him to the brink of suicide.

No matter how often or how casually we invade the private lives of artists we find unorthodox affective behavior which seems to bear some sort of relationship to their creative output. It is impossible even to think about a Michelangelo or a Hemingway or a Plath or an errant young Mozart and not be struck by their emotional turbulence; some might also identify *joie de vivre*. And one of the functions of a drive toward creative endeavor is to help the individual psyche collect this affective energy and somehow channel and control it for some psychologically advantageous function; whether constructive or destructive depends for the most part on the personality and peculiarities of the particular artist.

Virginia Woolf made an odd aside in her diary of September 1928, noting the manner in which her moods seemed to mesh with the strains of her writing:

> Often down here I have entered into a sanctuary; a nunnery, had a religious retreat; of great agony once; and always some terror; so afraid one is of loneliness; of seeing to the bottom of the vessel. That is one of the experiences I have had here in some Augusts; and got then to a consciousness of what I call "reality": a thing I see before me: something abstract; but residing in the downs

or sky; beside which nothing matters; in which I shall rest and continue to exist. Reality I call it. And I fancy sometimes this is the most necessary thing to me: that which I seek. But who knows—once one takes a pen and writes? How difficult not to go on making "reality" this and that, whereas it is one thing. Now perhaps this is my gift: this perhaps what distinguishes me from other people: I think it may be rare to have so acute a sense of something like that— but again, who knows? I would like to express it too. (130)

The search for the truth of her life and her relationship to the reality of the universe served to bridge the emotional distortions. A person with this sort of emotional, even spiritual awareness, and creative imagination, charged with an urge to relate experience, does find satisfaction in being able to express the feelings. Virginia Woolf found that release in writing about whatever absorbed her interest, fascinated her mind, challenged her thinking. The delicate balance of health may have been a source of her sensitivity, but it became a stumbling block to her work as an artist. Still, the tandem effect of the process cannot be denied. Virginia Woolf was driven to seek her truth among the emotion-charged, often distorted elements and fragments of her world and her life.

Leonard Woolf with his private code and years of note-taking on Virginia's mental and physical health was in a position to observe the constant interplay of her illness and her drive for writing. As he discovered, the drive to create is not at all times a benevolent dictator but can push the artist beyond his or her constitutional limits. When this occurs, some sort of breakdown is inevitable; either a somatic illness intervenes or a psychiatric disturbance or relief may be sought through alcohol or drugs. In the case of Virginia Woolf, there was the imminent threat of manic-depressive psychosis:

> It was mental and physical strain which endangered her mental stability; if she lived a quiet, vegetative life, she was well and sane. But to tell her, as doctors always did and I often had to tell her, that she must live a quiet, vegetative life, was absurd, terribly ironic. If she tired herself by walking too long and too far, if she sat up later than 11 two or three nights running, if she went to too many parties, the physical strain would very soon bring on the dangerous symptoms, the danger signals. . . . But the mental strain of her imagination or genius, of her own mind, was equally or rather more dangerous, and though you can tell a person like Virginia not to go for a walk or to a party, you cannot tell her not to think, work, or write. I have never known any writer work with such concentration and assiduity as she did. . . . Thus the connection between her madness and her writing was close and complicated, and it is significant that, whenever she finished a book, she was in a state of mental exhaustion and for weeks in danger of a breakdown. (*Beginning Again* 80)

Preparing a manuscript for publication was one thing, but Virginia Woolf never seemed able to prepare herself for the publication of a manuscript. Fears and anxieties would take charge of her mind. Too tired to force her emotions into more work and too weakened by the physical exhaustion of long periods of intense effort, she was at the mercy of a mental illness which today seems to be a hereditary disorder involving a biochemical malfunction in the active processes of the brain.

The inordinate stresses placed on the personality of this extremely shy and sensitive woman would push her to the breaking point. Physical problems such as fatigue and headaches would not be cured by rest as in most people but would escalate into weeks of insomnia, depression or mania, an all-pervading sense of guilt and worthlessness, and an almost paranoid fear of publication. This hypersensitivity to criticism was a particular problem for Virginia Woolf. It was usual for her to complete a novel and then suffer the rigors of the damned about throwing it to the public for scrutiny. Considering the torturous manner in which her mind attacked her writing and the personal identification she felt with her characters, this is in part understandable. An artistic integrity bound to the highest standards of writing allowed her to fear that the novel she had written and re-written was still not ready for public exposure and possible censure. But in reality the primary motivation behind this dread of criticism was a morbid fear of failure instilled in her as a child by her father. Throughout her life Virginia Woolf would suffer a neurotic dread of falling short of the level of perfection which her father set for her and the other members of the Stephen household, especially after his wife's death when he took over the daily lessons of Virginia and Vanessa. This stressor was not generated by the drive to create but was a by-product of her early emotional development.

Over and over in her diary Virginia Woolf made references to both the joy and release of writing as well as the strain that her own demands put on her. In *Downhill All the Way*, Leonard Woolf writes that for months after finishing *The Waves* Virginia would complain that her brain still felt numb from writing it. On July 10, 1933, she had completed *Flush* and was beginning *The Years* when she made these remarks in her diary about the despotic state of her mind:

> And then I was in "one of my states"—how violent, how acute—and walked in Regents Park in black misery and had to summon my cohorts in the old way to see me through, which they have done more or less, a note made to testify to my own ups and downs: many of which go unrecorded here though they are

less violent I think than they used to be. But how familiar it was—stamping along the road, with gloom and pain constricting my heart: and the desire for death, in the old way, all for two I dare say careless words. (196)

Leonard Woolf tells us that death was never very far from Virginia's mind. Having tried twice to commit suicide and having almost succeeded, she suffered from the desperate knowledge that depression might overwhelm her again or that mania might come down with its intense heat, robbing her mind of its reason. It was this memory of mental illness which must have made death seem an attractive alternative:

> When Virginia was quite well, she would discuss her illness; she would recognize that she had been mad, that she had had delusions, heard voices which did not exist, lived for weeks or months in a nightmare world of frenzy, despair, violence. (*Beginning Again* 79)

The memory of those days and nights must have remained terrifyingly real. Death was an outlet and thinking of death a way of controlling the awful build-up of tensions and anxieties; it might even have held the temptation of rest, an illusion which might free her from the physical complaints and exhausting insomnia. But, even more appropriately, death could be a way of escape from the imminent threat of insanity.

This was not all death meant to Virginia Woolf. More than a way out of suffering for the human being she was, death held its own age-old fascination for Virginia Woolf, the artist. "Death," as she once remarked to Vita Sackville-West, "is the only experience I shall never describe."

Death was in fact the enemy, her adversary. In this way her writings assume the quality of "everyman" facing the ultimate reducer of life. In the fall of 1940 bombs were falling all over England and death was as near Virginia Woolf as it was to every other person on the island. Leonard tells us her very human reaction was one of self-preservation. When a bomb struck beneath their window one night, she immediately turned to him and said: "I don't want to die yet" (*The Journey not the Arrival Matters* 72-73).

Recalling the incident for her diary, the artist took hold and we find her trying to imagine what it would be like to be killed by a bomb:

> Oh I try to imagine how one's killed by a bomb. I've got it fairly vivid—the sensation: but can't see anything but suffocating nonentity following after. I shall think—oh I wanted another 10 years—not this—and shan't, for once, be able to describe it.

Within six months on Friday, 28 March 1941, Virginia Woolf would decide to place the final punctuation to her life. She wrote two letters, one to her sister Vanessa, and the other to her husband of almost thirty years; and, placing them on the mantelpiece she walked across the downs to the River Ouse, filled her pockets with stones and drowned herself. On her writing table were the proof pages for her ninth novel, *Between the Acts*, a novel she had found more pleasant to write than any other of her career. She had already told Leonard the sketch of a new novel which was pounding in her mind. Why did she kill herself?

It seems the rational decision of a sane human being, an act committed as the shadow of insanity hung on the horizon like an enormous cloud, a dark spectre. The strongest drive in human beings is the drive to survive, yet for the artist survival without creative recourse in a world of madness or incapacity may seem synonymous with death, an emotional death. The drive to create is the drive to survive and death is its antithesis, but as we mentioned before Virginia Woolf had written out her mind and was facing a new inner landscape. Her underpinnings has been blown apart in the destruction around her; finding her moorings lost or shifting radically, she chose self-destruction. Believing she could not recover her sanity once more and realizing she did not have the strength to stave off the advancement of her illness, she made her choice. To Leonard she wrote:

Dearest,

I feel certain I am going mad again. I feel we can't go through another of those terrible times. And I shan't recover this time. I begin to hear voices, and I can't concentrate. So I am doing what seems the best thing to do. You have given me the greatest possible happiness. You have been in every way all that anyone could be. I don't think two people could have been happier till this terrible disease came. I can't fight any longer. I know that I am spoiling your life, that without me you could work. And you will I know. You see I can't even write this properly. I can't read. What I want to say is I owe all the happiness of my life to you. You have been entirely patient with me and incredibly good. I want to say that—everybody knows it. If anybody could have saved me it would have been you. Everything has gone from me but the certainty of your goodness. I can't go on spoiling your life any longer.

I don't think two people could have been happier than we have been.

V.

(The Journey not the Arrival Matters 93-4)

Works Cited

Jung, C.G. *Analytical Psychology: Its Theory and Practice*. New York: Random House, 1968.

Woolf, Leonard. *Beginning Again*. New York: Harcourt, Brace & World, 1963, 1964.

Woolf, Leonard. *Downhill All the Way*. New York: Harcourt, Brace & World, 1967.

Woolf, Leonard. *The Journey not the Arrival Matters*. New York: Harcourt, Brace & World, 1969.

Woolf, Virginia. *A Writer's Diary* (Ed. Leonard Woolf). New York: Harcourt, Brace & World, 1953, 1954 by Leonard Woolf, 1968 by The New American Library.

Woolf, Virginia. *The Waves*. New York: Harcourt, Brace & World, 1931, 1959 by Leonard Woolf.

PART IV:
Solutions and Answers and
a Higher Realm of Questioning

Chapter Thirteen
The Dilemma of Disease

A senseless roundabout of painful thought.

—*Anonymous*

Manic-depressive illness—bipolar disorder—can be thought of as a recurrent mood disorder that affects about one in every 100 people and has a mixed genetic, psychological, and social etiology. As noted in Chapter Nine, treatment with drugs and psychotherapy has come a long way in the past twenty-five years, especially since the advent of lithium maintenance programs. Modern psychiatrists identify two distinct phases of the disease and emphasize that over a period of time a person may exhibit symptoms of one or both phases. The manic state is a condition in which the person manifests extreme physical and emotional excitation, but in the depressive stage the opposite effect is observed.

The depressed person is typically in a state of emotional turmoil complicated by slowing mental processes, lethargy, and psychomotor complaints such as headaches, fatigue, dyspepsia, and delusional pains. There is an inability to concentrate as well as a gross lack of enjoyment of or interest in life, resulting in withdrawal from social contacts, feelings of worthlessness, guilt, and possibly thoughts of death or suicide. The depressive phase of bipolar disorder resembles major depression (*Harvard* 1-2).

Someone who displays over a period of time both phases of the disorder is said to be suffering from bipolar (referring to the extremes of the illness) disorder, but a person who shows a tendency for only one phase is termed unipolar. Among psychiatric circles often the bipolar disorder is designated Bipolar I and Bipolar II. In Bipolar II there are depressive phases with mild or hypomanic states in which the full mania may not be observed, but in Bipolar I the person alternates between mania and depression. The course of Virginia Woolf's illness indicates that she suffered from episodes of both phases, acute manic psychosis and depressive psychosis. Sometimes, in bipolar disease the cycling takes place rapidly during a course of the illness so that both mania and depression alternate. Today this form of the disorder is most likely to be treated with ECT and lithium. In Virginia Woolf's lifetime there was little effective therapy.

Mania is the rare form of this disease and hospital admissions have shown that many more people experience the problems of depression than the "high" elated feelings of mania. Unlike the depressed person who looks sick, who may be thin and old-looking, fatigued, the manic patient looks generally fit—at least until the effects of hyperactivity and lost sleep take their toll. The high level of activity is usually non-productive because the person is so easily distracted and overstimulated that he or she cannot focus on even the simplest goals. Sometimes this distractibility leads to an enormous feeling of helplessness even in the midst of grandiose displays of confidence and superiority. The mood is transient and can change abruptly from jollity to hilarity to wild excitement to rage to aggression to violence (*Harvard* 1-2).

The manic person has extreme likes and dislikes and passes judgment on others with cruel insensitivity. In fact the word "extreme" summarizes the manifestations of this side of the manic-depressive disorder. There is a childish lack of self-control which makes management of a manic person very difficult. Every action, no matter how ordinary, is exaggerated. Incoming stimuli are processed and intensified to an alarming degree until the manic person resembles a boiler about to explode from the heat of some undiscovered fire.

The stream of thought is rapid and talk becomes incessant and often incoherent. There is characteristically a "flight of ideas." However, under the apparently illogical flow there is usually one "trend" of thought. The attention is intense but fleeting. The manic person is totally absorbed, almost possessed by each thought, every impression, an idea, a sight, a sound, an object, but only momentarily so. In the worst attacks the person may not be able to complete a sentence or finish any task. The imagination is often carried away into delusions which range from playful fabrications to a conviction of persecution. The excitement can lead to confusion and the conscious state may resemble delirium.

Body weight decreases from the hyperactivity. Also, the person many times refuses food because he or she is distracted or because he or she feels persecuted. A very careful and tedious nursing is often required to get the person on a steady nutritional program which is essential to the healing process.

The depressed person is not hard to identify. He looks tired, self-concerned, preoccupied. His appearance may be unkempt, his eyes lackluster, his posture poor, and his attitude one of acute sadness. There is a retardation of responses, both verbal and physical. The depressive phase, characterized by ennui, fear, anxiety, guilt, and despair, only barely disguises the internalized feelings of rage—a rage which for whatever reasons the patient cannot openly express. These deep-seated feelings may be tied to unconscious convictions of persecution or expressions of inadequacy, guilt, or self-hatred. Usually, there is an over-concern about the body with many physical complaints from insomnia to neuralgia. Often, the depressed patient may imagine "blocked bowels" or an "empty organ" or maintain some other deluded malaise. He or she may even despair at explaining his or her malady and withdraw further into a stupor.

Suicide is a critical problem in depression. A suicide attempt is often the first and last symptom of a severe depressive illness. The attempt may be desperately earnest, planned, and executed. Sometimes, the depressed person kills a close relative, someone he or she loves, a child even. The objective is noble enough—to spare that loved one the suffering of life. Occasionally, a manic person will attempt suicide because he or she is delusional or feels omnipotent, but there is usually warning in the manic state since the symptoms are dramatic and easily recognizable. In depression, however, the symptoms may be "masked" to the point that the person seems to be functioning in society. For this reason every suicide attempt should be seen as a harbinger of a depressive psychosis or extreme neurosis. If the attempt is unsuccessful, therapy should be planned for the depressed person *and* his or her relatives.

The person suffering from depression is intensely aware of a failing ability to deal with life's demands. He feels hopeless, lost, unable to concentrate, unable to will his or her emotions, or to reach a decision. Everything about him takes on an aura of pain. He is painfully sad, and if a joyous occasion arises, he is painfully happy. The depressed person feels isolated in despair, unable to grasp the situation, and powerless to change it. He suffers from a "loss of self" which psychiatrists call depersonalization. Things are "unreal" or "unnatural." There may be confusion, anxiety attacks, or a complete withdrawal into a state of total inattention or paralysis.

The thought content in the depressed phase does not have much variety. Ideas are slow, fogged, unreal. An all-pervading sense of guilt combines with morbid, gloomy processing of external stimuli to produce a state of constant mental anguish. There are distortions of body image. She feels she has cancer or she thinks her brain may be melting. She is afraid her heart will not beat or she thinks she has tuberculosis. The chest may feel heavy and the body numb. The depressed person cannot sleep or eat or even cry.

As noted in earlier chapters, manic-depressive illness is a disorder known since ancient times, and there seems to be little change from early descriptions of the disease. Bellerophon in the Homeric epics suffered from melancholia. Hippocrates in his writing makes many references to both mania and melancholia, considering them to be separate but chronic states without much hope for recovery. In the first or second century A.D. a Roman physician, Aretaeus of Cappadocia, made exact and intensive observations about mania and melancholia, noting there seemed a connection between the two states. He also observed that young people seemed more prone to mania and that melancholia was more common in older people. He reported authoritatively the intermittent character of the disorder and described the same guilt-ridden attitudes of the depressed person which we observe today. He also contrasted this with the hilarity of the manic state (Arieti Vol. III).

Various physicians through the Middle Ages described the conditions of mania and melancholia and designed treatment measures. Very little improvement was made in these early diagnostic criteria until the late nineteenth century when the studies of Emil Kraepelin systematized psychiatric symptomology and classification. He was the first to distinguish that there was a single underlying process in manic-depressive illness (Ibid.).

Depression is the most common form of psychopathology. There are many kinds of depressions with as many causes. Dr. J. Mendels in an article published in 1968 suggested at least 14 primary divisions. Under the classification of depressive reactions he identified these major forms of depressive illness: psychotic, neurotic, reactive, psychotic-reactive, involutional, agitated, endogenous, psychogenic, symptomatic, pre-senile, senile, acute, chronic, and the depressive phase of manic-depressive psychosis (1549-1554).

The *DSM III-R* handles the classification by describing the symptoms and the two major categories—Major Depression and Dysthymia:

> The current state of Major Depression or Bipolar Disorder is described with a fifth-digit code. If the criteria for a Major Depressive or Manic Episode are currently met, the episode is subclassified as either: mild, moderate, severe without psychotic features, or with psychotic features. If the criteria are currently not met, the fifth-digit code indicates whether the disorder is in partial or in full remission. (214)

Then, a current Major Depressive Episode can be broken down into three sub-categories for possible treatment management: melancholic type, chronic, seasonal pattern. Other related disorders symptomatically are classified according to various standards explained in the manual. For example, "Uncomplicated Bereavement" is designated not a mental disease, unless there is a "morbid preoccupation with worthlessness, suicidal ideation, marked functional impairment or psychomotor retardation, or prolonged duration suggest[s] bereavement complicated by Major Depression" (222-3).

The determination of Bipolar Disorder is made if the person has had a Manic Episode or has regular variations in mood with periods of major depression interspersed with periods of hypomanic or somewhat elated functioning. In the bipolar disorder a person may go through the stages of despair followed by a period of neutral mood and then pass to the hyperactive, euphoric stage described as mania. Sometimes, however, the person switches directly to mania with no "normal" period. In most cases, however, the bipolar patient will enjoy years and maybe even a decade or more of normal living between attacks of either depression or mania:

> Most victims of bipolar disorder are normal between their periods of disordered mood, but some have residual symptoms. The more attacks of mania or depression a patient has suffered, the more likely another one is. If not treated, the episodes become longer and more frequent with age. (*Harvard* 2)

Recurrent mania has been demonstrated to be endogenous. Never in psychiatric history have physicians or chroniclers found any external rationale for the wild moods of mania. The early Greeks associated mania with moral disorders—drinking, carousing, and unwarranted revelry. Some recognized its unusual origin by claiming it was a visitation of evil inflicted on a person by the gods. During the Middles Ages a manic attack was proof of demon possession and required that the person be burned alive. The only sympathetic treatment used through the centuries has been isolation of the victim. Society has always feared the unknown origin of mania.

In the Gospels there is a famous account of the Gadarene maniac who had been exiled to live in a cemetery. Using the methods of the psychohistorian, we see many elements of mania represented in the Gospel accounts (Matthew 8:28-34; Mark 5:1-20). Both tell us the man cried night and day in a loud voice; he cut himself with stones; and he was so violent that people were afraid to travel through the area knowing even chains could not restrain the man. As Jesus approached the man, he fell down before him, begging his assistance. And Jesus rebuked the "demon" from whom the response came: "Jesus, Son of the most High God, don't torture me (us)!"

Could one interpretation be that this is a reflection of the intense paranoia which often accompanies the manic state? The man was healed, the "demons" cast out. The people of the community arrived to find the man clothed, sane, and talking to Jesus. They were afraid and asked Jesus to leave, regarding the mentally healthy man with genuine suspicion. And the Biblical record tells us that Jesus did leave, sending the man back to his own community and to his own family. But when the man returned to his hometown, his family and friends were as awe-struck at his divine cure as they had been convinced of the supernatural origin of the man's malady.

Socially we are not very far from that Gadarene countryside. A person who is identified as mentally ill is forever labeled in society and is looked upon with suspicion even after the symptoms of his disturbance have abated. With bipolar disorder, it is a fact, however, that in only the most severe states—catatonia (coma) or delirium—or in the most extreme cases is the manic-depressive patient out of touch with himself or the world around him. In most instances the manic or the depressed person is forced to observe what is happening to him during an attack and is able to recognize the unreality of his situation, but he is unable to adjust his thinking or control his behavior to any effective degree because his brain is suffering from a debilitating metabolic flux.

Modern researchers have established enough facts and accumulated sufficient evidence to prove that physiological changes in brain metabolism are responsible for these erratic disturbances of behavior. The body of research data is growing at such a rate that it is only a matter of time until the mechanisms, the genetics, and the environmental influences can be assessed and appropriate measures sought for the individual sufferer and his or her family.

On 6 May 1908 a young man named Clifford Beers along with several clergymen and businessmen founded the Connecticut Society for Mental Hygiene. The small group grew and served as the core for the later National Committee for Mental Hygiene. This was the beginning of the mental health movement in the United States which has developed into three major mental health programs: the National Association for Mental Health, The Mental Health Foundation, and the government-operated National Institute for Mental Health in Bethesda, Maryland.

Clifford Beers, however, was not simply a concerned businessman in 1908. He was an intelligent and capable human being who had lived through a psychotic nightmare of depression and then mania. He had survived over two years in a private hospital and then a public asylum to finally regain his mental faculties. In his chilling autobiography, *A Mind that Found Itself*, Clifford Beers gives us a view of the workings of the psychotic mind from the inside looking out. Although lacking the literary style of Virginia Woolf, his account of his illness contains many similarities to what we are told about Virginia Woolf's disorder. The book is a sane, well-written exposé of Clifford Beers' psychotic states and the treatment he received at the hands of early twentieth-century psychiatrists. The story of his madness brings the specter of mental illness within the comprehension of every rational human mind.

Clifford Beers was an 1897 graduate of Yale University, a cultivated, urbane young man who broke down in a state of psychotic depression at the age of twenty-four. For almost five years there had been nervous ups and downs, but the first real indication that he had crossed the barrier to insanity came when Beers tried to commit suicide by jumping from a fourth-floor window. Rushed to Grace Hospital in New Haven, Connecticut, where he was living at the time, he awoke in a delusional state of mind. Iron bars had been added to the second-story hospital window as a precautionary measure, but Beers' distorted thought processes interpreted the barred windows to be prison windows. Bruised and shaken from his suicidal leap with fractures of both ankles, Beers became convinced that he was a victim of police persecution.

Like Virginia Woolf, as his mind passed through the worst phases, Clifford Beers heard "voices." Sometimes these "voices" were mere vocal hums; at other times he recognized the "voice" of a friend. But most of the time the "voices" seemed to be "the unintelligible mumblings of individual persecutors." Also like Virginia, Beers had no appetite and believed his food was being poisoned because of his strange distortions of taste. And Clifford Beers describes in the book a vision of vivid beauty in which swarms of butterflies and large, gorgeous moths appeared all over his sheets in streams of motion. Somehow, it is difficult not to associate this with Virginia Woolf's first conception of *The Waves* which was originally dubbed *The Moths*. In June of 1927 she recorded her ideas for the book in her diary :

> Slowly ideas began trickling in; and then suddenly I rhapsodised (the night L. dined with the Apostles) and told over the story of the Moths, which I think I will write very quickly, perhaps in between chapters of that long impending book on fiction. Now the Moths will, I think, fill out the skeleton which I dashed in here; the play-poem idea; the idea of some continuous stream, not solely of human thought, but of the ship, the night, etc. all flowing together: intersected by the arrival of bright moths. . . . It is to be a love story; she is finally to let the last great moth in. The contrasts might be something of this sort; she might talk or think about the age of the earth; the depth of humanity; then the moths keep on coming. (109)

On Wednesday, 28 November 1929 Virginia makes another of many entries in her diary that refer to the inception of *The Waves*, still referred to here as *The Moths*:

> As for my next book, I am going to hold myself from writing till I have it
> impending in me: grown heavy in my mind like a ripe pear; pendant, gravid,
> asking to be cut or it will fall. *The Moths* still haunts me, coming as they al-
> ways do, unbidden, between tea and dinner, while L. plays the gramophone.
> (135)

Is it possible that vestiges of her psychotic thought inspired her mental reflection when she was working and writing during those periods of normal psychological functioning? Yes. Notice even in these two brief excerpts from her diary how Virginia depended on Leonard as the anchor and buoy by which to guide her ranging thoughts. She trips lightly enough over these creative musings but ties them firmly to such mundane references as "the night L. dined with the Apostles" or "while L. plays the gramophone."

Evidence of this very close connection between her subconscious mind and its influence on her conscious creative thinking was also noted by Leonard Woolf in *Beginning Again*:

> If, when she was well, any situation or argument arose which was closely
> connected with her breakdowns or the causes of them, there would sometimes
> rise to the surface of her mind traces or echoes of the nightmares and delusions
> of her madness, so that it seemed as if deep down in her mind she was never
> completely sane. (79)

Clifford Beers tells us that his sense of taste did not return to normal for a long time. This became a major source of many of his delusions. He thought he was being slowly poisoned or that a strange code based on what he ate indicted him with heinous crimes. For example he feared eating burned toast might implicate him in arson. He ate slowly or not at all, sometimes requiring two or three hours to ingest anything from his modest meals.

In comparison Leonard Woolf records that in the case of Virginia's breakdowns one of the most "troublesome symptoms" was her refusal to eat. He relates that for weeks in the depressive phase someone had to sit with Virginia at every meal for over an hour to persuade her to eat anything. Leonard Woolf theorized that there was a connection between Virginia's refusal to eat and the extreme guilt and self-loathing that accompanied her depressed states.

Another common factor described in Clifford Beers' account of the disorder as well as by Leonard Woolf in his memoirs was the reasonableness of irrational thought. In *A Mind that Found Itself* Clifford Beers wrote:

Most sane people think that no insane person can reason logically. But this is not so. Upon unreasonable premises I made the most reasonable deductions, and that at the time when my mind was in its most disturbed condition. (57)

And Leonard Woolf echoes this same sentiment in *Beginning Again*:

This excruciating business of food, among other things, taught me a lesson about insanity which I found difficult to learn—it is useless to argue with an insane person. What tends to break one down, to reduce one to gibbering despair when one is dealing with mental illness, is the terrible sanity of the insane. In ordinary life, as her writings, and particularly her essays, show, Virginia had an extraordinarily clear and logical mind; one of the most remarkable things about her was the rare combination of this strong intellect with a soaring imagination. . . . The point is that her insanity was in her premises, in her beliefs. She believed, for instance, that she was not ill, that her symptoms were due to her own "faults"; she believed that she was hearing voices when the voices were her own imaginings; she believed that the doctors and nurses were in conspiracy against her. These beliefs were insane because they were in fact contradicted by reality. But given these beliefs as premises for conclusions and actions, all Virginia's actions and conclusions were logical and rational; and her power of arguing conclusively from false premises was terrific. (163-4)

After almost two years in a depressive psychosis in which he hardly moved or took any interest in what was around him, Clifford Beers shifted in one day's time to a gregarious and excited nirvana—mania. For two years he had hardly communicated. Day after day he had sat and stared speechless and withdrawn, convinced that he was an innocent victim being brutally detained by the police. After the shift he talked, wrote, and had so many ideas that he could not sleep. He spent hours trying to catch his disorganized, red-hot thoughts on paper. Like Virginia Woolf would later write in her diary, Beers claimed words seemed to "fly ahead" and "thoughts stumble over one another." This is the way he described the switch to mania in his book:

. . . I had another most distinct sensation in the brain. It started under my brow and gradually spread until the entire surface was affected. The throes of a dying Reason had been torture. The sensations felt as my dead Reason was reborn were delightful. . . . It was a sensation not unlike that produced by a menthol pencil rubbed ever so gently over the fevered brow. (87-8)

Beers then described the weeks of sleeplessness that followed the change, a euphoric but animated suspension by night and by day, what seemed at the time hours of divinely inspired activity. During this period he was removed to the violent ward because his ebullient enthusiasm appeared to be getting out of hand. Reading through the pages of Beers' book as he sets down his experiences on the violent wards of two hospitals is like stepping into a chronology of horror. The cruel and vindictive treatment he received at the hands of orderlies and physicians alike served to intensify his delusional processing of events.

An incident he related tells about the use of mechanical "restraints" and is indicative of the attitude of asylum physicians at that time. Most of these doctors when frustrated by the difficult behavior of the very disturbed patient became cruel and hypocritical. Placed in restraints after a manic "joke" backfired, the doctor in charge "adjusted" the straight jacket to the point that Beers could not even take a complete breath and had absolutely no feeling or movement in his cramped fingers. Since he had offered no resistance to the procedure, Beers reported that he felt betrayed and asked that the jacket be loosened a little. In a fit of rage the doctor drew the cords even tighter:

> No incidents of my life have ever impressed themselves more indelibly on my memory than those of my first night in a strait-jacket. Within one hour of the time I was placed in it I was suffering pain as intense as any I ever endured, and before the night had passed it had become almost unbearable. . . . During the first seven or eight hours, excruciating pains racked not only my arms, but half of my body. . . . I even begged attendants to loosen the jacket enough to ease me a little. This they refused to do. (129-30)

Through Beers' eyes we are able to examine the type of treatment meted out to the insane person in the early part of this century. For days he was choked by attendants, strait-jacketed, and physically abused as if he were an animal. His primary fear was aroused that first night in restraints:

> Before midnight I really believed that I should be unable to endure the torture and retain my reason. A peculiar pricking sensation exactly like that of June, 1900, led me to believe that I might again be thrown out of touch with the world I had so lately regained. (130)

During the period of mania Beers was removed from the private hospital and admitted to a state asylum where the abuse he had received at the hands of orderlies and physicians was escalated with new and more rabid attacks launched against his floundering reason and already weakened body. After a short time on a moderately restricted ward with very little provocation, he was moved to the violent section of the state hospital.

Stripped of all clothing except underwear, Beers was at first secluded in an unventilated, unheated room with only a mat on the floor. To make matters worse, it was a cold New England wintertime. Bereft of his clothes, his dignity as a human being, and even the barest essentials of survival, he was treated with methods reminiscent of stories which come out of prisoner-of-war camps. Such conditions prevailed that even a sane man would have been driven to distraction. Beers minced no words in painting the image of what life was like in the state hospital "bull pen" (violent ward).

There was no type of therapy and no attempt was made to communicate with the disabled patients. Assaults on inmates by the illiterate and poorly paid attendants were commonplace. Attacks were more often than not unwarranted and unpredictable, the work of ignorant, sadistic men who were allowed to use any method to "control" patients. If the violent ward of the state hospital were survived at all, it was survived at the lowest level of biological existence. Clifford Beers was prompted to work for asylum reform because he almost did not survive his four months on the violent ward:

> That they (the attendants) had been trying to goad me into a fighting mood (by withholding his water) I well knew, and often accused them of their mean purpose. They brazenly admitted that they were simply waiting for a chance to "slug" me. . .

On the night of November 25th, 1902, the head attendant and one of his assistants passed my door. They were returning from one of the dances which, at intervals during the winter, the management provides for the nurses and attendants. While they were within hearing, I asked for a drink of water. . .

> "If I come there I'll kill you," one of them said.
> "Well you won't get in if I can help it," I replied as I braced my iron bedstead against the door. . .
> The door once open, I offered no further resistance. First I was knocked down. Then for several minutes I was kicked about the room—struck, kneed, choked. My assailant even attempted to grind his heel into my cheek. In this he failed, for I was there protected by a heavy beard which I wore at this time. But my shins, elbows, and back were cut by his heavy shoes; and had I not instinctively drawn up my knees to my elbows for the protection of my body, I might have been seriously, perhaps fatally, injured. As it was, I was severely cut and bruised. When my strength was nearly gone, I feigned unconsciousness. This ruse alone saved me from further punishment, for usually a premeditated assault is not ended until the patient is mute and helpless. When they had accomplished their purpose, they left me huddled in a corner to wear out the night as best I might—to live or die for all they cared. (160-1)

At the end of four months Beers was transferred to a room in a better ward and slowly his sanity began to return. This lucid account of manic-depressive illness and the pitiful arrangement of its treatment in the early 1900s is sobering. The events described by Clifford Beers are stunning not just for their content and perspective but for the lack of proportion apparent in human understanding and care of the insane. The actions and thoughts he recalled were the work of an insane mind, but the recounting of their misery is the appeal of a sensitive human being. Reform in the care of the mentally ill became the goal of his rational mind.

And there we have it—the state of psychiatry in 1902. And what about us and what about English literature if similar institutions had swallowed Virginia Woolf? And how many artists' lives will be wasted by ignorance and indifference to the problems associated with creativity and the drive to create?

Works Cited

American Handbook of Psychiatry. Vol. III (Ed-in-Chief Silvano Arieti, M.D.). New York: Basic Books, 1974.

Beers, Clifford. *A Mind that Found Itself*. Garden City, NY: Doubleday, 1908.

Diagnostic and Statistical Manual of Mental Disorders III-R. Washington, D.C.: American Psychiatric Assoc., 1987.

The Harvard Medical School Mental Health Letter (Ed. Lester Grinspoon, M.D.), 1985 Jan; 1(7): 1-3.

Hinsie, M.D., Leland E. and Robert Jean Campbell, M.D. *Psychiatric Dictionary*. New York: Oxford UP, 1960.

Mayer-Gross, M.D., F.R.C.P., W., Eliot Slater, M.A., M.D., F.R.C.P., D.P.M., Martin Roth, M.D., F.R.C.P., D.P.M. *Clinical Psychiatry*. London, Eng.: Casell, 1960.

Mendels, M.D., J. "Depression: The Distinction Between Symptom and Syndrome." *The British Journal of Psychiatry*, 1968; 114: 1549-54.

Works Consulted

Gold, M.D., Mark S. *The Good News About Depression*. New York: Bantam Books, 1986 by Mark S. Gold, M.D., 1987 by Villard Books, 1988 by Bantam.

Textbook of Psychiatry (Ed. John A. Talbott, M.D., Robert E. Hales, M.D., Stuart C. Yudofsky, M.D.). Washington, D.C.: American Psychiatric, 1988.

Chapter Fourteen
Women and Creative Drive

No use, no use now, begging Recognize!
There is nothing to do with a beautiful blank but smooth it.
Name, house, car keys,

The little toy wife—
Erased, sigh, sigh.
Four babies and a cocker! . . .

O sister, mother, wife,
Sweet Lethe is my life.
I am never, never, never coming home!

—Sylvia Plath, *"Amnesiac"*

Any book which analyzes creativity or uses Virginia Woolf as an example would be incomplete without some part of the work aimed at women, their problems, their possible solutions. Virginia Woolf has taken her place as an artist among us, not because she was a woman, or even because she was a woman artist, or even because she was a woman artist who committed suicide. Virginia Woolf is recognized for her art.

And this should be the goal of *any* woman struggling with the social changes of the twentieth century who has been endowed with a demanding internal drive for creative expression. At the risk of seeming pristine, it must be stated simply that women are different from men. Their history is different, their biology is different, their socio-economic functioning is different, and most significantly, their psychological make-up is different from their male counterparts. These are facts and in no way represent value judgments tied to the blurring of social and sexual identity today.

The woman artist inherits to one degree or another the same drive for creative expression, the same intense need, and the same pitfalls of adopting a creative lifestyle. But, set as she is and will be, regardless of her objections, against the backdrop of western civilization and the recent history of feminine restrictions, the woman artist will face other problems which the male artist does not. Her time, her financial resources, even in some instances, her personal identity are not her own; they must be purchased, invariably at some cost to her personal integrity and self-esteem, before she can consider the risk involved in her art.

In the general scheme of business or professional life a man is a man is a man (to parody Gertrude Stein), but a woman until she is able to prove otherwise is usually lumped into one of several stereotypical categories. Her individuality can be established with those for whom or with whom she works, but it is always an uphill battle and not only with males, but often with other women who have been reinforced by male thinking and control.

Freud was supposed to have exclaimed one day in utter dismay and frustration: "Woman! My God, what does she want?"

And the answer to that question is not really as complex and complicated as all the muddy water might seem to indicate. Clearly, as I see it, women want only the right and privilege to be individuals and to be accepted and treated as individual people rather than lumped together in some depersonalizing group. We would deny neither our history, our social concerns, our psychological make-up, nor our biological functions, but in the emotional crisis surrounding the modern feminist movement, more and more women seem willing to give up all sexual ties or identification in order to obtain recognition as individual human beings.

I have a personal anecdote that illustrates this point. Several years ago Dustin Hoffman starred in a movie called *Tootsie* in which he played the role of a desperate young actor who impersonates a woman (and actually creates a feminine personality) in order to get a steady job in acting. The role is the portrayal of an older woman on a TV soap opera. Not long after the movie came out, I was at a family gathering when the movie came up and my sister-in-law, Mary Purser Beeman, an attorney, and I fell into trying to explain to my father why the movie had struck such a chord with women. My father was an oilman and businessman from a very patriarchal background, but he was always interested in learning.

We were discussing the scene in which Dustin Hoffman as Dorothy is confronting the lecherous, domineering male director of the TV show. During the confrontation he/she asks the pertinent question: "Why is it Bob is always Bob, Ted is always Ted, Tom is Tom, but I'm Toots, Tootsie, Honey, or Sweetheart. I have a name, too. Why don't you call me by my name? It's Dorothy." (I took the liberty to paraphrase as I did during that family discussion.) Then the other actors on the set of the TV show applauded.

"You see, Dad," I had continued, "it took a man dressed as a woman to make that assertion. A woman wouldn't have done that, taken the risk to speak out like that."

"Most women today still just won't ask for that kind of respect," my sister-in-law Mary had added.

My father mused a moment and then red-faced admitted that he called the secretaries of the companies he dealt with "Sweetie" or "Honey" or some such and had never bothered to learn their names.

"Of course," he had said in his own defense, "if they are older ladies, I always call them Mrs. Jones or Mrs. Smith."

To his credit, he carried this realization over into his work and several times mentioned to me how he was making an effort to learn the names of the office workers—male and female. He had had an awakening. And this was a person who had taught me that the most important thing to learn on meeting someone was how to correctly pronounce their name and possibly how to spell it. He had often emphasized that a person's name was extremely important to them and that I should never forget that.

There have been a number of changes in our society since this book was first published. A woman judge now sits on the Supreme Court. Economic suffering has increased to the point that most households require the service of the wife and mother in the workforce, single-parent households have increased because the divorce rate is still sky-rocketing, and women are still impoverished—the preponderance of jobs available to women continue on the average to be lower-paying ones. More babies are aborted annually than servicemen have been killed in all our wars put together. The violence of society has turned especially toward the poor and disadvantaged, of whom women form the bleakest subsection. Minority women are the most abused and susceptible to abuse from the courts, the governmental agencies, and the labor market.

The *DSM III-R* states that Major Depression is diagnosed twice as frequently among women as men in all industrialized countries. Bipolar disorder is equally frequent among men and women (225;229). There must be other causes increasing the relative majority of women suffering from depression. Considering the familial inheritance and the importance we see now in nurture where nature has predisposed someone to an endogenous disorder, the status of women should be reviewed and upgraded. Only the future is at stake—the welfare of the young and their nurture.

A 1 September 1988 *Washington Post* editorial reported the recent Census Bureau statistics this way:

> The richest two-fifths of families now have the highest share of total income (67.8 percent) and the poorest two-fifths the lowest (15.4) in the 40 years the Census Bureau has compiled such statistics. . . . The rate last year went down for whites (to 10.5 percent) but up for blacks (to 33.1). For the elderly it was

lower than for the society as a whole; for children, much higher. A fifth of all children are now poor, and two-fifths of the poor are children. The rate for younger children is higher than for older ones. Of black children under 6 years of age, 49 percent lived in poverty last year; of white children under 6, just under 17 percent did so.

The causes, or some of them, are familiar. Wages in parts of the economy are weak. . . . A sixth of all families and more than 40 percent of all black families are headed by women. A third of these female-headed families are poor. Some benefits have also lagged; the government lifts relatively fewer people out of poverty than it used to. (*Editorials* 1024)

In a *New York Times* editorial the same week (3 September 1988) similar conclusions were drawn:

Poverty weighs heavily on the young, with profound consequences for the future. The overall poverty rate for children remained about the same, 20.6 percent in 1987 compared with 20.5 percent in 1986. But the number of black children under 6 who were poor in 1987 rose to 49 percent from 45.6 percent. And 39.8 percent of Hispanic children under 18 were poor, up from 37.7 percent. . . . Increased welfare benefits would especially help poor, single mothers. And increased health and education services would help give poor children a fair chance to succeed. (*Editorials* 1029)

No wonder women, especially poor and disenfranchised single mothers with young children, are susceptible to emotional disease or drug and alcohol problems. Unavoidably and in many cases, sadly, the woman artist must grope her way through the emotional cesspool of her own outrage, fear, and anxiety at being treated on the whole as a member of a stereotyped group in society rather than being recognized as an individual. All the problems of the creative lifestyle are doubly difficult and doubly debilitating because as an artist she must first establish herself as a person. Her view of the world, her concern for others, her drive for the tangible creative expression of the images in her mind are tangled with the inevitable negative, frustrating emotions which by their very nature drain her creative powers. One out of every 200 depressed women will likely die a suicide.

Unlike secondary sex characteristics, the drive for creative expression is no respecter of persons. Virginia Woolf in her feminist essay *A Room of One's Own* laments the paucity of women figures in literary history, but she describes graphically what the statistics imply:

When, however, one reads of a witch being ducked, of a woman possessed by devils, of a wise woman selling herbs, or even of a very remarkable man who had a mother, then I think we are on the track of a lost novelist, a suppressed

> poet, of some mute and inglorious Jane Austen, some Emily Bronte who dashed her brains out on the moor or mopped and mowed about the highways crazed with the torture that her gift had put her to. (50)

Poverty, lack of education, prejudice, and the limitations imposed quite naturally by a male-oriented and male-dominated society are a few of the reasons listed by Virginia Woolf in her essay for the lack of prominent women artists. But, never one to wail and moan or to piddle time and words on spilled milk, she forges positive challenges for women from the skullduggery of the past afflictions. Having been driven herself into madness and despair over her creative writing, having struggled more than once to regain her mental and physical capacities, she had "paid her dues," qualified as a survivor. From her own experience as a person, as a woman, as an artist, she had earned the right to lecture:

> For women have sat indoors all these millions of years, so that by this time the very walls are permeated by their creative force, which has, indeed, so overcharged the capacity of bricks and mortar that it must needs harness itself to pens and brushes and business and politics. But this creative power differs greatly from the creative power of men. And one must conclude that it would be a thousand pities if it were hindered or wasted, for it was won by centuries of the most drastic discipline, and there is nothing to take its place. It would be a thousand pities if women wrote like men, or lived like men, or looked like men, for if two sexes are quite inadequate, considering the vastness and variety of the world, how should we manage with one only? (91)

To the inherent tension involved in the creative life of any artist Virginia Woolf added another burden for women, gleaned from her own experience—the woman artist or generative creative person is in conflict with herself and the critical matter of her own integrity:

> And I thought of all the women's novels that lie scattered like small pock-marked apples in the orchard, about the second-hand book shops of London. It was the flaw in the centre that had rotted them. She had altered her values in deference to the opinions of others. (77)

Here is not a mere social preoccupation with second-class citizenship. Before the woman artist or creative person can give free rein to her creative vision, constructively channel her creative drive, she must come to grips with the terms upon which she herself will accept existence. Until she is a whole human being, independent, self-reliant, psychologically intact with full responsibility for her own health, physical welfare, and economic well-being, the artistic self will be secondary. Her poetic vision will be marred by her own incomplete self. No amount of name-calling, wishful thinking, legal maneuvering, or social matriculation through the feminist movement will take the place of attaining independent psychological functioning with everything that implies.

Entire books have been and will continue to be written on the subject of reaching psychic wholeness as a female person. The truth of the matter is, it is a private achievement, a personal triumph which no amount of social change will ever foster. If the individual women in a society change, then the society as a whole will of necessity be different. Some of the books which have influenced me in my journey include *A Room of One's Own*, Betty Friedan's *The Feminine Mystique* and *It Changed My Life*, and Dr. Karen Horney's *Feminine Psychology*. These are a few books that were written to share intellectually what it takes to develop the fully functional female self, but in the most real sense, each woman must find her own way emotionally, on her own.

The stringent requirements of art seldom tolerate the crusading viewpoint. Artistic integrity first burns away dross and refines the gold of human experience, making it relevant to every person regardless of sex, race, age, intelligence, or social position. For the very first time in history, it is possible for the woman artist to have what Coleridge called an "androgynous mind" capable of experiencing and transmitting the creative vision without preconceived notions of what she should feel or think or say. To have an androgynous mind capable of translucent thought separated from the havoc of extraneous emotional input is certainly the goal of the creative individual—male or female. As T.S. Eliot once remarked: "The more perfect the artist, the more completely separate in him will be, the man who suffers from the mind which creates."

For this kind of artistic integrity there are no rivals, no grudges, no guarantees, and no refunds. Until the individual woman artist sees and accepts herself as distinct from but equal to her male counterpart, she will never gain equal footing. Until she is at least amnesiac about the injustices of the past, she will still be bound to her "name, house, car keys, the little toy wife," etc. And from those stereotypical viewpoints so natural and integral to men, she will never be able to explain her innermost feelings or the suffering she has lived through, which is part of her past. After all, the commonality of suffering is part and parcel of the human condition and it is at this level that she is no longer only female: she is also personally human. What kind of commitment does this take? Virginia Woolf discovered through her suffering:

> When I rummage in my own mind I find no noble sentiments about being companions and equals and influencing the world to higher ends. I find myself saying briefly and prosaically that it is much more important to be oneself than anything else. (*A Room of One's Own* 115)

There is no reason, especially for the woman artist or generative thinker who must struggle with her own creative drive, for things to be otherwise just because for centuries it has not been so. Women should not be any more willing than men to sacrifice their art, their health, or their own very individual and personal vision for the mere sake of social compliance and convenience.

The future of the woman artist is open-ended, as is the future of the male artist who after centuries must come to terms with the havoc wreaked on the female psyche, who must also wend his way through a new world relating events and emotions on a more personal basis than before, who must re-evaluate his own uniqueness in light of the budding individuality of his female counterpart. Surely no one—male or female—would embark on such a difficult and painful passage if not driven to do so.

Virginia Woolf laid down her pen one day and committed suicide, but it is possible that her death can symbolize a beginning for women artists today. She has left to us the inordinate task of whittling out a responsible place in the arts and sciences, among scholars, educators, and artists:

> ... then the opportunity will come and the dead poet who was Shakespeare's sister will put on the body she has so often laid down. Drawing life from the lives of the unknown who were her forerunners, as her brother did before her, she will be born. As for her coming without that preparation, without that effort on our part, without that determination that when she is born again she shall find it possible to live and write her poetry, that we cannot expect, for that would be impossible. But I maintain that she would come if we worked for her, and that so to work, even in poverty and obscurity, is worthwhile. (*A Room of One's Own* 118)

Works Cited

Editorials On File 1988. New York: Facts on File, 1988.

Horney, M.D., Karen. *Feminine Psychology* (Ed. Harold Kelman, M.D.). New York: W.W. Norton, 1967.

Plath, Sylvia, "The Amnesiac." *Winter Trees*. New York: Harper & Row, 1972.

Woolf, Virginia. *A Room of One's Own*. New York: Harcourt, Brace & World, 1929, 1957 by Leonard Woolf.

Works Consulted

Hammen, C. "Self-cognitions, Stressful Events, and the Prediction of Depression in Children of Depressed Mothers." *Journal of Abnormal Child Psychology*, 1988 Jun; 16(3): 347-60.

Jaenicke, C., C. Hammen, B. Zupan, D. Hiroto, D. Gordon, C. Adrian, D. Burge. "Cognitive Vulnerability in Children at Risk For Depression." *Journal of Abnormal Child Psychology*, 1987 Dec; 15(4): 559-72.

John-Steiner, Vera. *Notebooks of the Mind: Explorations of Thinking*. New York: Harper & Row, 1985.

Chapter Fifteen
And What About the Children?

When life presents us with a problem it will be attacked in accordance with code of rules which enabled us to deal with similar problems in the past. . . . When the same task is encountered under relatively unchanging conditions in a monotonous environment, the responses will become stereotyped, flexible skills will degenerate into rigid patterns, and the person will more and more resemble an automaton, governed by fixed habits, whose action and ideas move in narrow grooves. He may be compared to an engine-driver who must drive his train along fixed rails according to a fixed timetable.

—*Arthur Koestler* The Act of Creation

Presumptuously, this chapter undertakes a subject which warrants volumes—the creative education of our children. As an educator and therapist, I have worked with children through the years in various capacities. Gradually from my experience, I have become convinced of several things about our educational process:

1) most of us do not understand what a child is;
2) most of us do not know what an adult is;
3) most of us do not understand what education is;
4) most of us are powerless to effect any real changes in the present system.

Let me mention in the closing chapters of this study of creativity and the creative drive some of the reasons I have come to these nihilistic conclusions about our system of public education. Our special concern in these pages has been the dilemma of the creative person in modern society and the plight of the artist who cannot do anything else except follow his internal drive for creative expression if he is to escape physical and psychological problems.

The purpose of this chapter is to point out that if a culture deserves that name, it will be vitally concerned with the nurture and care of its young. A society is also responsible for the cultivation of its artists at every level of their development. My mind shivers as I think of the waste and human carnage engulfing our children in our public school system (and some private institutions as well). It is hard to talk about education in the arts when so many children I have worked with are physically and emotionally, sexually, and psychologically abused, are neglected or abandoned, are used for ulterior gains by unscrupulous adults, or are treated as though their suffering mattered so little in the scheme of things. Incredible as it may seem, our standards of human rights have not extended down the age scale, regardless of what people want to believe about our being a child-oriented, youth-dominated society. We do not in the United States today have a nurturing society. Children are "to be seen and not heard." In some cases—for example, delinquents and the disturbed—they are not even to be seen.

This book is not a part of the genre dedicated to "crisis intervention" in our schools, although the time for that has come and gone several times over without causing much change in the quality of education. This chapter is only a quiet appeal from one voice representative of a small chorus anxiously anticipating new standards and ideals. Just as the real advancement in the status of women can only come through dedicated commitment by the individual women in our society, so it is in education. Since the largest proportion of educators are women, the course is laid.

A child comes into life, and if he is fortunate enough to be healthy and complete, he is endowed with an innate curiosity, an indescribable joy of discovery. At two years of age, the young child is beginning to bud; whenever limits are imposed on his rapidly expanding thirst for experience, he will scream in protest. Take any normal, healthy group of fifteen kindergarteners. Add a room full of growing plants, knobs, blocks, lights, colors, sound, paints, paper, chairs, stairs, etc., and you will see an entire universe of creative activity unfolding before your eyes. A drive for creative expression will at this age appear to be a drive for self-fulfillment that literally bursts from each little microcosm walking around the room. What happens?

Year after year the principle stated by Arthur Koestler in his book *The Act of Creation* takes its toll—"the same task is encountered under relatively unchanging conditions in a monotonous environment." Educators will rise up in arms to defend themselves, and I will admit that I have observed creative and generative teaching in our public schools (which I might also add usually went unnoticed by administrators). But, on the other hand, I have seen children—bright, imaginative, sensitive children—almost destroyed and many seriously handicapped for life because they are caught emotionally in the ebb and flow year after year of our standard public school environment.

We are concerned about the drop-out rate, especially among the poor and racial minorities, but I will tell you quite honestly that it would be a sign of mental illness for any child to willingly re-enter day after day, year in and year out, a situation in which he finds nothing but humiliation, ridicule, or psychological, emotional, physical, and sometimes even sexual abuse. It is time to revise our compulsory attendance laws so that children may enjoy the constitutional "freedom from cruel and unusual punishment" or change the system.

Not to be misunderstood at this point, I am advocating child-centered education, not child-dominated education. I am a strong advocate of discipline as a part of the learning process. However, the most effective discipline a child can learn is self-discipline. It is more "caught" than taught and can never be learned from immature, undisciplined adults, eager to indulge rather than nurture, to exploit rather than inspire.

Through my own teaching, in my other professional relationships, and with my own children, I have become convinced that there is no substitute for a basic human respect in all our dealings with our children. Most of us would speak to the most casual acquaintance with more apparent respect than to our own children or the children we work with in the classroom. Why? Because we do not have power over the near-stranger; because we have no ego-involvement with that person. And these are the two most compelling reasons why we should above all have respect for the basic human rights of our children or those children placed in our care.

Those of us in the pediatric professions who work with children on an hourly, daily, or even an annual basis should be willing to treat children with the same kind of respect we expect from them. Playing games of "uproar" or "one-up-manship" (to borrow from the Eric Berne and transactional analysis idiom) is much more understandable and forgivable in the immature than in adults in positions of responsibility toward children. Yet, sadly, I have seen adults repeatedly resort to such tactics when dealing with even very young children who could not possibly come up with *any* appropriate social response. The child in these cases is cruelly disadvantaged. Surely this kind of treatment compounds the insecurity of our position throughout the educational process as much if not more than any lack of skill or ignorance of subject matter.

Dhildren are individuals with certain rights and certain other responsibilities. Children are *not* adults, but like most adults, they operate psychologically and emotionally best in situations where they know what is expected and what consequences certain behaviors have, both good and bad. If children are made to feel good about themselves as people, if the children feel good about their ability to fulfill the requirements and expectations placed upon them, if children are rewarded unequivocally on the basis of the responses they make in the learning situation, and if children are made to feel secure in their expanding capabilities, then learning will be an exciting and stimulating experience which becomes a pleasant and successful lifetime of reward and personal achievement.

The problem with our traditional programs is really not too complicated, philosophically speaking. The processes involved in learning have been and are being studied, our standards and criteria in teacher education are being upgraded, our thinking about organization and administration of school programs is being challenged, even programs for the talented and gifted student have been added, but we have not yet learned the value and importance of professional ethics, humanitarian goals, and personal responsibility in all the integral areas of the complex social functioning required in the educational setting. Somewhere along the path from the one-room schoolhouse to the mega-systems of today we lost our hearts.

Quality education is compassionate education. We are not lacking in viable instructional material or sophisticated programs; but we are seriously deficient in well-trained, professional personnel at every level of administration who truly love children, have a fundamental grasp of their needs and problems, and are able under the present system to always put the best interests of the individual child ahead of any other consideration. This is sad commentary for the wealthiest, most technologically advanced nation in the world. Are we inexcusable? It is true we are the only country in western civilization to attempt universal education for all classes of society. Have we failed? Or, is it just that there is still so very much room for improvement? I vote to carry on.

Dr. Jean Piaget, the noted Swiss psychiatrist, has demonstrated over the past forty years or so how a child's thinking develops. In over forty volumes on child psychology and development, he has outlined the various aspects of that development. He has discovered, for example, that there is a sequential patterning of conceptual awareness and critical judgment in the growing child's intellectual functioning. It is a maturation process which follows definite stages throughout the period of childhood and into adulthood. We have ingested the Gesell Institute and its developmental studies, and yet in our schools we still do not give much more than lip-service to actual individual variance in psychological growth. Just as the Gesell norms set out signposts at various stages of physiological and behavioral development, so the work of Piaget shows us that each individual child also has his own timetable of maturation through various intricate stages in the overall process of the systems of thought and reason, affect and cognition.

Over and over, Piaget has shown that various ideas, concepts, or patterns of thought which are patently obvious to an older child and most certainly to an adult, are completely out of the range of intellectual capability for a much younger child. For example, in math reasoning children begin at a very concrete level of functioning. A five-year-old may be able to count to a thousand by rote, but there are very basic math concepts for which he simply cannot make mental judgments. One very simple but pointed example which is part of these developmental pathways is the concept of volume. Even on a concrete level, this can be demonstrated.

Take two glasses of equal volume which differ in height and shape only. One glass should be tall and thin, and the other, short and fat. Take two children for the experiment, one under five and the other around eight. Pour the juice into the glasses and ask the children to choose which glass they think holds more. The younger child will choose the tall glass, and even when juice is poured back and forth from the tall glass to the short one to show that they hold equal amounts, the five-year-old will still maintain that the tall glass holds more juice. The older child, however, will find the experiment delightful and ludicrous in most cases, because he understands the principle of conservation of mass in connection with the volume of the glasses.

The implications of such research are simple, direct, very positive, and very easy to apply—do not try to teach volume to five-year-olds; wait until they are seven or eight. Also, as a humane gesture, in nursery school and kindergarten always use glasses of equal size so that children do not think others are being favored for some mysterious reason. Do not expect very young children to be able to pour juice or milk from a large container into a glass without running the glass over and spilling the juice. The child simply does not have the concept of volume required to accomplish the task. It is a matter of development, not just learning experience. It would help to teach parents some of these simple concepts!

Each child has his own unique range of development and establishes himself in the due course of things at various levels of conceptual reasoning, but the progression of the stages and the more and more complex level of the tasks to be learned are more or less innate. To a very young child, for instance, the concept of one is represented by one ball, one marble, or one whatever object is considered. This is on a very concrete conceptual level. To a two-year-old one object always means *my* ball, *my* toy, *my* sweater, *my* car, etc. It is absurd to assume that emotionally or conceptually there could be any other meaning for the average or even bright two-year-old. Language can precede concepts, but rarely can it be substituted effectively for the natural development of the concept. This is why "talented and gifted" programs cannot achieve their ends on the promotion of verbal skill alone. Intellectual achievement should not be the primary goal of these programs. Creativity is much more; giftedness is not cumulative.

As a child develops, he begins to learn that problems can be solved with counting and then with mathematical manipulations. If given sticks, pennies, or dried beans, he can begin to understand functions—three pennies, take away two, and one is left. By seven or eight the child will usually have passed through the stages of concrete, one to one reasoning, and many may have arrived at semi-concrete or semi-abstract math reasoning; a few may be able to handle abstract arithmetic operations with little or no reference to concrete items. However, it is not uncommon at all for children in the lower elementary grades to count on their fingers in order to work their math pages. Bridging the abstract requires the capacity for abstract thought. One ball is one ball, one block is one block, but the number 1 as a concept and a unit is another whole step up the ladder to abstract reasoning.

Imagine the anxiety produced in a child when a stark page of blurry mimeographed or lightly copied (the copier is always on the blink near the end of school) numbers is placed in front of him near the end of the first year in public school. The child is told to "group" and "re-group" the basic facts or to "add" these numbers. If he has moved ahead toward more abstract thinking, with little or no assistance, he will be able to do the operations required. But, if for some reason—and there are as many reasons as there are children—his math conceptual development hasn't quite reached the semi-abstract level, he (or she) will only be able to do a few of the problems by rote or by using fingers or dots on the desk. The insecurity and fear which becomes part of overall psychological reaction as a result of a normal process of development being thwarted by a frustrating social situation and possibly an unsympathetic authority figure may convince him to hate math and resist math functioning for the rest of his school career. How many times have you heard a child say, "But, I'm not very good in math." What is it to be good in something that is a basic psychological function of rational development? From past experience that child has "learned" only a negative emotional response to what is as basic a matter of maturation as longer legs or stronger arms. There is no skill, no concept, no motor development which is bound to any magical chronological table. As much as most children are alike, they are different too.

Of course, you see where this discussion is leading. It is not even rational in light of these processes to require behavior from a child before he has developed the capacity for that behavior. Especially cruel and mentally unhealthy is a program of "education" which inflicts pain, embarrassment, or humiliation on a child as retribution for a periodic lag in development. Most children with classroom difficulties if given minimal emotional support and supplemental guidance will achieve within six months the levels of functioning of their more precocious peers.

For the exceptional child who is either very advanced or very retarded at a particular chronological age, our approach to his needs is equally illogical—we label him or ignore the problem. Many of our children have visual or auditory perceptual problems which disrupt and prolong the developmental processes, and yet they are bright, motivated children until habitual failure and disgrace overwhelm them. Thus the "sanity" of our system of rewards and restrictions seems monstrously self-perpetuating. We teach children *how* to fail, not how to be successful! Is it any wonder there is violence in the halls and classrooms of our secondary institutions?

I am sorry to state that in most instances in our more heterogeneous public school situations, the rigidity and inflexibility of both instructional programs and teacher expectations rises proportionately to the number and kind of social mixtures involved—bilingual students, racial and cultural diversity, economically advantaged and disadvantaged. What could be a valuable resource for our day-to-day system of education, a cornucopia of experience, becomes bedlam. If education's "sacred cow" of individual differences should be made a reality and used as a guiding principle in setting up and administering our instructional programs, there would be fewer disruptions, and better all-around education would be the result of the mixture. Fear prevents this. Fear and prejudice.

If we really loved our children we would have schools where their abilities and emotional needs were not assaulted and abused. How can we justify expecting children to function under pressures and anxieties the equivalents of which no adult would tolerate?

And the drive to create is a peculiarly difficult drive to squeeze into this mish-mash of educational mismanagement. Since it is singularly a drive for self-expression, in many children, it is hopelessly repressed at a very early age. For others it leads to rebellious and hostile behavior in later childhood and a predictably stormy adolescence. But under the hostile acts and negative emotional behavior and the layer after layer of ego defenses is the pain and frustration of a sensitively tuned human being with a need for a positive direction for his talents and a constructive outlet for his creative energies.

Music, art activities, poetry, drama, dancing, writing, building, sculpting, designing, planning, or just dreaming—there are many useful ways to augment and enrich the educational process. Imagine the difference (and this has been tried) if a child were rewarded for cooperative, disciplined work by being given equal time involving creative activities of his own choosing. (When my oldest son was eleven, he enjoyed Shakespeare and mythology; my nine-year-old son who is now 22 wanted to learn fencing.) The possibilities are geometrically expansive and creatively endless. Our creative writing instructors, drama critics, dance experts, and visual artists should not be bound to our college and university lecture halls, but they should regularly become a part of our elementary and secondary school programs. There should be no dichotomy where the arts are concerned; no segment of our population should be isolated or neglected either as audience or participant. Those of our artists who enjoy teaching should be accessible to young, creatively tuned minds.

Opportunity, freedom, skillful guidance, approval, acceptance, and emotional support will be the keys to open doors to a new society and a new way of life for the child genetically endowed with the "divine gift of creative fire." Just as Virginia Woolf found in the nursery her talent for story-telling and her creative outlet was secured, every child laboring under frustrating perception and compelling emotional energies must be channeled into learning situations where she can have freer access to the means of achieving creative expression. We must not burden her with our preconceptions without giving her a range of choices involving activities and the use of free time to a more satisfying and stimulating advantage.

Since this book was first published, the field of "talented and gifted education" has burgeoned. Colleges and universities now peddle degrees and credentials to "talented and gifted" teachers. There are state associations and annual conventions. Workshops are held regularly to inform faculties of their responsibilities to the "talented and gifted" student in the classroom. Ideas are still flourishing, but for the most part it is still "adults doing things to kids"!

The very heart of the creative process is self-expression, not delineation. When we transfer the concept of creativity to an educational framework and create a category for express creative functioning in a particular school-structured environment, then what we are actually talking about is called "training"—behavior modification. The success or failure of these programs depends on the kinds of expectations involved in their matriculation. At any rate, the students will *perform*. It's part of the structure. Whether or not any real creativity is fostered, encouraged, or evoked by "gifted and talented" educators is in proportion to the expectations of the programs: the designs and the products of that design—not necessarily the result of the creative process.

Any public library or nearby college or university can yield the interested reader a textbook or a course in education for the gifted child. Jean Piaget has published his work on the cognitive and affective development of the child. Studies based on the ten years of programs for the talented and gifted student are giving some ideas about how we are doing, where we are going, how well things seem to be working. It is probably too soon to be certain of much, but I am personally grateful that a new direction has opened up. There are two pertinent considerations that are still to be addressed, in my opinion:

1) Education for the obviously advanced and gifted is "special education," but all children are creative and deserve a creativity-enhancing program as a part of their regular school curriculum.

2) Because the link between creativity and the affective disorders has been clearly made, there is a new group of children whose special needs have not been but should be addressed—the emotionally disturbed.

In a very real sense, this is a crisis-level problem. Drugs and alcohol abuse are the symptom of a generation of blunted, lost children—many are artists, generative thinkers. They can be reclaimed. They can recover. The system can begin now to meet the needs of emotionally handicapped and vulnerable children, many of whom are creatively gifted children.

I hope to write an entire volume about the emotionally disturbed and their special educational needs. Art therapy is an important advance in the therapeutic approach. It belongs in the schools. It is especially useful in dealing with the results of social problems—divorces, abandonment, physical and sexual abuse. As noted, the famous student of Freud, Carl Jung, was probably the first modern psychiatrist to advocate art therapy. He regularly incorporated drawing, painting, and sculpting into his therapeutic regime for patients.

Art therapy should be a regular part of the school program, according to some United Kingdom specialists who collaborated recently on a book about the field—*Images of Art Therapy: New Developments in Theory and Practice*:

> More and more it is being realized that if young children are given the opportunity to experience some therapeutic intervention it may prevent future problems during early teens and adolescence. Encouraging specialist workers such

> as therapists and special-needs teachers to work within the normal school environment, and have regular contact with social workers and family clinics, can prevent the need for care and treatment orders, and the subsequent stigmatization that inevitably ensues by the removal from the "normal" institution. Removal sets up a course of treatment for "maladjustment" and it becomes increasingly difficult to readjust or return to the mainstream of "normal" life. With a view to this problem, Winnicott (1964) advocates the interesting idea of "educational diagnosis" which would follow the same lines as medical diagnosis in identifying the widely different needs of children in school. (Dalley, Case, Schaverien, Weir, Halliday, Hall, Waller 29)

Emotional problems seriously block intellectual development and classroom functioning. In most standard achievement tests the emotionally-disturbed child is easily identified—the pattern is common. He or she is the child whose verbal skills are average or better but whose math skills "bottom out." The math reasoning facility is the first to be blocked by repressed and unexpressed emotion. "Children must develop emotionally and intellectually, and when this gets out of phase and emotional needs are not met, the resultant blockage tends to arrest learning and general functioning" (33).

Seven or eight years ago I ran across a poem that says it all in a direct and tragic way. This poem has not been published anywhere as far as I know. It was given to me by a friend who thought I would appreciate it as a teacher. It is written anonymously and is attributed to a high school senior from southern California who committed suicide two weeks after he turned it in to his English teacher:

He Always

He always wanted to explain things.
But no one cared.
So he drew. Sometimes he would draw and it wasn't anything.
He wanted to carry it in a stone or write it in the sky.
And it would be only the sky and him and the things inside him that needed
    saying.
And it was after that he drew the picture.
He kept it under his pillow and let no one see it.
And he would look at it every night and think about it.
And when it was dark and his eyes were closed, he could still see it.
And it was all of him.
And he loved it.

When he went to school he brought it with him.
Not to show to anyone, but just to have it with him.

Like a friend.
It was funny about school.
He sat in a square brown desk,
Like all the other square brown desks.
And he thought it should be red.
And his room was a square brown room,
Like all the other rooms.
And it was tight and close.
And stiff.

He hated to hold the pencil and chalk, with his arms stiff and his feet flat on the floor.
STIFF.
With the teacher watching and watching.

The teacher came and spoke to him.
She told him to wear a tie like all the other boys.
He said he didn't like them.
And she said that it didn't matter.
After that they drew.
And he drew all yellow and that was the way he felt about the morning.
And it was beautiful.
The teacher came and smiled at him.
"What's this?" she said. "Why don't you draw something like Ken is drawing?"
"Isn't that beautiful?"

After that his mother brought him a tie.
And he always drew airplanes and rocketships like everyone else.
And he threw the old picture away.
And when he lay out alone looking at the sky it was big and blue and all of everything.
But he wasn't anymore.
He was square inside and brown.
And his hands were stiff.
And he was like everyone else.

And all the things inside him that needed saying, didn't need it anymore.
It had stopped pushing.
It was crushed.
STIFF.
Like everything else.

The ultimate goals of creativity education and therapy in the educational setting will inevitably dovetail since emotionally healthy functioning is a direct product of the free expression of the drive to create. The guidance and promotion of creative release will support mental health and creative adaptability. However, affective education is not always served by the "goals" of a "gifted" education program. Freedom within the creative process is invaluable. A truly gifted child does not have to be primed like an old-styled pump handle. On the other hand a stressful, performance oriented program can be unhealthy for the emotionally at-risk child.

Perhaps this list of practical suggestions for creativity education from a recent textbook makes that point:

1. *Provide a nonthreatening atmosphere.*
2. *Refrain from becoming the judge of the worth of all products in the classroom.*
3. *Model creative thinking and/or introduce other individuals who are able to illustrate the creative thinking process to the students.*
4. *Attempt to integrate activities and questions that encourage divergent production and evaluation into as many content areas as possible.*
5. *Make a conscious effort to remind students to be creative, to be original, to try to think of new ways to solve a problem, etc.*
6. *Systematically reward novel production.*
7. *Provide stimuli for as many of the senses as possible.*
8. *Make use of warm-up activities when moving from highly structured convergent or memory type activities to requiring students to engage in creative production.*
9. *Incorporate activities into the classroom instruction that require students to generate a large number of correct responses.*
10. *Instruct students in the principles of brainstorming, but incorporate strategies for self-evaluation of the quality of ideas.* (Gallagher 336-7)

Recently I was involved in a workshop for classroom English teachers as in-service training for the identification and management of the needs of the gifted student in the regular classroom. As an activity we were divided into groups of four or five teachers and given a group of profiles to analyze for recommendations to a talented and gifted program. From the list of ten or twelve, only three could be chosen—a statistically significant number, I think. At the conclusion of the exercise, each group of teachers made their recommendations arrived at by the consensus of the group. As it turned out, all the profiles were of famous talented and gifted Americans of the past—Abraham Lincoln, Will Rogers, Isadora Duncan, etc. The criteria were carefully imposed, but there were no "wrong" answers.

I had quite a struggle with one of the ladies in our group over a profile of a student whose abilities were so far above anything our public schools could offer I said he was not a candidate for a regular talented and gifted program but for some other program unavailable in the regular public school scope. I think it is very important to recognize the limitations of the public school system. We aim to educate the majority and aim toward the median with some emphasis on the extremes of the population of students, but realistically, the public school setting is not designed to handle all students—the very handicapped or the very exceptional. I stated my opinion and said I was in favor of special schools for the exceptionally gifted or very handicapped where their special needs can be met.

The other teacher took umbrage at what I said and argued adamantly for the boy whose profile I had said could not be served by a talented and gifted program. There was a compromise—the stuff of our public school teaching—and the other two teachers in the group suggested another choice to resolve the conflict. The discarded profile turned out to be Albert Einstein.

I rest my case.

In one of her essays about Lewis Carroll, author of *Alice in Wonderland* and *Through the Looking-Glass*, Virginia Woolf makes an appealing observation about the child's view of the world which she also claims in many cases is the view of the writer and artist. It is a reflection of the deep part emotion and emotional responses play in the world of the child, a sensitive part with which the artist must never lose touch for through it is found the mainspring of the energy produced internally by the drive to create:

> To become a child is to be very literal; to find everything so strange that nothing
> is surprising; to be heartless, to be ruthless, yet to be so passionate that a snub
> or a shadow drapes the world in gloom. (82)

Works Cited

Dalley, Tessa, Caroline Case, Joy Schaverien, Felicity Weir, Diana Halliday, Patricia Nowell Hall, Diane Waller. *Images of Art Therapy: New Developments in Theory and Practice*. London: Tavistock, 1987.

Gallagher, James J. *Teaching the Gifted Child* (3rd Ed.). Boston, MA: Allyn and Bacon, 1964, 1975, 1985.

Koestler, Arthur. *The Act of Creation*. New York: Dell, 1964.

Piaget, Jean, M.D. *The Child's Conception of Number*. New York: W.W. Norton, 1965.

Piaget, Jean, M.D. *The Language and Thought of the Child*. New York: New American Library, 1974.

Woolf, Virginia. "Lewis Carroll." *The Moment and Other Essays*. New York: Harcourt Brace Jovanovich, 1948.

Works Consulted

John-Steiner, Vera. *Notebooks of the Mind:Explorations of Thinking*. New York: Harper & Row, 1985.

Liebmann, Marian. *Art Therapy for Groups*. London, Eng: Croom Helm, 1986.

May, Rollo. *The Courage to Create*. New York: W.W. Norton, 1975.

Robbins, Arthur, Ed. D., A.T.R.. Linda Beth Sibley, M.P.S., A.T.R. *Creative Art Therapy*. New York: Brunner/Mazel, 1976.

Stein, Morris I. "Breakthrough and Trends: Lessons from the Second National Conference on Creativity and the Gifted/Talented." *Creativity Research and Educational Planning*. Ventura, CA:Ventura Co. Superintendent of Schools Office, 1982.

Chapter Sixteen
Genetics and the Future

The natural scientist's connection with the rest of humane learning is not familial but abstract, a little like our connection with humanity as a whole. . . .

The reality of separateness has existed since Kant, the last philosopher who was a significant natural scientist, and Goethe, the last great literary figure who could believe that his contributions to science might be greater than his contributions to literature. And, it should be remembered, it was not that they were philosopher and poet who happened to dabble in science, but that their writings were mirrors of nature and that their science was guided and informed by meditation on being, freedom and beauty.

—*Allan Bloom,* The Closing of the American Mind

We have sailed past 1984 and the images of "a brave, new world" may be consequently fading, but the reality of genetic engineering is more authentic today than ten years ago. The procedures of cloning cells and gene-splicing have improved significantly. Today babies are being conceived extra-utereo (in vitro), implanted, being born to very happy parents who otherwise could not have had children of their own. Sperm banks, gene banks, genetic counseling have become "buzz" terms. We now have the power if not in our hands, at least defined by technology, to manipulate the genetic building blocks of human destiny.

As we have seen from the research data for the manic-depressive illness, inheritance is not a simple, clear path of one dominant gene that needs correcting but a complex interaction of various factors dependent on population studied and attendant pedigrees. Also, the old nature versus nurture puzzle is not so puzzling anymore as we begin to see definitively that nurture really is as big a part of being human as we hoped it was. And, not surprisingly, what other animals do by instinct, even if in the great apes seemingly with some learning, we humans *must* learn, not having the great recourse to instinct that as a species we might have had at some point in our history.

I think it is time to get back to our books and work on our humanity as a society and as a culture, as well as individuals. Genetic engineering is not the only path to follow in the genetically predisposing mental illnesses. Perhaps in enzymatic disorders and most certainly in disorders such as Tay Sachs and Huntingdon's Chorea, the genetic and biochemical relief would be a welcome choice. However, the answers in human psychiatric disorders are not so simple. In the brain chemistry we can have some confidence; but, in the therapy and recovery from a psychiatric disorder, we must look to the social context.

And of course, having read this book and thought about the evidence presented here for an intricate relationship between creative drive and functioning and certain psychiatric illnesses, do you think you, as an individual, would be willing to take either the risk or the responsibility for eliminating that genetic quality from the human race? The possible effects are mind-boggling and discouraging. No more Virginia Woolf. No more affectively endowed artists plying their lowly trades. No more dogged visionaries to pull mass movements of social change (Nazi Germany, the Ku Klux Klan, McCarthyism, etc.) back onto the track of upward human development. No more serious disagreements as to just what is mentally healthy and what is insane. Would it really improve civilization, create a brave, new world?

Working the past twenty years as an educator and with emotionally disturbed children, I have come to the same conclusion as Carl Jung, who said that it was the intolerance of society which led to the incarceration and persecution of the mentally ill person. But the more disturbing question that haunts me is the social consciousness of our contemporary world which has imprisoned millions in jails, hospitals, work camps, and asylums. What do we have to fear from the truly unfortunate and the obviously ill?

If Virginia Woolf's psychiatric illness, which was extreme and critical in nature for most of her life and for which today we have effective treatment, could be managed by the care and concentration of one concerned, loving human being, then why must the rest of us demand exile or annihilation for similar people? Could it be that we simply do not want to be bothered—as with the ethical questions of the care of the elderly, the unwanted pregnancies, the troubled teenagers—or is it true that we do not want to be shaken from our material security by anyone or anything that questions our moral or spiritual values or attempts to prod us a little farther down the road toward human rights and human responsibility?

Creativity is one of our most hopeful possessions. The ability to extrapolate and formulate problems intimates the possibility of solutions. Envisioning that we have a problem is often the impetus to take the first step on the journey toward a solution. Yes, human beings really are like that. As beings of amazing complexity we do not have to work only on the level of taking things apart that we may not be able to fix—although legitimately that is one mechanistic approach. As beings of considerable variety capable of higher order thought, we can also intuit. Logic and rationality do not ever preclude intuition, but creatively speaking they should augment each other.

As beings with the power of choice, we can both initiate problem-solving and change courses if one solution isn't working—in mid-stream even, if necessary. The functional complexity of our existence is really an illusion fabricated by the incredible technology and metaphorical language so intrinsically but stridently set against the inevitabilities of existence. It is the illusion behind which as a civilization we have been trying to hide our vulnerabilities. It doesn't work. Denial of reality does not solve problems or change things. Illusion removes both choice and responsibility.

Never was this so imposed on me as when I stood a few years ago in a sophisticated modern hospital and heard those dreaded words about a sick family member: "There's nothing else we can do."

The enemy then was cancer. The battle was confined to tiny cells in the body that could not be controlled. In this age of world-wide, split-second communications, satellites, and space exploration, not to mention the trappings of computers and laser equipment, it is almost inconceivable that disease or accident can obliterate human beings who have been capable of such advanced mechanization. But it really is true. We are still, for the most part, coming into this life and leaving it the same way we have for thousands and thousands of years.

And, indeed, most of our problems are problems of the heart, not the head. The human spirit cannot transcend death by technology because what transcends death is life. The paradox of life is that to have it we must lose it. We must continually be in the process of letting go and reaching forward. This is what makes us, I believe, in the image of our Creator—this spiritual hunger to share who we are and what we are where we are when we can in whatever way we can. The drive to create. The opposite of growth and enlightenment is stagnation and death. We're either doing one or the other. If we are not living, we're dying—and this is not to mean the mere reduction of our physical selves. Creativity is what we curiously distinguish in the process as that human characteristic responsible for our mutual progress.

Now, this is not intended to be a self-help book, but if no help accrues to anyone from reading it, then I wasted my time and the press's money. There is a very hopeful thing going on in the world today, especially hopeful for those with problems of inordinate affectivity, mental disease, or addictive behaviors. Since the early thirties people have been quietly, anonymously banding together in small groups for mutual love, comfort, support, and enlightenment. It has not been an ostensibly religious movement, although many of our most devout religious people have been involved at times. It has as its core 12 steps of spiritual principles which apply almost universally to human progress. It was upon these 12 principles that two drunks—a stockbroker from New York and a doctor from Ohio—found they could stay sober and help other drunks like themselves stay sober. The kernel of this idea came from a spiritual experience the stockbroker had had in an asylum where he had been committed for chronic, hopeless alcoholism. Doctors had told him he would probably not live out the year.

For fifty-four years the program of Alcoholics Anonymous, which took its name from the book published in 1939 by the first 100 members of the society, has been amazingly effective in dealing with a disease for which no modern science or medicine had been able to find a cure. Today over 130 registered fellowships use the 12-step program to deal with all sorts of human problems. Groups deal with drug addiction (Narcotics Anonymous), gambling addiction (Gamblers Anonymous), food addiction—including anorexia nervosa and bulimia—(Overeaters Anonymous), mental and emotional disease (Emotions Anonymous) and family dysfunction (Al-Anon and Adult Children of Alcoholics and other Dysfunctional Families). (*Twelve Steps for Overeaters*, *The Twelve Steps for Adult Children from Addictive and Other Dysfunctional Families*, to mention only a few).

The new approaches in family systems therapy came about in large part as a result of the work in death and dying done by Elisabeth Kubler-Ross. Again, small groups of people with the common bond of a human problem of health or destiny came together for mutual love and support. The cancer societies, the hospice movement, the hundreds of support organizations and support groups representing all manner of human ills and suffering is a twentieth-century miracle. This miracle has begun in the very shadow of wars, death camps, and gas chambers. We are learning. Human beings are learning that we can do together what we could never do alone. There is hope for mankind. We are here together.

Even in the Soviet Union where a psychiatric diagnosis decried throughout world psychiatric circles for "sluggish schizophrenia" used to incarcerate political dissenters, a new era is beginning. The first six months of effective alcohol treatment has come through the newly formed Moscow

Alcoholics Anonymous Fellowship. And Dostoevsky was not being a fool or an effete dreamer when he said, "Beauty will save the world." The very essence of this movement among human beings is that we are worth saving.

As humans we are capable of surviving enormous personal as well as social holocausts if we can be linked up with other human beings who will be with us in our pain—share the load. The discovery is being made that we cannot eliminate all human suffering, but we can be here for each other. This is not to rebuke science for its benefits, the luxuries we have received from technological advancement, the comfort of certain kinds of knowledge. Knowledge, however, is not the same as awareness and neither knowledge nor awareness is a substitute for compassion. To think otherwise is to embrace the illusions of the stainless steel hospital and the lunar landing module. Inside both we still find a mortal whose beginning was a birth-wail and whose natural end is a cessation of breath. What happens in between depends on choice. Where that uniquely human choice has been denied, limited, or lost, it can be restored by participation in the healing group. We are social beings; we can learn to be here together—in love, not hate.

Let genetic research continue in its own way seeking to help mankind, but also let us continue gathering in small groups for mutual comfort and support. The weak can help the strong, the frail and doomed can recover, and a survival attitude will release victims. Let us continue walking from the darkness toward the light by the power of love, the reality of a Higher Power which gave a drunk 54 years ago a set of 12 spiritual principles that bring insight and awakening.

Amitai Etzioni in his book *The Genetic Fix* urged an informed and involved citizenry in the process of genetic engineering. His words are as sobering today as they were ten years ago:

> On the national level, Congress must be urged to set up a permanent National Health-Ethics Commission which will include members of a variety of disciplines, not just medicine, and representatives of the public, and which will be backed up by a research staff.
>
> Locally, each state, city, and town needs a local review Health-Ethics Board to oversee its hospitals and clinics, its medical healers and researchers.
>
> Individually, citizens and their leaders have to become better informed about new medical and genetic developments and the issues raised by their effects on matters of illness and health, life and death. The people must be the guards of the guards. . . . (203)

Works Cited

Alcoholics Anonymous (3rd Ed.). New York: Alcoholics Anonymous World Services, 1976.

Bloom, Allan. *The Closing of the American Mind.* New York: Simon & Schuster, 1987.

Elisabeth L. *Twelve Steps for Overeaters.* San Francisco: Harper & Row, 1982, 1983, 1988 by Hazelden Foundation.

Etzioni, Amitai. *The Genetic Fix.* New York: Macmillan, 1973.

Friends In Recovery. *The Twelve Steps for Adult Children from Addictive and Other Dysfunctional Families.* San Diego: Recovery Publications, 1987, 1989.

Mersky, H.; Shafran, B. "Political Hazards in the Diagnosis of 'Sluggish Schizophrenia'." *British Journal of Psychiatry*, 1986 Mar; 148: 247-56.

Works Consulted

Beattie, Melody. *Codependent No More.* New York: Harper & Row, 1987 by Hazelden Foundation.

Black, Claudia. *It Will Never Happen to Me.* Denver: Medical Administration, 1981.

Bradshaw, John. *Bradshaw on: The Family.* Deerfield Beach, FL: Health Communications, 1988.

Frankel, Victor. *Man's Search for Meaning.* New York: Washington Square Press, 1984.

Kritsberg, Wayne. *The Adult Children of Alcoholics Syndrome.* New York: Bantam Books, 1985.

Kubler-Ross, Elisabeth. *On Death and Dying.* New York: Macmillan, 1969.

Woititz, Janet G. *Adult Children of Alcoholics.* Hollywood, FL: Health Communications, 1985.

Chapter Seventeen
What About Men?

Every period has its bias, its particular prejudice, and its psychic malaise. An epoch is like an individual; it has its own limitations of conscious outlook, and therefore requires a compensatory adjustment.

—*C.G. Jung,* The Spirit in Man, Art, and Literature

What about men? This will most likely approach an essay rather than a reflection of any research. Ten years ago I was feeling the fallout of feminism in my life. I had been battered and divorced with two small sons, re-married and widowed, and re-married. On every hand things seemed out of hand. As noted in Chapter Fourteen, not much has really changed in the status of women. Some attitudes have mellowed, but as an example of the still divisive nature of the movement, angry demonstrators for pro-choice recently marched in Washington protesting any roll-back in abortion-on-demand. The Supreme Court ruled. Legislators—still mostly men—are debating biological destiny and either axing or accusing, acquiescing or accessing; the Equal Rights Amendment controversy drags on. Personally, I do not believe abortion should be birth control, and I have come to experience in my own life the truth that Virginia Woolf wrote that "it is more important to be yourself than to be anything else."

I think it is long past the time that men should study men—not just their achievements, ideas, or status as providers, warriors, protectors, defenders, power-brokers, role-models in the destinies of nations, epochs, and literature, but their psychology. Men, I am convinced, are the real victims of their own isolation, especially emotional isolation from other men and from women and children. All the great innovators in psychiatry and psychology have delved deep into the study of the feminine, but few have dared to even approach the intricacies of the male psyche—to set gender-specific criteria for certain investigations.

Apart from economics, women, I believe today, have the advantage—emotionally, psychologically, biologically, and as the beneficiaries of all the literature both scientific and fictional written about our sex. Men have written for centuries about who women are and what they think. In the past 100 years modern psychiatry and psychology have specifically explored the changing role and emerging consciousness of women. It seems that all this scrutinization has done is lead toward mere ruminations, more confusion, and some gross dishonesty. It seems this way if one looks only at the facts of female existence in society today and at the continuing "battle" promulgated in the wake of such information. It may be time to reach for a more balanced viewpoint. That will require certain honesty of investigation and the willing participation of men in the dialogue—not with women, but with each other.

Male psychiatric researchers are afraid to face the music or sit out. Surely, the male psyche deserves the same attention afforded the female, even if most of Freud's patients were women. Or, are most creative, generative male minds only consumed with world-order solutions to the planet-wide concerns of life? The truly androgynous mind cannot exist until men submit to the same sorts of clinical and research documentation that women have endured.

Our stages, our films, our poetry, our novels, our non-fiction draw such portraits of male moods and dramatic acts that it is hard to associate the "male image" or "ego" projections with the simple concept, "man." Does the term "mankind" *really* mean men *and* women? If so, why? If not, why not? Perhaps there is room for reflection, honest examination, open discussion, thoughtful examination, learning, and growth. Perhaps women can be a part of the process. Men, you really are not here alone, and it's okay. No matter what our roles and ills and projections and crimes, we are not your mothers; we're your sisters in this voyage of life. We can no longer fix you (not that you ever asked us to); we can't carry you or nurse you forever (not that most of us don't keep trying to). But, as more human than victim, we can stand with you, alongside you, in this amazing experience called "life." Is it possible for one woman writing a small volume about creativity and creative drive to give interested male readers permission to, as Virginia Woolf so aptly put it—"be yourself more than anything else"? Maybe you already are. But, if you find yourself trying to scratch an itch you didn't really know you had but now feel but can't find, here goes: BE YOURSELF MORE THAN ANYTHING ELSE.

Ten years ago I could not have done that, written that paragraph. I had been hurt and hurt deeply by what I perceived as a male-dominated, male-oriented, male-operated society. I was the epitomized victim of research studies and literature. Soap operas called me up for episodes! It was the fault of men and the patriarchy, and as a dependent person—the only role ever afforded me—I angrily wanted the male who was responsible for this state of things in my life to "fix me." When this never happened, I had to grow up. If I can grow out of the victim role and find a process of becoming a human being again, surely anyone can. And this is not my experience alone. In dialogue today, many women are sharing their stories in the hope that growth and freedom will be the legacy we leave to our sons and daughters.

Men who read this, thanks for carrying the enormous emotional burden all these centuries for our survival, for taking responsibility for wars, famines, and various persecutions and disasters. Even though some women were perpetrators, deceivers, or willing participants in the power-mongering, for the most part, when things went wrong you accepted the blame. "The buck stops here" didn't originate with Harry Truman.

We women have had a few years of independence, of self-reliance, of self-determination, if not personally, at least vicariously through the Woolfs, the Steinems, the O'Connors, the many achievers women can look at in the world today. We have read their biographies, enjoyed short stories, taken courses of study, developed ourselves intellectually, been excited to breathe the rare air of success and power. We have had a few equal opportunities, equal rights. And now we have ulcers, heart attacks, cancer, and failures in round figures to match your appreciable struggles. Forgive our resentments and accept the olive branch. Life *is* bigger than both of us.

As an older and a little more mature and happy woman, I can truthfully say that I cannot imagine a male joy or satisfaction more thrilling or fulfilling than to carry a child, nurse it, and live to see it leave the nest and have its own life to live. And this refers not solely to my own children, but to this work on creativity, my published poems, stories, and articles, as well. Achievements come and go. Life is good; life is wearisome; life is. Women have proven that biology does not have to be destiny. At this point in my life I find I can afford a new level of concern for and interest in my male counterparts in the world. Perhaps the pure and applied as well as the social scientists can begin to examine the male psyche and biology as intensely as they have perused the female since Freud.

Works Cited

Jung, Carl G. *The Spirit in Man, Art, and Literature* (Trans. R.F.C. Hull). New Jersey: Princeton UP, 1966.

Chapter Eighteen
Conclusion

*The essence of a work of art is not to be found in the personal
idiosyncrasies that creep into it—indeed, the more there are
of them, the less it is a work of art—but in its rising above the
personal and speaking from the mind and heart of the artist
to the mind and heart of mankind. . . .*

*Every creative person is a duality or a synthesis of
contradictory qualities. On the one side he is a human being
with a personal life, while on the other he is an impersonal
creative process. As a human being he may be sound or morbid
(ill), and his personal psychology can and should be explained
in personal terms. But he can be understood as an artist only
in terms of his creative achievement.*

—C.G. Jung, The Spirit in Man, Art, and Literature

This book has offered some evidence to support the theory of a drive
to create which is an inherent and critical factor in the creative functioning of any human being. The drive is an intrinsic aid to the affective balance a person needs in order to carry on the daily tasks of living. The intensity of the drive is directly related to the inheritance of affective disorders, especially the mood disorders—cyclothymia, hypomania, and
bipolar or manic-depressive illness. The greater the affective sensitivity
of the person, the greater the energy of the drive to create. In an artist we
see a person who is operating at a fairly high level of drive, and in the artist
there is a qualitative difference as well as quantitative because a specific
talent is available to the energy of the drive. Other driven individuals may
find different sources of release for their drive to create—business, law,
gardening, etc.

It is this inordinate drive to create that pushes the artist to develop
a creative lifestyle in order to accommodate his living circumstances to
his need for creative functioning. When this means of balance is destroyed
or restricted, the creative person—whether in the arts or sciences—becomes
emotionally disturbed. The emotional imbalance may take the form of an
affective psychosis or extreme neurosis or the person may seek relief in
drug or alcohol addiction. Examples of this effect have been noticed so
frequently among artists, writers, and other generative thinkers that a myth
of the insane artist or scientist has sprung up to explain the connection,

even though it is rationally accepted that insanity does not result in creative accomplishments.

What is this delicate, fragile thing we call "a life," and how is it that a quality defined as "creativity" is so highly valued among us humans? This book has sought to explore the dynamic process of human creative drive—an attribute that seems to be an inherent, instinctive ability to survive and explore solutions to real problems. Combined with learning and direction, this drive can be harnessed for the benefit of both the individual and society at large. Something new arises from the ashes of old efforts and failures in a most mystifying way, and all our science cannot tell how or when or to what degree the effects will be applied. Surely, this "wind of the spirit" is a gift and a treasure to be valued, developed, and dedicated to the benefit of the human community. This study has also suggested, based on continuing medical research and data, that to hopelessly afflict those with a high level of creative drive and talent is to reduce or lose the creative gift. In the individual the thwarting of creative drive may end in an array of physical or emotional dead-ends, and even, possibly suicide. The energy goes somewhere, either to creative work and solutions or into frustration and disease. To a great extent the individual must choose his own lifestyle and creative style, but in a broader sense the resource such people represent is a national and community treasure.

In a recent article published in the *Journal of Abnormal Psychology* researchers reported a higher incidence of creativity using the "Lifetime Creativity Scales" among manic-depressive patients and cyclothymic patients as well as their normal relatives as compared to control subjects who showed no sign of the disorder. The study concluded that liability for manic-depressive illness may carry advantages for creativity, perhaps particularly among those individuals who are relatively better functioning. In their summary, they made several observations important to the conclusions proposed by this study of creative drive and creativity:

> It is noteworthy that eminent artists and writers have described hypomanic symptomology during intense creative periods (Jamison, in press) and that manics and hypomanics have attributed both immediate and lasting effects on creativity to hypomanic episodes (Jamison, Gesner, Hammer, & Padesky, 1980; Kinney, Richards, Daniels, & Linkins, 1988). It will be important to distinguish between potential state versus trait characteristics that may enhance creativity. It would be fortunate if one such trait led to discovery of a biological marker that could track inherited bipolar liability through a pedigree in clinically unaffected as well as affected relatives. In addition, there would be major clinical implications if genotype-environment interactions could be identified that lead to enhanced creativity. Positive intervention might then not only prevent

the development of bipolar disorders but also foster creative talent and productive contribution to society. (Richards, Kinney, Lunde, Benet, Merzel 287)

I believe the drive to create is a "trait characteristic" that may enhance
creativity. Certainly the recognition of such drive in the young and its encouragement would promote both talent education as well as mental health.
If there were more public support of the creative—artists, teachers, scientists, inventors, generative thinkers—perhaps the toll in costs of alcohol
and drug treatment centers, mental hospitals, and general human carnage
would not be so high. The great need today is not so much for genetic
engineering as for humane and creative education. Somehow, the economics of supporting massive prisons, mental health clinics and hospitals, and
asylums for drug and alcohol abusers rather than providing for the educational and physical needs of our children and young people is hard to
justify if one considers the perspective of wasted creativity in the light of
the operation of the drive to create.

Creativity itself is a gift and the creative drive is a mechanism of homeostasis that governs the operation of that gift and directs its expression
toward the well-being of the individual. It is my personal belief that freedom from insanity, alcoholism, and addiction is a gift from a Higher Power,
a Creator, who has endowed humans with creative powers. It is man's
choice, and a very human one, to determine how these creative powers will
be administered—for good or ill. This choice is a process and a personal
one, but since we humans are also social beings—and not uniquely so; look
at the ants, for example—our choices affect the community and society
of the other beings on this planet.

Discussing the importance of the artist in society, Jung made these
observations. I believe his comments represent a description of the drive
to create:

> Art is a kind of innate drive that seizes a human being and makes him its
> instrument. The artist is not a person endowed with free will who seeks his own
> ends, but one who allows art to realize its purposes through him. As a human
> being he may have moods and a will and personal aims, but as an artist he is
> "man" in a higher sense—he is "collective man," a vehicle and moulder of the
> unconscious psychic life of mankind. That is his office, and it is sometimes
> so heavy a burden that he is fated to sacrifice happiness and everything that
> makes life worth living for the ordinary human being. (101)

On the significance of the artists in our midst, Carl Jung made this
assessment:

> Whenever conscious life becomes one-sided or adopts a false attitude, these images "instinctively" rise to the surface in dreams and in the visions of artists and seers to restore the psychic balance, whether of the individual or of the epoch.
>
> In this way the work of the artist meets the psychic needs of the society in which he lives, and therefore means more than his personal fate, whether he is aware of it or not. (104)

This study has attempted to outline a new theory of creative drive which cannot be neglected as part of the process of creative functioning. Operation of the drive, observation of both the results of intense creative drive and the effects of frustrated drive, and an example of an artist whose life portrayed the operation of the drive have been discussed. A writer was chosen to demonstrate the theory of creative drive because her insanity, her mental disorder (manic-depressive illness) is now identified with creativity and because her drive pushed her beyond her disease and into modern literary history. Medical research documents the role of affective diseases and their relationships to creative functioning. It suggests that responsible human choice is not only possible but essential to the business of restoration and healing of ourselves, our artists, and our planet.

Works Cited

Jung, C.G. *The Spirit in Man, Art, and Literature* (Trans. R.F.C. Hull). New Jersey: Princeton UP, 1966.

Richards, R., D.K. Kinney, I. Lunde, M. Benet, A.P. Merzel. "Creativity in Manic-Depressives, Cyclothymes, Their Normal Relatives and Control Subjects." *Journal of Abnormal Psychology*, 1988 Aug; 97(3): 281-88.

INDEX